THE GRAND CANYON
AND THE AMERICAN
SOUTH-WEST

D0813949

CONSTANCE ROOS

Dr Constance Roos was killed after being struck by lightning in Corsica on July 17th 1999, shortly after the completion of this book.

Constance Roos was 50. She was born in San Francisco, where she made her home and practised psychiatry. She received degrees from Stanford University and her MD from Case Western University. She was Assistant Clinical Professor of Psychiatry at the University of California, San Francisco. She had practised privately and was affiliated with Mount Zion, Pacific Presbyterian and Peninsula hospitals, was staff psychiatrist at the Community Crisis Centre, San Francisco, and assisted with emergency room work at San Francisco General and John George (Highland) hospitals.

Constance was an avid traveller, hiker and climber. She had explored and climbed in Africa, New Zealand, Bolivia, Mexico, Europe and Alaska as well as the western states. Her climbs included Mount Hood in Oregon, the Grand Teton in Wyoming, Mount Rainier in Washington, Huayna Potosi in Bolivia, Kilimanjaro in Africa, Popocatepetl in Mexico and many others.

Constance was in Corsica researching the Cicerone guide to the challenging GR20 route, perhaps the hardest of Europe's mountain treks. She has also written Cicerone guides to Norway and New Zealand.

Although I knew her for only a short period, I mourn the loss of a friendship that was young. I hope you enjoy using Constance's Grand Canyon guide as much as we enjoyed making it, and that we have done her last book justice.

Jonathan Williams

Cicerone Press
Milnthorpe, Cumbria

THE GRAND CANYON AND THE AMERICAN SOUTH-WEST

*TREKKING IN THE
GRAND CANYON,
ZION AND
BRYCE CANYON
NATIONAL PARKS*

by
Constance Roos

CICERONE PRESS
MILNTHORPE CUMBRIA LA7 7PY
UNITED KINGDOM
www.cicerone.co.uk

© 2000 Cicerone Press Ltd
ISBN 1 85284 300 4
A catalogue record for this book is available from the British Library
Route profiles, charts, area maps, legend and photographs by the author
Photo facing page 32: Walt Unsworth
Trail maps by Carto Graphics, San Francisco

Acknowledgements

This guide would not be complete without mention of all my friends who walked with me: Panos Antiochos, Dan Brooke and Cheryl Teuton, Jesse Brotz, Ute Dietrich, Bev Hedin, Terry Howard, Lynn Pelletier, Judy and Pete Sager, Tracy Shea, Betty Stanfield, and Mic Williams. Many thanks to the Grand Canyon Field Institute who shared with me their knowledge and expertise on several routes and trails described in this book.

A number of friends at home helped shape the book's final outcome. Trail maps were designed and produced by Kris Bergstrom and Shiela Semans of Carto Graphics, San Francisco. The United States Geological Survey provided the shaded relief used in the trail maps. Robert Shankland offered expert editorial guidance.

I am grateful to many thoughtful and friendly people, most of whose names I never knew, who went out of their way to make my visit in their home a pleasant one. Memories of my travels remain special because of their kindness.

Advice to readers

Readers are advised that whilst every effort has been taken by the author to ensure the accuracy of this guidebook, changes can occur which may affect the contents. It is advisable to check locally on transport, accommodation, shops etc but even rights-of-way can be altered.

The publisher would welcome notes of any such changes.

Other Cicerone guides by the same author:
Classic Tramps in New Zealand
Walking in Norway

Front cover: Zion Canyon National Park

CONTENTS

General Map...12
Map Legend 13

INTRODUCTION 14

1   **USING THIS BOOK**
    Summary of contents...16
    Fact panels..17
    Distances and time estimates 17
    Trail rating..17
    Maps..18
    Direction 18
    Water 19
    Long distance route recommendations..............19
    Route profiles...19
    Summary tables 20

2   **VISITING THE SOUTH-WESTERN
    UNITED STATES**
    Travelling to the South-Western United States.......................21
    Passports and visas 21
    Customs and duties 21
    When to go 23
    Getting around...23
    Entrance fees 23
    Time zones 24
    Currency 24
    Traveller's cheques and credit cards 25
    Insurance 25
    Sales tax 25
    Lodging and camping 25
    Business hours 26
    Telephone..26
    Toll-free numbers 26
    Post 26
    Laundry 27
    Weights, measures and temperature 27
    Electricity 27
    Smoking...27
    Tipping...28
    Helpful phone numbers 28

3   EQUIPMENT AND SPECIAL HAZARDS
Equipment 29
Shelter...29
Sleeping bag...29
Stove and fuel 29
Food...30
Clothing 30
Boots...30
Miscellaneous..31
Special hazards 31
Water requirements..31
Heat and sun..31
Rockfall 32
Cold 32
Flash floods 32

4   VISITING GRAND CANYON NATIONAL PARK
Introduction..33
Getting there 33
Getting around - shuttle services...34
Weather and seasons..35
Lodging...35
Camping 38
Visitor services 38
Interpretative programmes 39
Grand Canyon Association...39
Grand Canyon Field Institute..39
Other facilities...39
Time zones..39

5   WALKING IN GRAND CANYON NATIONAL PARK
Introduction..40
Overnight backcountry permits and procedures 40
Fees 42
Groups...42
Day hiking..42
Trip planning..43
Corridor trails 43
First-timers on cross-canyon trips 44
Lodging at Phantom Ranch 45
Shuttle services 45
Maps..46
Backcountry Management Zones 46
Trail categories 47
Waymarking...48

Camping regulations 48
Water sources 49
Search and rescue 49
Visiting archaeological sites......................................51
Tour aircraft and river-runners 51
Mules 52
Insects, reptiles and mammals 52
Heat 54
Other Grand Canyon dangers...................................54
Warning..54

**6   GRAND CANYON NATIONAL PARK:
     SOUTH RIM, RIM TO RIVER TRAILS**
Introduction...56
Table of trails...56
South Bass Trail 57
Boucher Trail..60
Hermit Trail..64
Bright Angel Trail...67
South Kaibab Trail..71
Grandview Trail..75
New Hance Trail...78
Tanner Trail 81

**7   GRAND CANYON NATIONAL PARK:
     NORTH RIM, RIM TO RIVER TRAILS**
Introduction...84
Table of trails...85
Thunder River and Bill Hall
   Trails, with Deer Creek Extension 85
North Bass Trail 90
North Kaibab Trail 94
Nankoweap Trail..98

**8   GRAND CANYON NATIONAL PARK: TRANS-
     CANYON TRAILS, NORTH AND SOUTH RIM**
Introduction 103
Table of trails (South Rim) 104
Escalante Route: Tanner Canyon to New Hance Trail
   at Red Canyon 104
Tonto Trail: New Hance Trail at Red Canyon to
   Hance Creek...107
Tonto Trail: Hance Creek to Cottonwood Creek 108
Tonto Trail: Cottonwood Creek to South Kaibab Trail 109
Tonto Trail: South Kaibab Trail to Indian Garden 111

Tonto Trail: Indian Garden to Hermit Creek...........................112
Tonto Trail: Hermit Creek to Boucher Creek.........................113
Tonto Trail: Boucher Creek to Bass Canyon 115
Table of Trails (North Rim) 116
Clear Creek Trail..116

9 GRAND CANYON NATIONAL PARK: SOUTH AND NORTH RIM TRAILS

Table of trails (South Rim)...119
Rim Trail..119
Shoshone Point 122
North Rim Trails: introduction..122
Table of trails (North Rim)..123
Cape Royal Trail 123
Cliff Springs Trail 124
Cape Final Trail..126
Ken Patrick Trail 127
Bright Angel Point Trail..129
Transept Trail 129
Widforss Trail..130
Uncle Jim Trail 131

10 GRAND CANYON NATIONAL PARK: LONG DISTANCE ROUTES

Introduction..132
Table of routes 132
Boucher Trail to Hermit Trail Loop 133
Hermit Trail to Bright Angel Trail Loop 135
Cross-canyon: North Kaibab Trail to
    Bright Angel Trail...137
South Kaibab Trail to Bright Angel Trail 139
Grandview Trail to South Kaibab Trail....................................142
Escalante Route: Tanner Trail to Grandview Trail 142
Kanab Canyon to Thunder River Route...................................144

11 VISITING ZION NATIONAL PARK

Introduction..153
History 153
Getting there 154
Getting around..154
Zion valley transportation 154
Weather and seasons...155
Lodging..157
Camping 157
Visitor services 157

Zion National History Association..157
Interpretative programmes...157
Other facilities...158
Time zones..158

12   WALKING IN ZION NATIONAL PARK
Overnight permits and fees...159
Day-walking..159
Hiking the Narrows..159
Shuttle services...160
Groups..160
Maps..160
Weather and seasons..160
Minimum impact..162
Water sources..162
Waymarking...162
Flash floods...162
Insects, reptiles and mammals...163

13   ZION NATIONAL PARK:
        KOLOB CANYONS TRAILS
Introduction...164
Table of trails..164
Timber Creek Overlook...164
Middle Fork of Taylor Creek Trail..165
La Verkin Creek Trail..166
Kolob Arch Trail...169
Willis Creek Route..170
Hop Valley Trail..172

14   ZION NATIONAL PARK:
        WEST RIM TRAILS
Introduction...176
Table of trails..176
Connector Trail...176
Wildcat Canyon Trail...177
Northgate Peaks Trail...181
West Rim Trail...182

15   ZION NATIONAL PARK:
        ZION CANYON TRAILS
Table of trails..189
Gateway to the Narrows or Riverside Trail...........................189
Up the Narrows to Orderville Canyon....................................190
Weeping Rock..191

Hidden Canyon and Observation Point...................................193
Angels' Landing via Scout Lookout...195
Emerald Pools...197
Court of the Patriarchs 199
Sand Bench Horse Trail 199
Par'us Trail 200
The Watchman 202

16   ZION NATIONAL PARK:
        EAST RIM TRAILS
        Table of trails...203
        Canyon Overlook Trail 203
        East Rim Trail...204
        East Boundary to Echo Canyon Trail 207
        East Mesa Trail...208
        Stave Spring Junction to Cable Mountain
          and Deertrap Mountain Trails.....................................209

17   ZION NATIONAL PARK:
        SOUTH-WEST DESERT TRAILS
        Introduction...211
        Table of trails...211
        Chinle Trail 211
        Huber Wash...215

18   ZION NATIONAL PARK:
        LONG DISTANCE ROUTES
        Table of routes...216
        Across Zion via Hop Valley and the West Rim 216
        The Zion Narrows...219
        East Rim Trail via Cable and Deertrap Mountains...............225

19   VISITING BRYCE CANYON NATIONAL PARK
        Introduction...227
        Getting there 227
        Getting around...228
        Weather and seasons...228
        Lodging...230
        Camping 230
        Visitor services 230
        Interpretative programmes...230
        Bryce Canyon Natural History Association....................230
        Other facilities...231
        Shuttle services 231
        Time zones..231

20   WALKING IN BRYCE CANYON NATIONAL PARK
Introduction..232
Walking permits 232
Groups..232
Maps...232
Weather and seasons..234
Water sources 234
Waymarking..234
Flash floods 234
Insects, reptiles and mammals 234

**21   BRYCE CANYON NATIONAL PARK:
       CANYON AND RIM TRAILS**
Table of trails..235
Fairyland Loop 235
Queen's Garden Trail...238
Navajo Loop...242
Rim Trail 242
Peekaboo Loop 244
Bristlecone Loop 245
Riggs Spring Loop..248

**22   BRYCE CANYON NATIONAL PARK: LONG
       DISTANCE AND CONNECTING TRAILS**
Table of trails (long distance) 249
Under the Rim Trail 249
Connecting trails: introduction 255
Table of trails (connecting)..255
Sheep Creek Connecting Trail 256
Swamp Canyon Connecting Trail..256
Whiteman Connecting Trail...256
Aqua Connecting Trail 257

APPENDICES
A Long distance routes summary tables...............................258
B Useful addresses..266
C Local facilities 270
D Author's favourite walks...272
E Index of charts and route profiles....................................274
F Index of maps...276

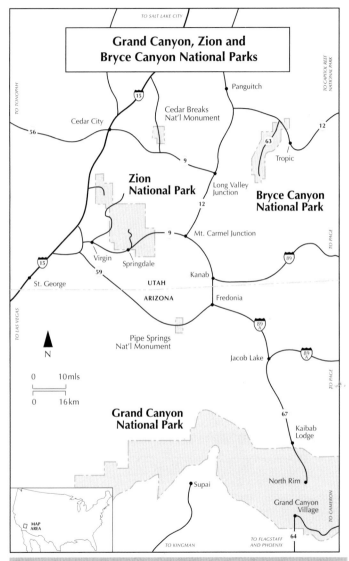

Grand Canyon, Zion and Bryce Canyon National Parks

TO SALT LAKE CITY

TO CAPITOL REEF NATIONAL PARK

TO TONOPAH

Panguitch

15

Cedar Breaks Nat'l Monument

Cedar City

56

9

63

12

Tropic

Zion National Park

Long Valley Junction

Bryce Canyon National Park

12

9   Mt. Carmel Junction

TO PAGE

89

15

Virgin

Springdale

59

Kanab

St. George

UTAH

ARIZONA

Fredonia

89A

TO LAS VEGAS

Pipe Springs Nat'l Monument

N

Jacob Lake   89A

TO PAGE

0   10 mls

0   16 km

67

Grand Canyon National Park

Kaibab Lodge

Supai

North Rim

Grand Canyon Village

TO CAMERON

MAP AREA

TO KINGMAN

TO FLAGSTAFF AND PHOENIX

64

Legend

··········	Trail
········	Route
··················	Other trail
—— 9 ——	Highway
————	Main road
————	Secondary road
—FR232—	Unpaved road
▪▪▪ ▪ ▪▪▪ ▪ ▪	National Park boundary
▪▪▪ ▪ ▪ ▪▪▪ ▪ ▪	State boundary
🏠	Ranger Station
■	Building / Resthouse
▲	Campground
☍	Picnic Area
Ⓟ	Parking / Trailhead
◍	Spring / Perennial water

INTRODUCTION

The price of wilderness still includes eternal vigilance.
Colin Fletcher

The south-western corner of the United States, dotted with national parks and monuments, wilderness areas, state parks and recreational areas, boasts of a seemingly endless variety of deep canyons, high and low desert, snow-capped mountains and raging rivers. Within this area Grand Canyon National Park, Zion National Park and Bryce Canyon National Park encompass some of the most extraordinary scenery in the United States. Though Grand Canyon National Park is well known world-wide, Zion and Bryce Canyon National Parks are less so. Yet the parks offer such splendid scenery that each merits a visit of its own.

Come and view this magnificent corner of the United States. Join me in touring these parks on foot. Walk the high country of Zion and veer down into the valley from atop its towering red walls. Weave amidst the hoodoos of Bryce and descend into the hidden depths of the Grand Canyon. Walkers can easily steer clear of crowds and enjoy the backcountry in relative isolation.

I have tried to present material and information as accurately as possible. But how quickly things change! Paths can be re-routed; new buildings are built and others are removed; bridges are washed away. Changes in the landscape occur due to storms, flooding, rockfall and other natural causes. Be prepared for sudden changes in weather, wide fluctuations in temperature and unexpected obstacles blocking routes and trails.

Many of my trips to foreign countries have been inspired by guidebooks that I first studied from home. I hope this book will aid in planning a trip into this special area of the United States and, once you have arrived, help to make your visit a pleasant and meaningful one. I have presented travel and park information and trail descriptions in a style that I hope will be useful and practical yet not overload you with too much detail.

Plan to arrive a day or two before your walk to get up-to-date information from the National Park Service. Without thoughtful planning many of these trips are dangerous or life threatening. Bring along your common sense and good judgement and you will enjoy the trip of a lifetime.

May you grow to love this section of the American South-West as I have. Have a great trip!

Constance Roos

CHAPTER 1

USING THIS BOOK

Every time I go anywhere out in the desert or mountains
I wonder why I should return.
Someday, I won't.
Edward Abbey

Summary of contents

Introductory sections 1–3 discuss general guidelines on how to use this book. Section 2 outlines travel information and how to get around in the United States. Section 3 guides you on equipment necessary for overnight or day-walks.

The following sections provide trail descriptions and recommended long distance walks for walkers and backpackers for all three parks. Grand Canyon National Park, covered in sections 4–10, begins with an overview of the park, followed by information on walking in the Grand Canyon along with permit procedures. Trails and routes from the South Rim, North Rim, Trans-canyon Rim and long distance walks are then described in each successive section. Associated fact panels, trail maps, charts and route profiles are provided. Zion National Park, covered in sections 11–18, covers trails in Kolob Canyons, West Rim and East Rim and Zion Canyon walks. Bryce Canyon National Park, included in sections 19–22, covers Bryce Canyon and Rim walks as well.

All of the walking trails in Zion National Park and Bryce Canyon National Park are described. In Grand Canyon National Park, all of the maintained and non-maintained rim to river trails and rim trails are described as well. All of the walks described follow known trails or established routes along canyon bottoms or beside rivers.

You are provided with information on how you can link together several trails to convert day-walks into long distance walks. Choices of long distance walks in all three parks are offered. Route profiles of the elevation gains and losses of the walks and summary tables with walking time estimates are included. Appendices present succinct information on walking times of long distance walks, local facilities, helpful addresses and phone numbers, and my favourite walks in each park.

Fact panels

Fact panels, preceding each trail description, list the distance of the trails in miles and kilometres, the starting and ending elevations, average time to walk the trail, the maps needed, the best time of year to walk the trail and other related information.

Distances and time estimates

The National Park Service (NPS) publishes trail distances. When these distances are unavailable I have estimated trail length from the United States Geological Survey (USGS) 7.5 minute topographical maps. Distances are noted as one-way or a loop. A car shuttle may be necessary, but other transport options such as van, shuttle or taxi services often exist.

Time estimates, which include rest stops, vary widely especially in Grand Canyon National Park. Times depend on the direction travelled (ascent or descent), terrain, season, temperature and condition of the trail, as well as the strength of the party. Time estimates provided for the long distance walks (sections 10, 16 and 19) allow additional time for carrying a full backpack. Fact panels indicate whether the time estimates provided are for backpackers or day-walkers.

Trail rating

I've presented an overview of each trail by noting its difficulty, steepness and obstacles, such as creek crossings, snow, rocks or talus. Some trails or routes may be designated as one grading (eg. Easy) even though a few sections could lift its rating into a more demanding category (eg. Moderate). "Easy" would then refer to the route as a whole and not to an atypical section. In addition, these ratings refer to the challenges of the route itself, exclusive of its length.

Sections are graded along the following guidelines:

Easy. You will encounter no major difficulties or obstacles on the trail. Level or gently undulating terrain predominates; elevation gains and losses are minimal. Beginners and visitors with children will find these walks suitable. This designation applies to rim walks in Grand Canyon National Park and Bryce Canyon National Park and Zion Canyon walks in Zion National Park.

Moderate. Gains and losses in elevation exceed those in the "Easy" category. The path may be rocky with some steep ascents or descents although no scrambling is involved. In general, elevation gains and losses are more gradual and not as steep as in the "Strenuous" category. In spite of their large changes in elevation, Corridor Trails in Grand Canyon National Park rate as moderate.

Strenuous. These trails, for experienced walkers in good physical condition, may present some rough and rocky terrain with exposure, scrambling, rocks, talus or scree. Parties with novices or small children should not attempt these trails. In Grand Canyon National Park, elevation gains and losses may be as great as 5,000 feet (1,524 metres). River walks in Zion National Park (eg. The Narrows) involve exposure to very cold water, swift currents and flash flood dangers.

Extremely Strenuous. Only experienced canyoneers and backpackers in excellent physical condition can attempt these unmaintained trails or routes. Talus-hopping and scrambling is necessary; exposure may be extreme. Water sources are scarce to non-existent. You need to be sure-footed, unafraid of heights, and able to use a map and compass.

Maps

You may purchase topographical maps locally or by mail from the addresses listed in Appendix B. Topographical maps are published by the United States Geological Survey 7.5 minute series (USGS), Trails Illustrated (TI) and Earthwalk Press (EP). The United States Geological Survey no longer publishes the 15 minute series.

Direction

Most of the trails in this book can be walked in either direction. If a particular direction is preferred, this is noted in the text.

In Grand Canyon National Park, the following directions are preferred: Trans-canyon, North Kaibab to South Kaibab or Bright Angel Trails; Kanab Canyon - Thunder River, counter-clockwise from Sowats Point to Indian Hollow; Boucher to Hermit Loop, counter-clockwise descending the Boucher Trail and ascending the

Hermit Trail; South Bass to Hermit Trails, descending the South Bass and walking east on the Tonto Trail and ascending the Hermit Trail; Escalante Route, travelling west from the Tanner Trail to the New Hance or Grandview Trails.

In Zion National Park the following directions are preferred: The Narrows, south from Chamberlain's Ranch to the Temple of Sinawava; West Rim Trail, south from Lava Point to the Grotto picnic area; East Rim Trail, East Entrance to Weeping Rock; Across Zion, east from Lee Pass to the Grotto picnic area.

With respect to rivers, 'true left' and 'true right' apply to the sides of a river while looking downstream.

Water

Know your water sources before you start out. Check with the Backcountry Ranger Office (BRO) at Grand Canyon National Park and visitor centres in Zion Canyon or Kolob Canyons and Bryce Canyon National Park before you depart. Year-round sources are noted on the route profiles and fact panels. Seasonal water sources are mentioned in the text.

Long-distance route recommendations

Several multi-day long-distance routes are suggested. Route profiles, trail maps, fact panels, average walking times and an overview of the walks are included. You will find both the route profiles and book maps useful for planning your trip. However, neither should be relied on for walking - be sure to purchase topographical maps that cover your route.

Route profiles

This book includes route profiles for most of the trails described and for each long distance route. Route profiles indicate important trail markers, elevations, and year-round water sources or springs. Trail steepness can be gauged at a glance. The horizontal distance on the trail is represented on the horizontal axis and not by the length of the profile line. The steeper a segment on the profile line, the more this segment will exaggerate the true distance between the points. The book's limited page length make some segments of the trail drawn on the route profile appear steeper than they truly are. This vertical exaggeration becomes especially apparent for longer routes.

Summary tables

Summary tables in Appendix A estimate how long it will take to walk from point to point along each long distance route. Estimates assume you will be carrying a backpack of approximately 40 pounds (18 kilograms).

CHAPTER 2

VISITING THE SOUTH-WESTERN
UNITED STATES

This land is your land, this land is my land
From California to the New York Islands
From the redwood forest to the Gulf Stream waters,
This land was made for you and me.
Woodie Gutherie

Travelling to the South-Western United States
The airports at Las Vegas and Salt Lake City, Nevada and Phoenix, Arizona are closest to the parks in this book. At the time of writing, non-stop flights from Great Britain were not available. You can reach Las Vegas, Salt Lake City or Phoenix easily on connecting flights from any major American city. Popular connecting cities are San Francisco, Los Angeles, Denver, Dallas/Fort Worth, Chicago, Washington DC, or New York. Fares vary widely depending on class of service, level of airline competition and the time of year. Summer and the Christmas holidays are the most expensive times to fly.

Passports and visas
British visitors staying less than 90 days need a full passport rather than a British Visitor's Passport. You should be able to show that you have sufficient funds for your stay, approximately $350 per week.

The date stamped on your passport and your immigration form specify the last date you should leave the United States. Don't overstay your visit. Instead get an extension from the United States Immigration and Naturalization Service (INS).

Customs and duties
Customs allows 200 cigarettes and one litre of spirits to be brought into the United States free of charge. You may not bring any fresh food or freeze-dried meat. Your backpacking gear, especially boots and tents, should be free of soil.

When to go

If you have the freedom to choose the time and season of the year to visit, the spring and autumn win without contest. Although the weather can be fickle from mid-April to late May, temperatures are generally pleasant. Spring marks the revival of the green leaves and trees, along with torrents of water and a colourful array of wildflowers. Be sure to carry some warm clothes in case a wave of cold weather arrives. Temperatures begin to warm up in Zion and the Grand Canyon by late April but not until late May in Bryce Canyon.

Autumn, from September into late October, marks the best time of year in the canyon country. Gone are the summer crowds, thunder showers, and scorching temperatures. Weather may remain stable for days on end. Crystal clear blue skies, cool nights and the turning of the leaves to yellow and reds accent the canyon foliage. In the summer, unbearable heat, often over 100 °F (38 °C), stifles the Grand Canyon and Zion Valley. The rim areas of Grand Canyon remain somewhat cooler due to their elevation over 7,000 feet (2,133 metres). Bryce Canyon National Park, still plagued by overcrowding, never reaches too great a temperature due to its high elevation.

Serious crowding in the United States national parks begins after the Memorial Day holiday, the last Monday in May, and extends to Labour Day holiday weekend, the first Monday in September. Another major holiday, Independence Day on the 4 July, compounds summer congestion. Lodging or camping near any national park may be impossible during the summer. Limited access at viewpoints makes finding a parking spot a major accomplishment.

Getting around

The most practical way to get around is to rent a car at the airport. No public transportation operates into Zion National Park, Bryce Canyon National Park, or the North Rim of the Grand Canyon. A small airport, bus and taxi service, and a car rental agency serve the South Rim of the Grand Canyon (see section 4).

Entrance fees

All national parks in the United States charge entrance fees. A Golden Eagle Pass entitles the holder entrance into all national parks and monuments for one year. If you plan to visit more than one or two parks, this makes a wise purchase. A Golden Age Passport, for visitors over 62 years of age, costs a one time minimal lifetime fee. Golden Access cards are available for disabled visitors. Golden Age and Golden Access holders may receive discounts at campgrounds. Visitors arriving on foot or bicycle pay a reduced fee.

Time zones

The continental United States spreads over four time zones, with additional zones for Alaska and Hawaii. The Eastern Zone, 5 hours behind Greenwich Mean Time (GMT) and 6 hours behind Great Britain, covers the eastern seaboard and extends inland to the Great Lakes and Appalachian Mountains. The Central Zone, 7 hours behind Great Britain, extends from Chicago to western Texas and the Great Plains. The Mountain Zone, 8 hours behind Great Britain, stretches across the Rocky Mountains, the American South-West, and the states of Utah and Arizona. The Pacific Zone, 9 hours behind Great Britain, spans the Pacific States and Nevada. Alaska operates 1 hour and Hawaii operates 2 hours behind Pacific Time.

Time changes in this corner of the United States cause considerable confusion. The neighbouring states of California and Nevada are in the Pacific Time Zone, and Utah and Arizona are in the Mountain Time Zone. Nevada and California operate on Pacific Standard time (PST) and push ahead 1 hour to Pacific Daylight Time (PDT) from the first week in April to the last week in October. Utah operates on Mountain Standard Time (MST) and pushes ahead to Mountain Daylight Time (MDT) from early April to late October.

Unlike the neighbouring states of Utah, Nevada, and California, Arizona does not convert to Daylight Savings Time (DST) and ignores the usual summer time change. Grand Canyon National Park, located entirely in the state of Arizona, remains on Mountain Standard Time (MST) all year. Thus during the summer, Utah operates 1 hour ahead of Arizona even though they are in the same time zone.

The United States indicates time using "am" and "pm" (eg. 6am and 6pm) and not military time (eg. 0600 and 1800).

Currency

United States currency can be found in denominations of $1, $2, $5,

$10, $20, $50, $100 and $500. One hundred cents (¢) make up a dollar and coins come as 50¢ (a half-dollar), 25¢ (a quarter), 10¢ (a dime), 5¢ (a nickel) and 1¢ (a penny). One dollar coins (Susan B. Anthony dollars) turn up in states that allow gambling (eg. Nevada). Two-dollar and $500 bills are rare. The popular quarter operates telephones, laundry machines, parking meters, and so on.

Traveller's cheques and credit cards

Traveller's cheques in United States dollars provide the safest and most convenient way to carry money. Almost everyone accepts them if your passport proves your identity. Places of business and banks accept traveller's cheques at face value although there may be a charge for converting them at change bureaux. You can also exchange your foreign currency at change bureaux at airports and in larger cities at American Express and Thomas Cook offices. Accepted everywhere, credit cards can be used to pay for goods and services or to receive cash from an automated teller machine (ATM). You cannot rent a car without one.

Insurance

The United States offers no national health insurance. Be sure you purchase travel insurance. A hospital stay can set you back thousands of dollars in expenses.

Sales tax

A state sales tax increases charges on purchases, rental cars, hotel and motel bills. The rate varies from state to state but averages around 8%. A few states do not charge sales tax.

Lodging and camping

All three national parks offer hotels, motels, and campgrounds within their borders or nearby communities. Reservations are highly recommended for lodging in all three parks. Phantom Ranch (see section 4), at the bottom of the Bright Angel Trail along the Colorado River, should be reserved at least one year in advance especially if you wish to visit between spring and autumn. Winter reservations at Phantom Ranch can sometimes be obtained at short notice.

Camping is available all year long in all three parks. Reservations are essential from May to October for North Rim Campground, at Mather Campground on the South Rim and Watchman Campground in Zion National Park. Desert View

Campground, open in summer, at the South Rim of Grand Canyon National Park and campgrounds at Bryce Canyon National Park and South Campground at Zion National Park operate on a first-come first-served basis. Campgrounds fill early in the day in summer. See Appendix B for information on making campground reservations.

Business hours
Standard business hours run from 9am to 6pm. Hours are often extended into the evening near National Parks during the busy summer season.

Telephone
You will find public telephones everywhere (eg. bus and train stations and street corners). Coins or phone cards may be used for local calls. For operator assistance, dial 0. If a call costs more than the amount deposited an operator will ask for more. Calls made from hotels and motels are more expensive than calls from either public or private phones. The lowest rates are available between 6pm and 7am and all day on Sunday. Calling cards save on charges.

You can make an international call by dialling 011 + country code + city code + the number. If you need help the international operator (dial 00) will provide assistance.

Toll-free numbers
Many agencies, private and public companies offer toll-free numbers within the United States. You call them at their expense by dialling the prefix 1-800 and then the number.

Post
Post Offices, located in small towns as well as large cities, usually open from 9am to 5pm on weekdays and 9am to 1pm on Saturdays. Small towns are proud of their Post Office. Blue, waist-high mail boxes stand in front of Post Offices and on selected street corners. You will find a Post Office in Grand Canyon Lodge at the North Rim, next to Babbitt's General Store at the South Rim of the Grand Canyon, in Zion Lodge, and in Bryce Lodge. Letters addressed with the zip code may be sent c/o General Delivery to any Post Office and will be held for no more than thirty days. Airmail to Europe takes about one week. The United States Postal Service boasts some of the lowest postal rates in the world.

The last line of letters addressed to the United States should include the name of the city, the state abbreviation and the postal code. States are abbreviated with two capital letters (eg. California is CA). Postal codes or zip codes direct a letter to a particular section of the city to which it is addressed. Codes contain five digits and follow the state abbreviation (eg. San Francisco, CA 94118). If you are unsure of the state abbreviation you can spell out the state name (eg. San Francisco, California 94118). Post Offices have zip code directories. Letters without the zip code will be delayed and may be lost.

Laundry
Laundromats with coin-operated washing machines and dryers can be found in many small and medium-sized towns. They provide the most efficient and economical way to take care of this essential chore. Self-service laundries are available inside Bryce Canyon National Park at the General Store, at the South Rim of the Grand Canyon next door to Mather Campground, and at the North Rim of the Grand Canyon next to the service station and campground. For visitors to Zion National Park, you will find a laundromat in Springdale, Utah. A dry-cleaning service may be available at hotels or through independent dry-cleaners.

Weights, measures and temperature
United States distance measurements are recorded in inches, feet and miles; weight is noted in ounces and pounds. Distance signs for walkers in the National Parks list distances in miles and height in feet although the metric system is occasionally used as well. Temperature in the United States is noted commonly in degrees Fahrenheit (°F) but, especially in Grand Canyon National Park, temperatures are also given in degrees Centigrade (°C).

Electricity
Electric plugs support two prongs with 110V AC.

Smoking
Smoking is a declining habit in the United States. In hotels and motels some rooms may be designated as non-smoking. Domestic aeroplane flights and some public buildings, outdoor stadiums and restaurants forbid smoking. Throwing a burning cigarette out of an automobile can result in a large fine in areas at risk from forest fires.

Tipping

Tips are given to service providers, eg. waiters and waitresses or taxi drivers, at the discretion of the customer, depending on your satisfaction with their service. Tips are usually given at 15% of the total charge. Baggage handlers often receive $2 per bag carried. Many workers' livelihoods depend on tips.

Helpful phone numbers

Local operator: 0
Local calls within your area code: the seven-digit phone number
Outside your area code: 1 + area code + phone number
International telephone operator: 00
Emergencies: 911
Local directory information: 411
Long distance directory information: 1 + area code + 555-1212
Directory information for toll-free numbers: 1-800-555-1212

CHAPTER 3

EQUIPMENT AND SPECIAL HAZARDS

I am glad I shall never be young without wild country to be young in.
Of what avail are forty freedoms without a blank spot on the map!
Aldo Leopold

EQUIPMENT

For your overnight trips in Zion, Bryce and the Grand Canyon you will need equipment similar to what is essential for most backpacking trips in other parts of the world. During summer and late spring, hot to scorching temperatures dominate your concerns in Grand Canyon National Park and in Zion National Park. In winter, in all three parks, you will need extra cold-weather gear. General gear requirements are outlined below.

Shelter

In summer, I carry a lightweight tent; others prefer a ground cloth and tarpaulin. A tent guards against unexpected night time visitors such as scorpions, ringtail cats, tarantulas, ants and mice. In spring, winter and autumn a heavier tent offers more protection. Be prepared for sudden changes in weather at any time of year. Snow can fall from September to May. Summer thunder showers often deluge the South-West.

Sleeping bag

A lightweight sleeping bag (or light blanket in summer only) offers more than enough warmth in the heat of summer. In spring, winter and autumn, I carry a warmer bag, adequate in freezing weather. A sleeping pad adds to my comfort and warmth.

Stove and fuel

You must carry a camping stove since backcountry fires are prohibited. White gas and kerosene are available at most outdoor sporting goods stores. Butane or propane cartridges can be difficult to locate. Do not count on finding your special brand.

It is a violation of federal law to carry any fuel (eg. gas, kerosene, or butane cartridges) on aeroplanes. Stoves with an attached receptacle for fuel or separate fuel bottles may be confiscated at United States airports and not returned. Fuel containers must be free of fuel and gas fumes.

Food

Grocery stores near all three parks stock dehydrated and lightweight foods. High carbohydrate food provides invaluable energy. Electrolyte replacement drinks restore lost electrolytes in hot weather. Carry extra food in case you are delayed for any reason (eg. bad weather, illness and poor road conditions).

Never leave your food out unprotected. Be sure to guard your food supply from uninvited visitors. Squirrels, mice or other rodents may eat through the outside pockets of packs. Hang your packs empty, away from your tent, with the zippers and pockets open. Never store or sleep with food in your tents.

Established campsites in Grand Canyon National Park on the Corridor Trails and the Hermit Trail are especially vulnerable to these raids; use overhead wires for hanging food. Mice and squirrels have been known to chew at ropes used for hanging food so that the food bag falls to the ground. Outwitting these rodents challenges many a canyon hiker.

Clothing

Pack clothing that will keep you warm when wet. Layers of synthetic or wool clothing, waterproofs with full-length side zippers, and a warm hat and gloves are necessary any time of year. Be prepared for fickle weather and varying temperatures especially in spring and autumn.

In summer, I carry a long-sleeved synthetic shirt, cotton shirt and shorts, and a fleece jacket. Loose fitting, light-coloured cotton clothing shield from the sun and allows for air flow. During the autumn and spring when it can turn cold, I wear synthetic long underwear under the shorts and carry another synthetic mid-weight long sleeved shirt. In winter, I pack another heavier synthetic shirt and trousers, overmitts, a balaclava, extra fuel and food, a heavier tent and a warmer sleeping bag and pad.

Boots

Medium to lightweight boots with a lug sole will serve you well.

Trainers provide inadequate ankle support. Carry several changes of socks. Woollen socks are warmer than synthetic ones, but dry more slowly.

In winter and early spring, in Grand Canyon National Park, instep crampons may be necessary to negotiate the icy upper sections of some trails as you descend off the rim. Gaiters protect your feet and socks from snow. Snow and ice may not be gone from the Grand Canyon South Rim trails until May, the North Rim until June, the Zion high country until May and the Bryce Rim until June.

Miscellaneous
Do not forget your map and compass, signal mirror, extra food, water purification tablets or pump, more water than you think you will need, pocket knife, nylon cord for hanging food or hauling packs, toilet items, camera and film. Medical kits should include general first aid supplies, an ankle wrap and blister care materials. A walking stick helps with balance on the steep trails; some find them too cumbersome. You will also need plastic bags for trash, some sort of pack cover or strong large plastic bags to line your pack, electrolyte replacement drinks, salty snacks, matches or lighter, trowel, whistle, flashlight and extra batteries.

SPECIAL HAZARDS

Water requirements
Remember to drink as much water as you can before you leave camp in the morning. Know your water sources before you depart and plan ahead. Carry up to one gallon of water a day or more in high summer. Treat all water either with a filter or with tablets. Filters clog easily from dirty water. Electrolyte replacement drinks such as ERG® or Gatorade® help to prevent dehydration in hot weather. Urine colour should be pale yellow and output should be copious.

Heat and sun
Pay close attention to sun protection. A hat with a wide brim shades your face and head; a bandanna shields your neck. You must have sunglasses that block UV light and strong sun block (SPF 15 or higher) for your skin. White cotton shirts absorb less heat. Long sleeves protect your arms and provide more sun protection.

Rockfall

Humans cause much of the rockfall danger. Cutting trails leads to erosion and increases the chance of kicking loose debris and rocks on walkers below. Watch where you place your hands and feet.

Cold

Sudden changes in weather bring snow, rain and anything in between. Hypothermia, commonly known as the "killer of the unprepared", strikes most commonly between 30 °F and 50 °F (0 °C and 10 °C). Snow can fall between September and May; rain is possible anytime of year. You should always be prepared with several layers of synthetic or wool clothing, shelter, full waterproofs, warm hat and gloves, and extra high-energy foods.

Flash floods

Flash floods present a serious hazard in narrow canyons especially in the Grand Canyon and Zion. In summer, large amounts of rain, often in thundershowers, fall in the higher elevations many miles from the park. The water rushes through tributary creeks eventually overloading distant small run-off creeks. Stay out of side creeks during the high flash-flood season from July to early September. Several deaths occur each year due to flash floods.

Grand Canyon from Desert View, South Rim (photo Walt Unsworth)

Mules on Bright Angel Trail, Grand Canyon National Park

CHAPTER 4

VISITING GRAND CANYON
NATIONAL PARK

*It is unique. It stands alone...it is one of the few things
that man is utterly unable to imagine
until he comes in actual contact with it.*
George Wharton James, 1910

Introduction

Over five million people from all over the world visited Grand Canyon National Park in 1999. Known as Kaibab or "mountain lying down" to the Indian Piute tribe, no amount of pictures, reading or photographs will prepare you for what you will see. The park extends over one million acres of land. The Grand Canyon spans 18 miles across at its widest and 1.5 miles across at its narrowest. The Canyon's 10 mile wide central section measures 1 mile deep.

From the accessible South Rim Grand Canyon Village, walkers can choose from eight splendid rim to river trails, all direct and fast routes to the Colorado River. Far away from the crowds of the south, the cooler and higher North Rim Village receives 10% of the number of visitors that go to the South Rim Village. The North Rim's magnificent viewpoints indent the canyon walls in finger-like projections that boast sweeping views of the upper inner canyon. Superlative day-hiking on the rim awaits walkers at the North Rim Village, although only the North Kaibab Trail provides access into the Inner Canyon.

Getting there

Located entirely within the state of Arizona, the Grand Canyon Village at the South Rim is easily reached from Phoenix, Las Vegas or Salt Lake City. Located 59 miles north of Williams, Arizona on Highway 64 and 78 miles north of Flagstaff, Arizona via Highway 180, Grand Canyon National Park is 310 miles from Bryce Canyon National Park, 272 miles from Zion National Park and 215 miles from the North Rim of the Grand Canyon. In addition it is 440 miles from Death Valley, California, 649 miles from Los Angeles, California and 334 miles from Tucson, Arizona.

Commuter airlines fly to the Grand Canyon Airport (South Rim) from Las Vegas, Phoenix and Flagstaff. Poor weather can ground these small sightseeing planes. Airport buses (Tusayan Shuttle) run hourly between Grand Canyon Village and the airport. Grand Canyon airport operates one car rental agency. Nava-Hopi Tours runs buses from Flagstaff to Grand Canyon Village on the South Rim. Amtrak train, Greyhound bus lines and several commuter airlines serve Flagstaff, Arizona.

The best way to reach the North Rim of Grand Canyon National Park is by car; no public transportation serves this remote location. The closest major airports are Salt Lake City, Nevada, 379 miles away or Las Vegas, Nevada, 276 miles away. Small commuter airlines and rental car agencies serve Page, Arizona, 119 miles away.

Getting around - shuttle services
Parking is limited at all viewpoints and near the hotels. Trailheads with rim to river trails are found at Hermits' Rest (Hermit and Boucher trails), near Bright Angel Lodge and Kolb Studio (Bright Angel Trail), Yaki Point (South Kaibab Trail), Grandview Point (Grandview Trail), Moran Point (New Hance Trail) and Lipan Point (Tanner Trail).

Parking, traffic and smog present serious problems in the summer months. The National Park Service encourages use of their spring and summer shuttle services. On the South Rim, buses serve the West Rim Road to Hermits' Rest, East Rim Drive to Yaki Point and the Village Loop. The Village Loop Shuttle stops at all major facilities within Grand Canyon Village. On the North Rim, a limited shuttle service runs between Grand Canyon Lodge.

A light rail system, planned to open in 2002, will serve Grand Canyon Village at the South Rim. Alternative fuel buses will connect you to viewpoints and some trailheads.

From May to October, Transcanyon Shuttle provides a bus service for the 215 mile, 4–5 hour trip between the North and the South Rim. The Transcanyon Shuttle bus leaves the North Rim in the morning and the South Rim in the early afternoon. Reservations (see Appendix B) are highly recommended.

Weather and seasons

The main seasons at the Grand Canyon are only loosely defined. The South Rim at 7,000 feet remains open all year and receives 15 inches of precipitation per year. Roads may be closed by snow from October to April due to treacherous icy sections. It can get very cold on the rim in winter, although mild temperatures predominate in the canyon. The least amount of precipitation falls during May and June. Weather patterns are fickle; snow may come and go, or it may stay on the ground all winter. Pleasant temperatures predominate on the rims in the late spring and autumn. Inner canyon temperatures begin to soar by late spring.

The North Rim, located at over 8,000 feet (2,438 metres), opens only from mid-May to late October. Mid-July to late-August thunderstorms mark the rainiest season; flash-flood dangers reach their peak during this time of year. The North Rim receives over 25 inches of precipitation in the average year and during the winter over 10 feet of snow may accumulate. You will need warm clothes in the evening anytime of the summer. When the hotel and concession services close in mid-October, day visitors are allowed until snow blocks the access road.

At the Colorado River at 2,400 feet (732 metres), only 8 inches of rain reach the canyon bottom each year. Raindrops often evaporate before they reach the ground. Unbearable temperatures reign in the Inner Canyon in summer and late spring. Early spring and autumn mark the most pleasant walking season. Winter can be pleasant and not too cold although the days are short and many trees lack their leaves.

Lodging

Reservations for camping or lodging on either the North or South Rim should be made months in advance. Don't expect to find lodging if you arrive without reservations. Especially during the spring, summer and autumn the Grand Canyon (particularly the South Rim) is overcrowded with people. Lodging and camping sites are very limited on the North Rim; it's a long drive to alternative accommodation. Contact AmFac Parks and Resorts for lodging reservations on the North or South Rim (see Appendix B).

On the South Rim, the Fred Harvey Company manages several choices of accommodation. You can choose between seven different

Average South Rim Temperatures and Precipitation
Grand Canyon National Park

	Max °F (°C)	Min °F (°C)	Precp ins (cm)
January	41 (4)	18 (-8)	1.3 (3.3)
February	45 (7)	21 (-7)	1.6 (4.1)
March	51 (10)	25 (-4)	1.4 (3.6)
April	60 (16)	32 (0)	0.9 (2.3)
May	70 (21)	39 (4)	0.7 (1.1)
June	81 (27)	47 (9)	0.4 (4.6)
July	84 (29)	54 (12)	1.8 (4.6)
August	82 (28)	53 (11)	2.2 (5.6)
September	76 (25)	47 (9)	1.6 (4.1)
October	65 (18)	36 (2)	1.1 (2.8)
November	52 (11)	27 (-2)	0.9 (2.3)
December	43 (7)	20 (-7)	1.6 (4.1)

Average North Rim Temperatures and Precipitation
Grand Canyon National Park

	Max °F (°C)	Min °F (°C)	Precp ins (cm)
January	37 (2)	16 (-9)	3.2 (8.1)
February	39 (3)	18 (-8)	3.2 (8.1)
March	44 (7)	21 (-6)	2.6 (6.6)
April	53 (11)	29 (-2)	1.7 (4.3)
May	62 (17)	34 (1)	1.2 (3.1)
June	73 (23)	40 (4)	0.9 (2.3)
July	77 (26)	46 (8)	1.9 (4.8)
August	75 (25)	45 (7)	2.8 (7.1)
September	69 (20)	39 (3)	2.0 (5.1)
October	59 (16)	31 (-1)	1.4 (3.6)
November	46 (8)	24 (-4)	1.5 (3.8)
December	40 (4)	20 (-7)	2.8 (7.1)

lodges in Grand Canyon Village: El Tovar Hotel, Bright Angel Lodge, Kachina Lodge, Maswik Lodge, Thunderbird Lodge and Yavapai Lodge. You'll find Moqui Lodge in Tusayan just outside the gate to the south entrance. The recently upgraded El Tovar Hotel, the canyon's masterpiece of architecture, sits majestically near the start of the Bright Angel Trail in the centre of Grand Canyon Village. Bright Angel Lodge and Maswik Lodge offer separate rustic cabins as well as lodge rooms. Several hotels and motels operate in Tusayan.

On the North Rim, the stately Grand Canyon Lodge provides lodging near the Rim. Designed by the architect Gilbert Stanley Underwood in 1928, this magnificent structure offers panoramic canyon views with luxury accommodation. Reservations should be made at least one year in advance.

Camping

The South Rim Mather Campground in Grand Canyon Village on the South Rim remains open all year. In summer, a first-come first-served campground operates at Desert View and a National Park Service campground opens in Tusayan, just outside the South Entrance.

North Rim Campground, 3 miles north of Grand Canyon Lodge near the General Store, opens from mid-May to mid-October. This pleasant, shaded campground offers a good alternative to a fully-booked hotel. Trans-canyon walkers are allowed to stay at North Rim Campground without a reservation.

Reservations are advised for Mather Campground from April to October and essential at North Rim Campground all summer.(See Appendix B for information on camping reservations.) Additional campgrounds are located a short drive away at Kaibab Lodge and 30 miles south in Jacob Lake, Arizona.

Visitor services

The South Rim Visitor Centre, 3 miles north of the South Rim Entrance Station, opens its bookstore daily and presents numerous slide shows. The Yavapai Museum at Yavapai Point chronicles a geologic history of the Grand Canyon. Tusayan Museum, near Desert View, presents an archaeological history of the Grand Canyon.

On the North Rim, the National Park Service Visitor Information Centre office and a bookstore run by the Grand Canyon Association operate next to Grand Canyon Lodge.

Interpretative programmes
The National Park Service offers several daily talks by rangers and junior programmes. *The Guide*, the National Park newspaper available when entering the park, lists specific hours and location of programmes.

Grand Canyon Association
The Grand Canyon Association, a non-profit organization, aids research, interpretation and education at the Grand Canyon National Park. Membership entitles you to their quarterly newsletter, discounts on purchases at all National Park visitor centres and on Grand Canyon Field Institute classes.

Grand Canyon Field Institute
The Grand Canyon Field Institute, a non-profit organization sponsored by the Grand Canyon Association and Grand Canyon National Park, presents educational programmes in the park. The Institute offers courses on geology, ecology, photography, human history, wilderness studies as well as women's classes. Many classes cater to backpackers, although some courses use mules or llamas to transport gear. Expert instructors, some known the world over for their knowledge of the Grand Canyon, lead trips.

Other facilities
The Grand Canyon Village on the South Rim supports a fully stocked general store, Babbitt's, a Post Office, dog kennel, medical clinic, visitor centre, trailer village, and the Backcountry Ranger Office (BRO). Summer automotive services include a petrol station, an automobile mechanic and towing services. A petrol station at Desert View opens in summer only. Nearby Tusayan supports year-round petrol stations and automobile repair shops.

On the North Rim, you will find a small general store, laundry and showers (near the campground), a Post Office in Grand Canyon Lodge, a petrol station, and a Backcountry Ranger Office (BRO).

Time zones
Grand Canyon National Park, entirely in the state of Arizona, remains on Mountain Standard Time (MST) all year.

CHAPTER 5

WALKING IN GRAND CANYON NATIONAL PARK

Leave it as it is. You cannot improve on it.
The ages have been at work on it, and man can only mar it.
Theodore Roosevelt

Introduction

One of the world's greatest scenic wonders, there is no other place on earth like the Grand Canyon. Most enjoy the park only from its viewpoints. The park's 1.2 million acres protect the canyon's 277 mile length. However, only walkers can truly experience and appreciate this great park.

Gone are the days when we can walk freely in many of the wilderness areas of the United States. The National Park Service strictly regulates backcountry visitation. Though the rules in the Grand Canyon National Park may seem excessive, this system allows miles of the canyon to remain as wilderness. Today's solitude in the backcountry exists because of these regulations.

Overnight Grand Canyon trips require careful planning. You must thoughtfully consider the amount of water and food needed, altitude gain and loss and water sources available. For many, canyon-walking will be a new experience and different than any you have enjoyed in other parts of the world. Many, caught under the Canyon's spell, return again and again.

Overnight backcountry permits and procedures

In order to prevent congestion and overuse of certain areas in the Grand Canyon National Park, a permit system has been established to regulate overnight hiking below the rim. Obtaining this permit requires considerable advance planning. The National Park Service issues approximately 16,000 permits for backpacking each year. Requests for permits exceed the number issued.

Write to the Backcountry Ranger Office (BRO) for the *Backcountry Trip Planner* to obtain up-to-date procedures on obtaining a permit

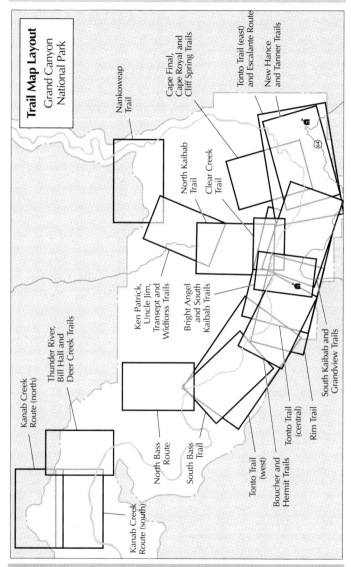

Trail Map Layout
Grand Canyon
National Park

Nankoweap Trail

Cape Final, Cape Royal and Cliff Spring Trails

Tonto Trail (east) and Escalante Route

New Hance and Tanner Trails

North Kaibab Trail

Clear Creek Trail

Ken Patrick, Uncle Jim, Transept and Widforss Trails

Bright Angel and South Kaibab Trails

Kanab Creek Route (north)

Thunder River, Bill Hall and Deer Creek Trails

North Bass Route

South Bass Trail

Tonto Trail (west)

Boucher and Hermit Trails

Tonto Trail (central)

Rim Trail

South Kaibab and Grandview Trails

Kanab Creek Route (south)

41

and help you with filing an application. Because changes in these procedures are made from time to time, only a general outline of how to obtain a permit will be included here.

At the time of writing, requests for backcountry permits are considered no earlier than the first day of the month, four months prior to the proposed starting date of your walk. Fax your request to the Backcountry Ranger Office (BRO) for your backcountry reservation on the first day of the correct month to ensure the maximum opportunity of obtaining the permit you wish (eg. for April permits write on December 1). To increase your chances of obtaining your permit, offer alternative starting dates and routes.

The Grand Canyon National Park web site can be found at www.thecanyon.com/nps, and provides limited information on permit procedures. This includes only the permit procedure for the popular Corridor trails and does not give information on how to obtain a permit in any other part of the Grand Canyon National Park.

A limited number of Corridor permits are available from the BRO on a last minute, "in-person" basis. They are available on a first-come first-served basis to anyone waiting in line at 8am at the BRO. The wait for a permit can be several days.

Fees
In 1997 the National Park Service instituted a backcountry use fee system for overnight camping below the rim. An initial charge for your permit and a small fee per person per night must be paid when you apply for your permit. The fee system covers the cost of longer hours at the BRO, additional patrols on Corridor trails, improved search and rescue services and educational displays.

Groups
Individual permits are issued for 1–6 people and large group permits for 7–11 people. Large groups are allotted fewer campsites than smaller groups.

Day-hiking
Day-hiking does not require a permit. For day-walking try the Hermit Trail to Dripping Springs or Santa Maria Spring, the Grandview Trail to Horseshoe Mesa and the South Kaibab Trail to Cedar Ridge or Skeleton Point.

The scenic South Kaibab Trail, much less crowded than the

neighbouring Bright Angel Trail, supports superb views from its ridge line. For day-walkers in good condition a superb 6–7 hour, 13.4 mile day-walk descends the South Kaibab to the Tipoff, turns west on the Tonto Trail past Pipe Spring and continues west for 4.2 miles to Indian Garden. Ascend to the South Rim on the Bright Angel Trail.

Limited day hiking above the South Rim is confined to the 9 mile Rim Trail and a shorter, but splendid, walk to Shoshone Point.

From the main North Rim Village only the North Kaibab Trail, following a creek bed with limited views, drops below the rim. Several North Rim day-walks such as the Widforss or Cape Final Trails provide a cooler alternative to the North Kaibab Trail. Do not miss the short walks to the spectacular viewpoints of Cape Royal and Bright Angel Point. See section 9 for a description of the Grand Canyon Rim Walks.

Trip planning

Though summer is the most popular time to visit the Grand Canyon, it is not the optimal season for a visit. American family and European vacation visitors peak at this time. In addition to the unbearable heat, trails, hotels, parking and access roads are horribly overcrowded. Spring and autumn bring fewer visitors and cooler temperatures. Winter trips are less popular. Although winter inner canyon temperatures are reasonable, heavy rain or snow can make canyon access difficult or dangerous. Corridor Trails offer the safest routes into the inner canyon during the winter.

Corridor trails

The three Corridor trails, the North and South Kaibab and Bright Angel trails, make up the only maintained and patrolled trails in the canyon. They are linked by the Black Bridge and the Silver Suspension Bridge that span the Colorado River near Bright Angel Campground and Phantom Ranch.

Wild camping is not allowed along the Corridor trails. If you are planning to stay at Bright Angel Campground (next to Phantom Ranch). Indian Garden, or Cottonwood Campground you must have a backcountry permit. These heavily used Corridor campsites, with water, toilets, telephones, buildings and rangers in residence, detract from the wilderness experience of walking in the Grand Canyon.

First-timers on cross-canyon trips

The National Park Service recommends that first time walkers in the Grand Canyon use the Corridor trails (North and South Kaibab and Bright Angel). One of the most popular walks from the South Rim descends the South Kaibab Trail to Bright Angel Campground and Phantom Ranch and ascends back to the South Rim via Indian Garden on the Bright Angel Trail (South Kaibab to Bright Angel Trail). The South Kaibab is recommended for descending to Phantom Ranch due to its quick access and splendid ridge views. The longer but more gradual Bright Angel Trail eases your ascent back to Grand Canyon Village. There is no water on the South Kaibab Trail but the Bright Angel Trail supports year-round water sources. (See section 6 for descriptions of South Rim, Rim to River trails.)

Popular trips from the North Rim descend the North Kaibab Trail to Phantom Ranch and Bright Angel Campground, cross the Colorado River on one of the suspension bridges and ascend on the Bright Angel Trail to Grand Canyon Village on the South Rim (North Kaibab to Bright Angel Trail). This cross-canyon venture is only possible from May to October when the North Rim is open. May, September and October are the best months for this trip; summer can be unbearably hot. Ironically, this overcrowded cross-canyon trip uses two of the canyon's least scenic and busiest trails. Transcanyon Shuttle services (see below under Shuttle Services) connect the South and North Rims.

Other overnight trips into the Canyon from the North Rim Village descend to Cottonwood Campground. A recommended layover day can include a trip to Ribbon Falls or, for the hardy, a walk all the way to the Colorado River. On the third day ascend back to the North Rim.

Although the National Park Service recommends that first time walkers use the Corridor Trails, I feel that experienced walkers can handle some non-maintained trails in the Grand Canyon. Try the Hermit to Bright Angel Loop or the Grandview to South Kaibab trails (see section 10, Grand Canyon National Park, Long Distance Trails). A day-walk on any of the Corridor trails tests your ability to handle one of these more difficult alternatives.

Lodging at Phantom Ranch

Phantom Ranch, located near the Colorado River at the junction of the South Kaibab, North Kaibab and Bright Angel trails, can be reached by mule or on foot. Offering the only accommodation inside the canyon, reservations for cabins and same-sex dormitories should be reserved up to one year in advance through AmFac Parks and Resorts. Space is extremely limited. Phantom Ranch provides meals, towels, bedding and pillows, soap and shower facilities. Meals must be reserved in advance. You do not need a backcountry permit if you are staying at Phantom Ranch.

Children are welcome at Phantom Ranch, but are discouraged during summer and winter due to extreme temperatures and its remote location. Families with children up to five years of age are limited to cabin use only.

Snacks, beverages, and very limited supplies are sold at the Phantom Ranch canteen. Phantom Ranch is thought to sell the best lemonade in the Canyon. Summer high temperatures average 103 °F (40 °C) but can reach 120 °F (48 °C). Mail sent from Phantom Ranch is postmarked "Mailed by mule from the bottom of the Canyon". For a fee, mules will transport your duffels out of the canyon between Phantom Ranch and the South Rim Village. Reservations for duffel transport can be made at the Bright Angel Lodge on the South Rim or at Phantom Ranch.

Shuttle services

On the South Rim, distant East Rim trailheads such as Grandview Point (Grandview Trail), Moran Point (New Hance Trail), and Lipan Point (Tanner Trail) can be reached by private car, taxi, or Fred Harvey bus tours. Shuttle buses serve Yaki Point (South Kaibab Trail). From spring through to autumn, you must take the West Rim Drive shuttle bus service to Hermits' Rest. During the rest of the year you can reach Hermits' Rest by private car, bus tours and taxi. From the Grand Canyon Lodge at the North Rim, a hiker's shuttle serves the North Kaibab car park. Contact Transcanyon Shuttle (see Appendix B) for information on rim to rim transportation.

Maps

Maps are published by the United States Geological Survey (USGS) and several private publishers. The larger scale USGS 7.5 minute maps are useful for off-trail hiking. The USGS no longer publishes the 15 minute map series; some old-timers still use them. Other maps available are the Trails Illustrated Grand Canyon National Park (TI)(1:73530), Earthwalk Press Grand Canyon National Park (EP)(1:48000) and Bright Angel Trail Hiking Map and Guide (EP)(1:24000). The waterproof and tear proof Trails Illustrated map shows the Backcountry Management Zones (see below). The Kaibab National Forest, North Kaibab Ranger District Map published by the United States Forest Service (USFS) is essential for reaching Sowats Point and Indian Hollow Campground (Kanab Canyon to Thunder River trailheads), Saddle Mountain (Nankoweap Trailhead), and Swamp Point (North Bass Trailhead). Use the Kaibab National Forest, Tusayan District (USFS) map to reach the South Bass trailhead.

USGS maps are available at Babbitt's General Store at the South Rim in Grand Canyon Village, neighbouring outdoor shops in Flagstaff and Page, Arizona, and Willow Bank Bookstore and Bureau of Land Management (BLM) in Kanab, Utah. United States Geological Survey (USGS) maps may also be purchased from their office in Denver, Colorado (see Appendix B). The Grand Canyon Association, North Rim and South Rim visitor centres and many local stores carry the Earthwalk Press (EP) map, Trails Illustrated (TI) map, and the Bright Angel Trail Hiking Map and Guide (EP) but do not stock the USGS maps. The Kaibab National Forest Service map (USFS) is available at neighbouring outdoor shops and petrol stations, at the North Kaibab Ranger Station in Fredonia, Arizona or at the Tusayan Ranger Station in Tusayan, Arizona.

Backcountry Management Zones

The National Park Service has developed a system of backcountry 'zones' to classify areas of the park by accessibility and usage. Each use area allows for a defined number of overnight campers depending on its size, topography, number of available camps and ecological sensitivity. You will need to designate use areas when you apply for your permit.

The National Park Service notes the zones as follows:

Corridor zone:	recommended for first time hikers. Purified water. Paved roads to trailheads. Toilets, signs, and emergency stations.
Threshold zone:	for experienced Grand Canyon hikers. Dirt roads to trailheads. Water needs purification. Pit toilets.
Primitive zones:	for highly experienced Grand Canyon hikers. Non-maintained roads and routes, "four-wheel drive" roads to trailheads. Occasional developments.
Wild zones:	only for very fit and highly experienced Grand Canyon hikers. Indistinct to non-existent routes require route finding ability. Water may be non-existent. No development.

Primitive and Wild zones are not recommended for use during the summer due to high temperatures and lack of reliable water sources.

Trail categories

Trails vary from the maintained Corridor trails to rocky, slippery and steep non-maintained trails. In the early days, these trails were used by Indians to transport metal from mines. Later the white man would guide tourists on the trails from the rim to the river. Years ago these same trails were used so little that they were faint and difficult to find. Today with more walkers in the remote areas of the Grand Canyon, these same trails are now maintained by the walkers who use them.

I have classified each trail according to the following criteria:

Rim Trail:	these easy, well-signed, and busy trails are on either the North or South Rim. There is little to no elevational change. These high-use trails may be paved or have wheelchair access.
Corridor Trail:	the Corridor trails (Bright Angel and North and South Kaibab trails) are maintained, busy and patrolled backcountry trails and make up

the main cross-canyon trail system. Paths are wide, well-signed and often have emergency telephones, water (North Kaibab and Bright Angel trails only) and rangers in residence. These trails are recommended for walkers without previous Grand Canyon experience.

Wilderness Trail: these unmaintained trails are not patrolled and require route-finding, map and compass and scrambling skills. Moderate exposure exists on trails. Prior Grand Canyon-hiking experience is recommended.

Route: these off-trail routes are indistinct, difficult to follow, require scrambling and may be obscured by brush. Extremely rugged terrain predominates. Use of ropes or other aid may be necessary. Water may not be available. A high level of fitness, extensive Grand Canyon-walking experience, and careful pre-trip planning is required.

Waymarking
Waymarking is excellent on the maintained corridor trails. On unmaintained trails in the primitive and threshold zones, signposts may be lacking and trails faded or non-existent.

Camping regulations
I have summarized the following park regulations from National Park Service literature:

1   Your permit is valid only for the date, time, leader and size indicated on the front. To request changes in the permit you must return it to the Backcountry Ranger Office (BRO).

2   You must use a backcountry stove; no fires are allowed.

3   In the summer, carry 1 gallon (4 litres) of water per person per day. All water sources must be purified.

4   Keep food away from animals. Use food storage tins at Cottonwood, Bright Angel, and Indian Garden Campgrounds.

5   Pack out all trash. "Pack it in, pack it out."

6   Use toilets where available.

7   If toilets are not available, defecate at least 100 feet (30 metres) from water. When near the river, urinate directly into the river.

8   An Arizona state fishing license is required for all fishing.

9   No pets are allowed in the backcountry or below the rim.

10   Do not alter campsites in any way. Choose previously used sites. Do not camp in drainage during the rain/flood season.

11   Stay on the main trails; do not cut switchbacks.

Water sources
Except along Corridor trails water can be scarce to non-existent. In hot weather, carry the minimum of 1 gallon (4 litres) or more of water per person per day. Primitive and Wild zones are not recommended for use during the summer due to high temperatures and lack of reliable water sources.

On Corridor trails, purified drinking water is available at Phantom Ranch, Bright Angel Campground, and Indian Garden all year. Seasonal water can be found from May to October at Cottonwood Campground and Roaring Springs on the North Kaibab Trail and at Mile-and-a-Half Resthouse and Three Mile Resthouse on the Bright Angel Trail. All other water, including that obtained from the Colorado River and Bright Angel Creek, should be purified.

Always ask the BRO about available water sources. Depending on the year, some usually reliable water sources may be dry. Pay attention to their advice.

Search and rescue
The Corridor trails make up the Canyon's only patrolled trails. Most of the 400 rescues per year involve first time canyon walkers on Corridor trails. Over 1,000 visitors each year are treated for heat related illness; many more incidents go unreported. Take a close look at the temperature chart (see Grand Canyon National Park: Average Rim Temperatures and Inner Canyon Temperatures) before

Year Round Water Sources
Grand Canyon National Park

Boucher Creek
Bright Angel Creek
Buck Farm Creek
Clear Creek
Colorado Creek
Crystal Creek
Dripping Springs
Garden Creek
Grapevine Creek
Hance Creek
Haunted Creek
Havasu Creek
Hermit Creek
Little Colorado River

Kanab Creek
Miner's (Page) Spring
Monument Creek
Nankoweap Creek
Olo Creek
Pipe Creek
Phantom Creek
Royal Arch Creek
Santa Maria Spring
Shinumo Creek
Tapeats Creek
Thunder River
Vasey's Paradise

departing on your walk. Avoid the heat between 10am and 4pm; take advantage of shade. Carry 1 gallon (4 litres) of water per day or more in the summer months. Remember it takes twice as long to hike out of the canyon as it does to hike into the canyon. Do not plan on being rescued and travel prepared.

Visiting archaeological sites

As you explore the Grand Canyon, you may come across old archaeological sites invaluable to the understanding of long-ago inhabitants of the Grand Canyon. Vandalism or theft of park cultural or archaeological resources is a violation of federal law. The following House Rules are taken from National Park Service (NPS) literature:

1   Keep your feet off the furniture. Archaeological sites are fragile.
2   Don't eat in the living room. No picnicking at or near archaeological sites.
3   No slumber parties. Camping in ruins or sites is forbidden.
4   Don't touch the paintings. Human oils damage the pictographs.
5   Don't pee in the parlour – or any other site.
6   Don't go in if you're not invited. Many sites are closed to visitors.
7   Don't rearrange the furniture or mess with the knick knacks. Leave everything as you found it.
8   Tell mum if you see anything wrong. Contact a ranger if you see any violation of these rules.

Tour aircraft and river-runners

Intrusions into the quiet of the Grand Canyon occur mainly from tour aircraft. On a nice day, few parts of the canyon are safe from engine noise. The Boucher and the Nankoweap trails lie below main airway routes. Through the years there have been many complaints about noise from engine drone of the flights above the canyon. Flights below the rim were banned some years ago. The National Park is working to try to limit flights and restore some of the canyon's natural quiet.

You may share a beach with river-runners. Private rafters have waited several years and paid high fees for the privilege of running the canyon. Commercial rafts vary from the huge motor-powered "banana" boats to quieter and smaller oar-powered boats. Many clients on these commercial trips are enjoying their first wilderness experience. River-runners often share beer and food with hungry backpackers and can sometimes provide emergency assistance. It is fun to stop and chat with these visitors. Remember, you are all here for the same reason.

Mules

Mule trains will pass you on Corridor trails. Large steps are built into these trails to minimize erosion from the hooves of the animals. Trails used by mules are dusty in summer, muddy in winter, and smelly all year long. When you see mules approaching stand quietly on the uphill side of the trail, give them the right of way and obey the instructions of the lead rider.

Insects, reptiles and mammals

Several species of rattlesnake call the Grand Canyon home. The rose colour of the pink rattlesnake, endemic to the Grand Canyon, may have been developed to help them blend in with the red canyon walls. Walkers can surprise rattlesnakes when the creatures are resting in the shade under a bush or rock trying to escape the midday heat. Do not place your hands or feet in places you cannot see; be careful when stepping over boulders or trees.

Scorpions can enter the warmth of your boots, clothes, or sleeping bag; shake them out before using. Be sure to wear shoes in camp and do not leave your boots outside your tent at night. Stinging red ants follow crumbs of food; irritating bites are common. Camp away from anthills and refrain from throwing scraps of food around.

Rodents such as squirrels and mice bite into packs. Be sure to protect packs by hanging them with their pockets open on the overhead wires or using metal boxes provided at Corridor campgrounds. Over recent years these troublesome rodents have become increasingly bold sometimes chewing through ropes with sacks of food hanging from them. Never store or sleep with your food inside your tent.

Inner Canyon Temperatures and Precipitation
Grand Canyon National Park

	Max °F (°C)	Min °F (°C)	Precp ins (cm)
January	56 (13)	36 (2)	0.7 (1.8)
February	62 (17)	42 (6)	0.8 (2.0)
March	71 (21)	48 (9)	0.8 (2.0)
April	82 (28)	56 (13)	0.5 (1.3)
May	92 (33)	63 (17)	0.4 (1.0)
June	101 (38)	72 (22)	0.3 (0.7)
July	106 (41)	78 (26)	0.8 (2.0)
August	103 (38)	75 (25)	1.4 (3.6)
September	97 (37)	69 (20)	1.0 (2.5)
October	84 (29)	58 (14)	0.7 (1.8)
November	68 (20)	46 (8)	0.4 (1.0)
December	57 (13)	37 (3)	0.9 (2.3)

Heat

Grand Canyon temperatures at the river in July average over 106 °F (41 °C). At times temperatures peak as high as 120 °F (48 °C). Heat will increase as you descend; generally it is 20 or 30 °F (11 °C) warmer by the river than at the rim. There can be little to no shade. In hot weather, try walking early in the morning and early evening and rest in the shade during the hottest part of the day. Better yet, do not visit in summer. Spring and autumn bring fewer visitors and moderate temperatures.

Other Grand Canyon dangers

You can accidentally be stabbed by the painful spines of yucca and cactus plants. Especially in the late summer months, flash flood danger exists in the canyon. Thunder clouds unleash intense storms miles away leading to torrents of water rushing down side canyons. Canyon bottoms should not be used as campsites during flash-flood season, from July to early September. Flash floods are known to occur at other times of year. In this book, areas prone to flash flood dangers are: Jumpup Canyon, Kanab Creek, the side canyons to Bright Angel such as Phantom Canyon, and the creek beds along the Escalante Route. In September 1997, two people were killed in Phantom Creek near Phantom Ranch and Bright Angel Campground was evacuated due to concern about rising waters.

Warning

The Grand Canyon supports one of the harshest, most unforgiving environments in the world. Every year hikers die in the Grand Canyon. Temperatures soar to the extremes; water is scarce to non-existent. Even for experienced hikers, slippery, steep trails provide treacherous footing. Be careful in planning your trip; heed all warnings in this book; obey National Park Service rules and regulations; use common sense. Always carry a map and compass; know how to use them. Do not expect the park service to rescue you. Be responsible for your own safety and you will enjoy the trip of a lifetime.

Deer Creek Canyon, Grand Canyon National Park

CHAPTER 6

GRAND CANYON NATIONAL PARK: SOUTH RIM, RIM TO RIVER TRAILS

The Grand Canyon seems a gigantic statement for even nature to make.
John Muir

Introduction

Two maintained rim to river trails, the South Kaibab and the Bright Angel trails and six other unmaintained rim to river trails provide the major access from the South Rim into the Grand Canyon. These trails are described here from east to west from the South Bass Trail to the Tanner Trail. The Grandview, not a true rim to river trail, provides poor access to the Colorado River. Horseshoe Mesa, at the end of the Grandview Trail, makes splendid destination for an overnight hike.

In order of increasing difficulty the trails are: Bright Angel, Grandview, South Kaibab, Hermit, South Bass, Tanner, Boucher, and New Hance. Trails described are accessible and reasonable to walk all year only if there are available water sources on the way.

SOUTH RIM, RIM TO RIVER TRAILS

Trail	Distance Miles One way	Distance Kilometres One Way	Rating	Difficulty
South Bass Trail	8.0	12.8	Wilderness	Strenuous
Boucher Trail	10.5	16.5	Wilderness	Ex. strenuous
Hermit Trail	8.9	14.2	Wilderness	Moderate
Bright Angel Trail	8.9	14.2	Corridor	Moderate
Grandview Trail	3.0	4.8	Wilderness	Moderate
Hermit Trail	8.9	14.2	Wilderness	Moderate
South Kaibab Trail	6.3	10.1	Corridor	Moderate
South Bass Trail	8.0	12.8	Wilderness	Strenuous
Tanner Trail	9.0	14.4	Wilderness	Ex Strenuous
Boucher Trail	10.5	16.5	Wilderness	Ex. Strenuous
New Hance Trail	8.0	12.8	Wilderness	Ex. Strenuous

The Hermit Trail and Bright Angel trails, with perennial (year-round) water sources, are described as "all year" trails. If there is no water available along the way, I recommend foregoing summer trips, such as the South Kaibab Trail. Time estimates vary widely depending on the direction travelled (ascent or descent), terrain, season, temperature and condition of the trail, as well as on the strength of the party.

SOUTH BASS TRAIL

Start:	South Bass Trailhead at Bass Camp (6,650 feet/2,027 metres)
End:	Bass Rapids (2,250 feet/686 metres)
Distance, one way:	8 miles (12.8 kilometres)
Times, one way:	4–5 hours down, 5–7 hours up
Maps:	Havasupai Point (United States Geological Survey 7.5'); Grand Canyon National Park (TI); Kaibab National Forest: Tusayan, Williams, and Chanlender Ranger Districts (United States Forest Service)
Season:	spring and autumn
Water:	Colorado River
Rating:	strenuous

William Bass, best known for his tireless trail building in the 1880s, prospected the area around the South Bass Trail. Bass improved an original Indian trail and extended it to the river in order to take tourists across the river to the north side.

The South Bass Trail starts at Bass Camp, 29 miles west of Grand Canyon Village on Rowe Well Road and 4 miles north of Pasture Wash Ranger Station on Forest Service Road 328. The drive takes about 2–3 hours from Grand Canyon Village. You will find the Kaibab National Forest map indispensable. This unmaintained, rutted road can flood any time of year; high clearance four-wheel drive vehicles are mandatory.

From West Rim Drive proceed 0.1 mile south of Bright Angel Lodge and turn left onto Rowe Well Road. If West Rim Drive is closed, drive from Bright Angel Lodge to Maswik Lodge and then

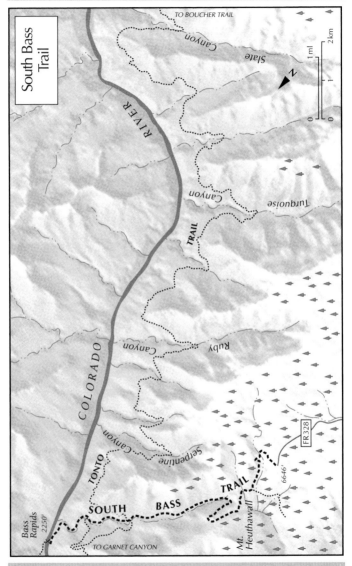

South Bass Trail

TO BOUCHER TRAIL

Slate Canyon

2 km

1 ml

N

COLORADO RIVER

Turquoise Canyon

TRAIL

Ruby Canyon

Serpentine Canyon

TONTO Canyon

SOUTH BASS TRAIL

Bass Rapids 2250'

TO GARNET CANYON

Mt. Heuthawall

Heuthawall

6646'

FR 328

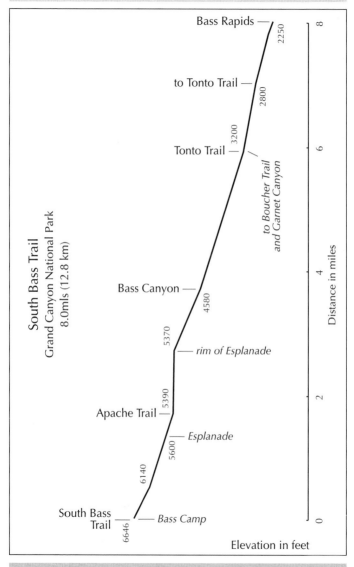

South Bass Trail
Grand Canyon National Park
8.0mls (12.8 km)

Bass Rapids — 2250

to Tonto Trail — 2800

3200
Tonto Trail — 3200

to Boucher Trail
and Garnet Canyon

Bass Canyon — 4580

5370
— rim of Esplanade

5390
Apache Trail — 5390

5600
— Esplanade

6140

South Bass Trail — Bass Camp
6646

Distance in miles

Elevation in feet

to the Kennels. Take several right 90° turns to reach Rowe Well Road heading south. Or, from Tusayan just south of Moqui Lodge turn west onto FR 328 and go west to Rowe Well Road.

Back on Rowe Well Road the pavement soon ends as you enter Kaibab National Forest. Follow this road across several railroad tracks. In 1 mile meet FR 328 and turn right to Pasture Wash. Drive almost 16 miles from the FR 328 intersection, enter the Indian Reservation and proceed for 1.8 miles. Turn right onto a poor dirt road to Pasture Wash. Exit the Indian Reservation and re-enter Kaibab National Forest and, as the road deteriorates even more, pass by the unstaffed Pasture Wash Ranger Station. The road continues 3.5 miles farther to the South Bass trailhead. You can camp at the road head if you have obtained a backcountry permit for this use area.

Directions
From Bass Camp head east through the Kaibab and Toroweap formation to reach an eastern drainage. Descend steeply through the Coconino Sandstone to the terraced Esplanade. The Apache Trail joins from the west 1.5 miles from the start. Following the cairns, continue 1 mile north across the flat Esplanade to the east of Mt. Huethawli. Turn south and descend steeply off the Esplanade through the Supai to the head of Bass Canyon. Next, double back through the Redwall.

Criss-crossing a wash, remain east of the Bass Canyon drainage and follow the bushy trail to the Tonto Trail junction. Drop down to a creek bed just before the Tonto Trail turn-offs. First the Tonto Trail branches west and shortly another turn-off veers east. Another mile down the creek you cross another connecting trail that turns west to join the Tonto Trail. Continue down the creek bed to lower Bass Canyon. Pools of water can be found here in the spring. Nearer the river your route turns west from the drainage and reaches a cairn that marks your descent to a beach above Bass Rapids. The map shows a route that heads farther west for 0.5 mile to a beach at the head of Shinumo Rapids. Both beaches are popular with river-runners.

BOUCHER TRAIL

Start:	Hermit Trailhead at Hermits' Rest (6,640

	feet/2,023 metres)
End:	Boucher Rapids (2,320 feet/707 metres)
Distance, one way:	Hermits' Rest to Boucher Rapids, 10.5 miles (16.9 kilometres)
Times, one way:	6–8 hours down, 8–10 hours up
Maps:	Grand Canyon (United States Geological Survey 7.5'); Grand Canyon National Park (TI); Grand Canyon National Park (EP)
Season:	autumn, winter and spring
Water:	Dripping Springs, Boucher Creek, Boucher Rapids
Rating:	extremely strenuous

The Boucher Trail was originally named the Silver Bell Trail by its founder Louis Boucher who lived near the river along Boucher Creek. He built a cabin at Dripping Springs and prospected granite in the 1890s.

The Hermit Trail, which connects to the Boucher Trail, starts at the far west end of the Hermits' Rest car park, 9 miles along West Rim Road from Grand Canyon Village. In summer, shuttle buses ferry you to Hermits' Rest. Drive your car to the road head during other times of the year.

The Boucher Trail, one the Canyon's steepest and grandest, starts 2.5 miles from Hermits' Rest along the Hermit Trail. The Boucher Trail itself measures 8 miles from it start near Dripping Springs to the Colorado River. If you start walking from Hermits' Rest and plan to go all the way to the Colorado River, you've got a long 10.5 mile day ahead of you. The popularity of canyon-walking has changed a faint route into an obvious trail. Only experienced, sure-footed and fit walkers should attempt this trail.

Directions

To reach the Boucher Trailhead, descend the Hermit Trail into the Hermit Basin down the rocky steps for 1 mile until the Waldron Trail branches south. Continue straight ahead or west on the Hermit Trail and descend 0.5 mile more to reach the Dripping Springs Trail Junction. Here the Hermit Trail bends north. Turn west on the Dripping Springs Trail and continue for 1 mile to the junction of the Boucher and the Dripping Springs Trail. This part of the trail passes

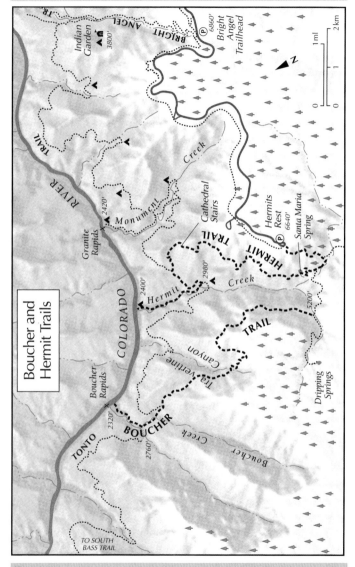

Boucher and
Hermit Trails

BRIGHT ANGEL TR.

Indian
Garden
3800'

6860'
Bright
Angel
Trailhead

Creek

RIVER TRAIL

Cathedral
Stairs

Monument

2420'

Granite
Rapids

HERMIT TRAIL

Hermits
Rest
6640'

Santa Maria
Spring

COLORADO

2400'

Hermit

2980'

Creek

5200'

TRAIL

Travertine Canyon

Dripping
Springs

Boucher
Rapids

2320'×

BOUCHER

TONTO

2760'

Boucher Creek

TO SOUTH
BASS TRAIL

N

2 km
1 ml
1
0
0

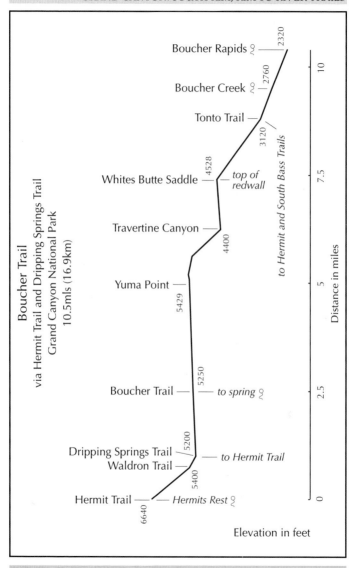

Boucher Rapids ⚲ ― 2320

Boucher Creek ⚲ ― 2760

Tonto Trail ― 3120 / *to Hermit and South Bass Trails*

Whites Butte Saddle ― 4528 / *top of redwall*

Travertine Canyon ― 4400

Yuma Point ― 5429

Boucher Trail ― 5250 / *to spring* ⚲

Dripping Springs Trail ― 5200 / *to Hermit Trail*

Waldron Trail ― 5400

Hermit Trail ― 6640 / *Hermits Rest* ⚲

Boucher Trail
via Hermit Trail and Dripping Springs Trail
Grand Canyon National Park
10.5mls (16.9km)

Distance in miles

Elevation in feet

10

7.5

5

2.5

0

high above Hermit Creek on a long and lovely traverse. An excellent 6 mile round trip day-hike from Hermits' Rest goes to Dripping Springs.

The Boucher Trail officially starts from the Dripping Springs Trail junction. Dripping Springs, 300 vertical feet and 0.5 mile from this trail junction, supports the only water near the trail. Since the round trip to Dripping Springs will take you 45 minutes, you may wish to carry all your water you will need from the start.

From the start of the Boucher Trail, follow the Supai formation 2.5 miles to Yuma Point. Not for the acrophobic, this spectacular section merits special care in winter due to ice. There is no true exposure although some steep cliffs grace the eastern edges of the trail. You will find a fine, dry camping spot on Yuma Point just where the trail circles around the point and turns south-west.

For the next mile cross west around Yuma Point before you descend steeply on a very rocky trail through the Supai. Some short sections before Travertine Canyon require scrambling. The trail continues to the west of Travertine Canyon and ascends to Whites Butte, a fine but dry camping spot.

Pass west of Whites Butte and north-west of the saddle and descend steeply through the loose Redwall scree for your last jarring descent to meet the Tonto Trail. From this junction, turn west and continue 0.3 miles to the camping area at Boucher Creek. Continue 1.5 miles farther down rocky Boucher Creek to reach Boucher Rapids at the Colorado River.

HERMIT TRAIL

Start:	Hermit Trailhead at Hermits' Rest (6,640 feet/ 2,023 metres)
End:	Hermit Rapids (2,400 feet/732 metres)
Distance, one way:	8.9 miles (14.2 kilometres)
Times, one way:	5–6 hours down, 6–7 hours up
Maps:	Grand Canyon (United States Geological Survey 7.5'); Grand Canyon National Park (TI); Grand Canyon National Park (EP)
Season:	all year

Kanab Creek at the Colorado River, Grand Canyon National Park

Thunder River Trail, Grand Canyon National Park

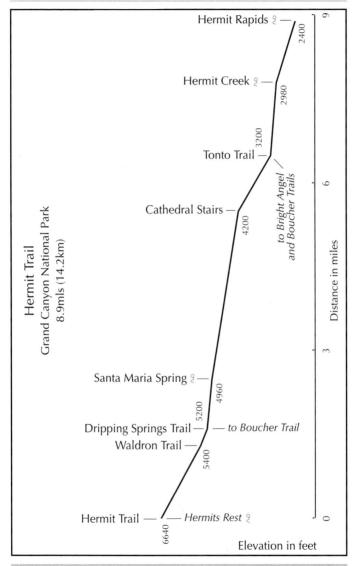

Hermit Rapids ⚲ — 2400

Hermit Creek ⚲ — 2980

3200

Tonto Trail —

to Bright Angel and Boucher Trails

Cathedral Stairs — 4200

Santa Maria Spring ⚲ — 4960

5200

Dripping Springs Trail — *to Boucher Trail*

Waldron Trail — 5400

Hermit Trail — — *Hermits Rest* ⚲ 6640

Hermit Trail
Grand Canyon National Park
8.9mls (14.2km)

Distance in miles

9 6 3 0

Elevation in feet

Water: Santa Maria Spring; Hermit Creek, Colorado River

Rating: moderate

The Hermit Trail was originally constructed in 1896 and improved with cobblestone inlay in the early 1900s. It was extended in 1913 to bypass the tolls charged by Ralph Cameron on the Bright Angel Trail. The Santa Fe railroad built an overnight station at Hermit Camp. You will find remains of the camp in spite of the National Park Service plan to remove the partially torn down stone corrals and cabins.

Walkers with some canyon-walking under their boots on the Bright Angel or Kaibab Trails often graduate to the Hermit Trail. The well-graded, wide and rocky but heavily travelled Hermit Trail resembles a maintained trail, although rock slides on the path of the trail require scrambling in several sections. The Hermit, Tonto and Bright Angel trails connect into a popular overnight trip. More experienced walkers will enjoy the more remote Boucher to Hermit Loop.

Directions

The Hermit Trail starts from Hermits' Rest, 9 miles west of Grand Canyon Village along the West Rim Road. Shuttle buses serve Hermits' Rest during the summer.

From the directional sign at the west end of the Hermits' Rest car park the trail switchbacks west down a rocky staircase to the Hermit Basin. Here the trail, constructed in cobblestone switchbacks known as White ZigZags, passes through the Coconino Sandstone. In a little over 1 mile, and a 1,300 foot drop, the Waldron Trail branches south. The Hermit Trail continues east and in 0.3 mile you reach the Dripping Springs and Hermit Trail junction at the head of the Hermit drainage.

Proceeding north-east from the junction, descend through the Supai over several long traverses to Santa Maria Spring, 2.5 miles from Hermits' Rest. This rewarding day-walk presents you with tremendous views down the Hermit drainage. The 1913 shelter provides welcome shade and water during the summer. In autumn, check with the BRO regarding water at Santa Maria Spring. Late in the year, the amount of water available may be just a trickle. The Redwall Narrows of Hermit Creek are visible 1,000 feet below the spring. To the west you can see Yuma Point, Dripping Springs and the general route of the Boucher Trail.

Continue to descend farther through the Supai to the top of Cathedral Stairs. Many boulders and rock slides block the trail in this section and you will have to scramble through piles of rocks. The trail remains easy to follow.

Next criss-cross through the Redwall on the switchbacks to Cathedral Stairs to below Cope Butte. The descent lessens as you reach the Tonto Trail junction. Turn west and go 1 mile to the designated campsites at Hermit Creek. Hermit Creek, south of the campsites, merits exploration with its pools, waterfalls and spring wildflowers.

Back on the Tonto Trail, a sign just before Hermit Creek Camp ground directs you to a short cut to Hermit Rapids. If you are lucky to have a reservation for Hermit Rapids, follow the creek bed north from Hermit Creek Campground or from the Tonto Trail sign, around 1.5 miles to the Colorado River. The high waves of Hermit Rapids provide one of the Canyon's best rides.

BRIGHT ANGEL TRAIL

Start:	Bright Angel Trailhead at Kolb Studio (6,860 feet/2,091 metres)
End:	Silver Suspension Bridge at the Colorado River (2,440 feet/744 metres)
Distance, one way:	8.9 miles (14.2 kilometres)
Times, one way:	4–5 hours down, 5–7 hours up
Maps:	Phantom Ranch, Grand Canyon (United States Geological Survey 7.5'); Grand Canyon National Park (TI); Grand Canyon National Park (EP)
Season:	all year
Water:	Indian Garden, Colorado River, Bright Angel Campground (year round). Mile-and-a-Half Resthouse and Three Mile Resthouse (May to September only)
Rating:	moderate

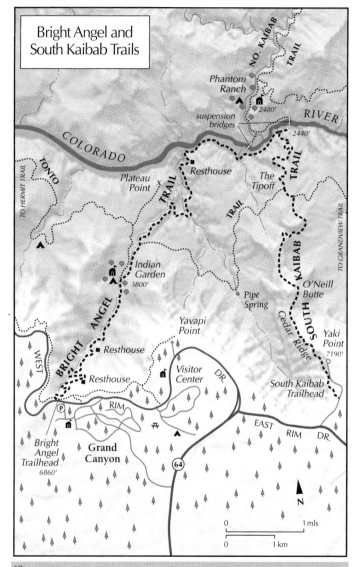

Bright Angel and
South Kaibab Trails

NO. KAIBAB TRAIL

Phantom
Ranch
2480'

suspension
bridges

COLORADO

RIVER
2440'

TONTO TRAIL

TO HERMIT TRAIL

Plateau
Point

Resthouse

The
Tipoff

TRAIL

TO GRANDVIEW TRAIL

Indian
Garden
3800'

Pipe
Spring

KAIBAB

O'Neill
Butte

Yavapi
Point

Cedar Ridge

SOUTH

Yaki
Point
7190'

BRIGHT ANGEL

WEST

Resthouse

Resthouse

Visitor
Center

DR.

South Kaibab
Trailhead

P

RIM

EAST RIM DR.

Bright
Angel
Trailhead
6860'

Grand
Canyon

64

N

0   1 mls

0   1 km

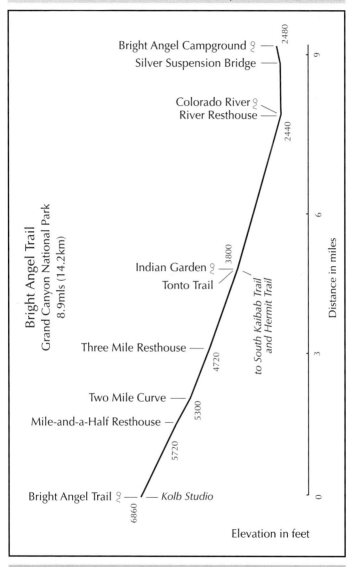

Bright Angel Trail
Grand Canyon National Park
8.9mls (14.2km)

Bright Angel Campground — 2480

Silver Suspension Bridge —

Colorado River — 2440
River Resthouse —

Indian Garden — 3800
Tonto Trail

to South Kaibab Trail
and Hermit Trail

Three Mile Resthouse — 4720

Two Mile Curve — 5300

Mile-and-a-Half Resthouse —

5720

Bright Angel Trail — Kolb Studio
6860

Distance in miles

9

6

3

0

Elevation in feet

Following the Bright Angel Fault, the Bright Angel Trail was originally used by Indians to reach the springs at Indian Garden. Indian pictographs grace a rock face just above Two Mile Corner. Prospectors improved the original trail in 1890s. In 1903, when owner Ralph Cameron started charging each visitor for usage, trails were built in other parts of the canyon to avoid the toll. In 1928 ownership of the trail passed to the National Park Service and was renamed the Bright Angel Trail in 1937.

Well marked for its entire length, this popular trail provides the easiest access to the river from any point on the rim. Warning signs recommend the appropriate clothing and water requirements. Overcrowded with 10,000 people per year, the trail supports one of the main mule routes into the canyon. If you dislike crowds, look elsewhere either for a day-walk or overnight trip.

In the summer, with Inner Gorge temperatures hovering around 100 °F (38 °C), to walk the round trip from rim to river in one day is not recommended. When the temperatures are more moderate during other seasons of the year, an experienced and fit walker can complete the round trip. In this case your best route descends the South Kaibab Trail and ascends the Bright Angel Trail.

The majority of the 400 canyon rescues per year are for heat-related illnesses suffered on the Bright Angel Trail. Though it is the "easiest" of rim to river trails, you still must be fit. Visitors who have underestimated the difficulty of climbing out of the canyon in scorching heat are prone to exhaustion and dehydration. On a day-walk in winter, be sure to carry warm clothing and adequate food and water.

Directions

From the trailhead west of the Kolb Studio and Bright Angel Lodge in Grand Canyon Village, the Bright Angel Trail begins its descent into the canyon with steep switchbacks. Dropping 3,000 feet for the first 3.1 miles, the trail follows Garden Creek until it meets Pipe Creek just past Indian Garden. From the start, you can't miss Indian Garden with its lush green campsites shaded with cottonwood trees.

You pass shelters, One-and-a-Half Mile Resthouse and Three Mile Resthouse, built in the 1930s by the Civilian Conservation Corps, offering water from May to September, shade, and emergency telephones. Just after Three Mile Resthouse the trail levels off until it reaches Indian Garden (camping, water, corrals, toilets, shade). An overnight stop at Indian Garden, 4.6 miles from the start, offers far from a wilderness experience. A 1.4 mile side trail goes north from Indian Garden to Plateau Point, a fine day-hike from the rim, offering splendid views of the Inner Gorge.

If you are planning to take the Tonto Trail west toward Monument Creek, camp your first night at Horn Creek. If you plan to turn east on the Tonto Trail toward the Grandview Trail and Horseshoe Mesa, the South Kaibab Trail presents a more scenic and direct descent into the canyon.

From Indian Garden, the Bright Angel Trail descends north through the Tapeats Narrows until it reaches the Devils Corkscrew. Here the trail switchbacks through the Vishnu Schist to reach the River Resthouse at Pipe Creek. Turn east on the River Trail for 1.5 miles to reach the Silver Suspension Bridge. Cross here for the fastest way to Bright Angel Campground and Phantom Ranch. Continuing east on the River Trail, still south of the Colorado River, in 1 mile you meet South Kaibab Trail at the Kaibab Suspension Bridge.

SOUTH KAIBAB TRAIL

Start:	South Kaibab Trailhead near Yaki Point (7,190 feet/2,192 metres)
End:	Kaibab Suspension Bridge at the Colorado River (2,440 feet/744 metres)
Distance, one way:	6.3 miles (10.1 kilometres)
Times, one way:	3–5 hours down, 5–7 hours up
Maps:	Phantom Ranch (United States Geological Survey 7.5′); Grand Canyon National Park (TI); Grand Canyon National Park (EP)
Season:	autumn, winter and spring
Water:	Colorado River
Rating:	strenuous

Built by the National Park Service in 1924, the South Kaibab Trail soon became an alternative to the Bright Angel Trail. At that time a toll was charged on the neighbouring Bright Angel Trail or Cameron Trail. To build

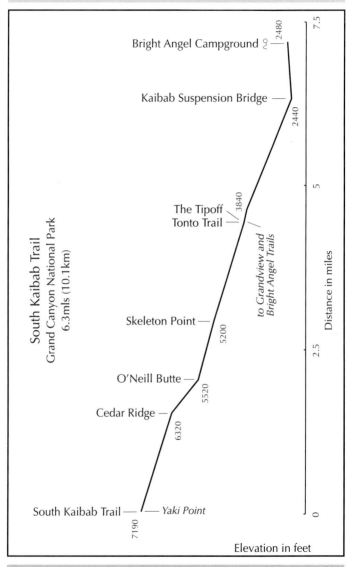

South Kaibab Trail
Grand Canyon National Park
6.3mls (10.1km)

Bright Angel Campground — 2480

Kaibab Suspension Bridge — 2440

The Tipoff
Tonto Trail — 3840

*to Grandview and
Bright Angel Trails*

Skeleton Point — 5200

O'Neill Butte — 5520

Cedar Ridge — 6320

South Kaibab Trail — — *Yaki Point*

7190

Distance in miles

Elevation in feet

the Kaibab Suspension Bridge that crosses the Colorado River at the bottom of the South Kaibab Trail, workers carried the gigantic steel cables from the rim to the river. In 1928 the National Park Service completed the cross-canyon system of trails known today as the Corridor trails.

Since the South Kaibab Trail follows a ridge, rather than a depression between two ridges, it provides some of the finest Grand Canyon views. This wide mule-travelled trail, easy to follow all the way to the Colorado River, makes a fine outing for either day-walkers or backpackers. Many day-walkers descend the short distance to Cedar Ridge. A more rewarding outing continues to Skeleton Point before the uphill return trip. You will meet mule trains ascending the South Kaibab Trail. Mules have the right of way; stand quietly on the uphill side of the trail and allow them to pass.

If you are walking cross-canyon from the North Kaibab Trail during the summer, consider ascending the Bright Angel rather than the South Kaibab Trail. The Bright Angel Trail, though longer, ascends more gradually than the South Kaibab Trail and provides year round water sources not available on the South Kaibab Trail. During the cooler months of the year, you may wish to consider ascending the more scenic and less crowded South Kaibab rather than the Bright Angel Trail. If you decide to ascend the more scenic South Kaibab Trail, leave before dawn and carry at least 1 gallon (4 litres) of water per person.

Directions

After turning onto Yaki Point Road, 1.2 miles east of the junction of Highway 64 and East Rim Drive, turn left into the trailhead car park. During the summer, shuttle buses from Grand Canyon Village serve the South Kaibab trailhead and Yaki Point. When the shuttle bus is not operating, a bus service links Bright Angel Lodge with Yaki Point. The National Park Service is considering eliminating all automobile access to the South Kaibab trailhead and Yaki Point.

From the South Kaibab trailhead switchback down the wide trail 1.5 miles and 800 vertical feet through the Kaibab limestone, the Toroweap and the Coconino to reach the Hermit shale of Cedar Ridge. From Cedar Ridge you get fine views west towards Plateau Point, Pipe and Burro Spring on the Tonto Trail leading into Indian Garden from the east.

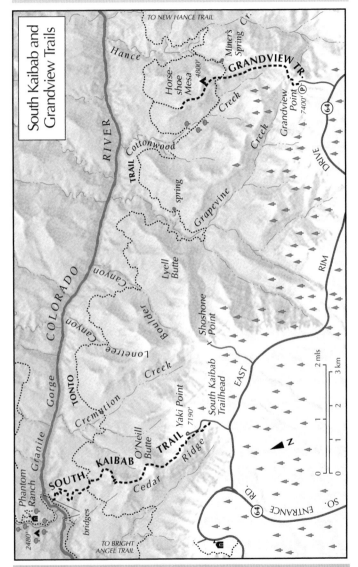

South Kaibab and
Grandview Trails

TO NEW HANCE TRAIL

Hance

Miner's
Spring Cr.

GRANDVIEW TR.

Horse-
shoe
Mesa
4800'

Grandview
Point
7400' P

64

RIVER

Cottonwood

Creek

Grapevine Creek

TRAIL

spring

DRIVE

COLORADO

Canyon

Boulder

Lyell
Butte

Shoshone
Point

RIM

Lonetree Canyon

Creek

TONTO

Cremation

South Kaibab
Trailhead

EAST

2 mls

3 km

Yaki Point
7190'

Granite Gorge

KAIBAB

O'Neill
Butte

TRAIL

N

Phantom
Ranch

SOUTH

Cedar Ridge

2480'

bridges

SO. ENTRANCE RD.

TO BRIGHT
ANGEL TRAIL

64

Descending east off Cedar Ridge through the Supai you proceed along a lengthy 1 mile traverse with fantastic views east. You can see the Tonto Trail as it meanders east across the Tonto Platform past Newton Butte and across Cremation Canyon. From here the Tonto Trail leads to Horseshoe Mesa and the Grandview Trail. Reaching Skeleton Point you get fine views both towards the east and west Tonto platforms.

Next you begin a steep descent on switchbacks through the Redwall and in 1 mile past the Skeleton you arrive at the Tipoff. If you turn west from the Tipoff you will pass Pipe Spring, a perennial water source, and in 4.6 miles reach Indian Garden. Turn east along the Tonto Trail and a 2 day, 23 mile trip brings you to the Grandview Trail and Horseshoe Mesa.

From the Tipoff the South Kaibab meanders north. After 10 minutes the descent angles steeply down into the Inner Gorge and you are rewarded with fine views of the river's suspension bridges. Bright Angel Creek and Phantom Ranch are soon obvious along with the wide Colorado River below. After zigzagging through the Tapeats you reach the Kaibab suspension bridge 2 miles from the Tipoff. Cross the Colorado River on the bridge and continue ahead to Phantom Ranch and Bright Angel Campground.

GRANDVIEW TRAIL

Start:	Grandview Trailhead at Grandview Point (7,400 feet/2,256 metres)
End:	Horseshoe Mesa (4,800 feet/1,463 metres)
Distance, one way:	3 miles (4.8 kilometres)
Times, one way:	2 hours down, 3 hours up
Maps:	Grandview Point, Cape Royal (United States Geological Survey 7.5'); Grand Canyon National Park (TI); Grand Canyon National Park (EP)
Season:	autumn, winter and spring
Water:	none (Miner's Spring)
Rating:	moderate

In 1895 the Grandview Hotel offered horse trips into the canyon to visit

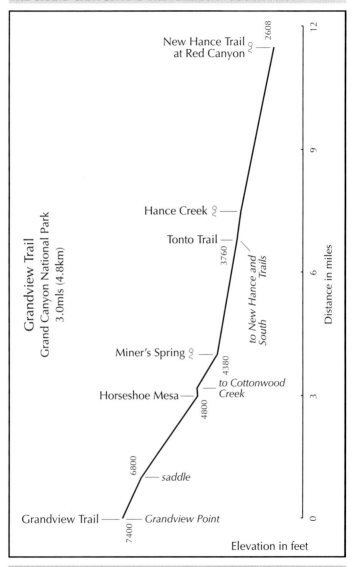

Grandview Trail
Grand Canyon National Park
3.0mls (4.8km)

New Hance Trail
at Red Canyon
2608

Hance Creek

Tonto Trail
3760

to New Hance and
South Trails

Miner's Spring
4380

Horseshoe Mesa
4800

to Cottonwood
Creek

6800
— saddle

Grandview Trail —
Grandview Point
7400

Elevation in feet

Distance in miles

the mines on Horseshoe Mesa. However, when the El Tovar Hotel was constructed across from the railroad station in 1902 in Grand Canyon Village and easier access into the canyon became available, the Grandview Hotel quickly lost its attraction.

The copper mines of the Grandview Area, especially the Last Chance Mine, were mined from the late 1800s until 1910. Burros were used to bring the ore to the rim. Relics of this historic area, such as wheelbarrows, nails and pots, still dot the canyon near the mines. The mines are considered unsafe to enter due to danger of collapse and high levels of radon.

If this is your first overnight trip into the Grand Canyon, Horseshoe Mesa provides a spectacular introduction to canyon-walking. Superior views of the canyon greet you; side canyon walls do not constrict your views. The Mesa offers expansive canyon views. Not a true rim to river trail, the Grandview is impractical if you wish to reach the Colorado River.

Horseshoe Mesa also makes a fine base camp trip although you probably will have to make the 500 foot descent east to Miner's (Page) Spring for water. A fine day-walk from Horseshoe Mesa descends east to Miner's Spring, joins the Tonto Trail, traverses the north side of the Mesa, and then returns back to the Mesa directly south up the front of the west wing of the Mesa and past the Cave of the Domes. A longer outing passes Cottonwood Creek and the dry O'Neill spring and ends with a steep, crumbly ascent 500 feet back up to your camp on the Mesa.

Directions

The Grandview Point road turns north from East Rim Drive, 9 miles east of the junction of East Rim Drive with Highway 64. The Grandview Trail descends into the canyon from the north end of the turnout.

Several sections of steep wooden-braced steps and pavement characterize the top rocky, steep section of the Grandview Trail. Unrestricted views to Horseshoe Mesa and across the Colorado River present themselves from this upper section. After 1 mile the trail crosses a saddle between Grapevine and Hance Canyon. Heading east for a short section, the trail flattens out but soon drops north switchbacking at an even steeper angle. The descent becomes more gradual as the Supai is traversed all the way to the southern section of Horseshoe Mesa. The trail to Miner's (Page) Spring veers off to the east. If you are spending the night, continue north across the Mesa for 5 minutes to the designated campsites near the abandoned building.

NEW HANCE TRAIL

Start:	New Hance Trailhead near Moran Point (7,040 feet/2,133 metres)
End:	Hance Rapids at Red Canyon (2,608 feet/ 795 metres)
Distance, one way:	8 miles (12.8 kilometres)
Times, one way:	6–7 hours down, 8–9 hours up
Maps:	Grandview Point, Cape Royal (United States Geological Survey 7.5'); Grand Canyon National Park (TI)
Water:	Colorado River
Season:	autumn, winter and spring
Rating:	extremely strenuous

The Hance Trail had long been considered one of the Canyon's most difficult trails. The Hance Trail, following an old Indian route, was built by John Hance around 1900 to accommodate the growing number of tourists wanting to reach the bottom of the canyon. Steep, slippery, rocky and torn with boulders, in the 1880s tourists originally lowered on ropes down some sections. Today little remains of the original Hance Trail. After the original trail washed away, the New Hance Trail was relocated to the east of the original trail, to its current location in Red Canyon. The New Hance Trail also boasts the reputation of being the most difficult of the South Rim, rim to river trails.

Parking for the New Hance Trail is at Moran Point, 14.9 miles east of the junction of Highway 64 and East Rim Drive. Walk 1 mile west from Moran Point along the rim to the trail sign for the New Hance Trail. If you are planning to link the New Hance Trail with other rim to river trails, it is always easier to descend rather than ascend the New Hance Trail.

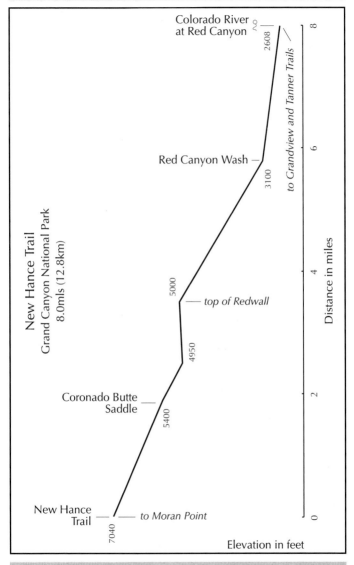

New Hance Trail
Grand Canyon National Park
8.0mls (12.8km)

Colorado River
at Red Canyon

2608

Red Canyon Wash

3100

5000

top of Redwall

4950

Coronado Butte
Saddle

5400

New Hance
Trail

to Moran Point

7040

to Grandview and Tanner Trails

Distance in miles

Elevation in feet

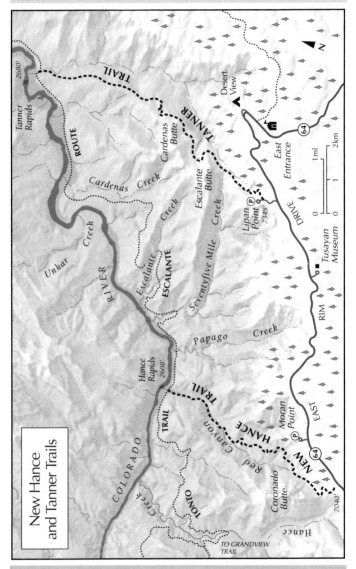

New Hance and Tanner Trails

Directions
From the trailhead immediately descend very steeply, switchbacking down the drainage east of Coronado Butte. Follow the trail as best you can through rocks and washouts. Coronado Butte rises on the west. This upper section may be covered by snow and ice during the winter. Once reaching Coronado Butte Saddle the trail turns north-east and traverses the Hermit Shale, Sandstone and Supai, continuing up and down through several rocky draws. Be careful in this section and visually locate the top of the Redwall and its large cairn.

Descend through the rocky and loose Redwall above two drainages and cross the Tonto Platform. Enter the eastern drainage, which flows south-east below Moran Point, and follow the creek all the way to Hance Rapids at the Colorado River.

TANNER TRAIL

Start:	Tanner Trailhead at Lipan Point (7,349 feet/ 2,240 metres)
End:	Tanner Rapids (2,680 feet/819 metres)
Distance, one way:	9 miles (14.4 kilometres)
Times, one way:	6–7 hours down, 8–9 hours up
Maps:	Desert View (United States Geological Survey 7.5'); Grand Canyon National Park (TI)
Season:	autumn, winter and spring
Water:	Colorado River
Rating:	extremely strenuous

The Tanner Trail, initially used by the early Indians in the sixteenth century, was maintained by the Spanish looking for gold. In the late nineteenth century the Mormons improved the trail in order to mine copper along the Colorado River. In later years, horses stolen in Utah were herded down the north slopes of the Colorado River on the Nankoweap Trail and forded across the river. After brands were changed, they were driven up the Tanner Trail and resold. The Tanner Trail became known as the Horsethief Trail.

The Lipan Point car park can be found 20 miles east of the junction of Highway 64 and East Rim Drive. The Tanner Trail begins 100 yards east of the car park, near the information sign.

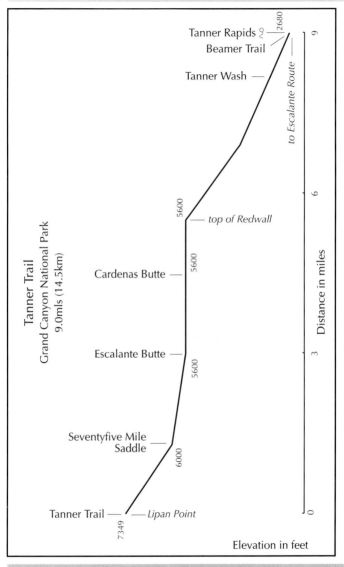

Tanner Trail
Grand Canyon National Park
9.0mls (14.5km)

Tanner Rapids
Beamer Trail
2680

Tanner Wash —

to Escalante Route

5600 — *top of Redwall*

5600

Cardenas Butte —

Escalante Butte —

5600

Seventyfive Mile
Saddle —

6000

Tanner Trail — — *Lipan Point*
7349

Distance in miles

Elevation in feet

Directions

From the Tanner trailhead follow the west side of Tanner Canyon for the entire route to the river. Descend very steeply down the initial series of switchbacks in and out of the trees to the base of Seventyfive Mile Saddle, your first good camping spot. From the saddle, contour around the base of both Escalante and Cardenas Buttes for 3 miles through the Supai Sandstone. Fine camping spots exist here along the flat contour line.

Next the trail descends steeply again through the Redwall formation toward the bottom of Tanner Canyon. After the 45 minute jarring descent, the trail veers northward for 1 hour remaining high along a low ridge on the west side of the creek. You are rewarded with fine views of the Unkar Delta and the Colorado River. The descent on the east side of the ridge continues for another hour through the Dox formation and becomes more gradual as you approach the canyon bottom. Continue through the Tanner Wash for 10 minutes to the river at the Tanner Rapids. Camping is prohibited in the high sand dunes at the river on either side of Tanner Wash.

If you've time for a day-hike, the Beamer Trail heads east up the river contouring in and out of many drainages for 9.5 miles to meet the Little Colorado River and Marble Canyon.

CHAPTER 7

GRAND CANYON NATIONAL PARK: NORTH RIM, RIM TO RIVER TRAILS

Some element of fear probably lies at the root
of every substantial challenge.
Colin Fletcher, *The Man Who Walked Through Time*

Introduction

North Rim Village, located 45 miles north of Jacob Lake, Arizona on Highway 67, hosts 10% of the number of visitors to Grand Canyon Village on the South Rim. Several cool alternatives to unbearably hot inner canyon temperatures in summer are available for walkers. Paths wind through cool conifer forests leading to views of far away deserts and the Inner Canyon. Several viewpoints display the finest of Grand Canyon vistas.

While the South Rim trailheads into the Inner Canyon centre around Grand Canyon Village, North Rim trailheads, except for the North Kaibab, are accessed from remote entry points at the end of miles of dirt roads. These remote trailheads require lengthy drives over secondary or unpaved roads. In spite of extra planning needed to reach these distant trailheads, these North Rim trails are well worth the effort. Advance planning, previous experience on South Rim unmaintained trails, knowledge of map and compass use and thoughtful judgement are absolute requirements before you attempt these trails.

As the North Rim is over 1,000 feet higher than the South Rim, the elevation gain and loss to the Colorado River are greater and the ascents and descents more severe than on the Canyon's south side. North rim to river trails in order of increasing difficulty are: North Kaibab, Thunder River, Bill Hall, Nankoweap and North Bass. Easily reached from the North Rim Road, north of the visitor centre, the North Kaibab Trail provides the North Rim's only maintained or Corridor Trail into the Inner Canyon.

Trail	Distance Miles One way	Distance Kilometres One Way	Rating	Difficulty
Thunder River Trail	16.0	25.6	Wilderness	Ex. Strenuous
Bill Hall Trail	12.0	19.2	Wilderness	Ex. Strenuous
North Bass Trail	13.5	21.6	Route	Ex. Strenuous
North Kaibab Trail	14.2	22.9	Corridor	Moderate
Nankoweap Trail	14.5	23.2	Wilderness	Ex. Strenuous

THUNDER RIVER AND BILL HALL TRAILS, WITH DEER CREEK EXTENSION

Start:	Thunder River Trailhead at Indian Hollow (6,380 feet/1,945 metres) or Bill Hall Trailhead at Monument Point (7,050 feet/2,148 metres)
End:	Lower Tapeats at the Colorado River (1,980 feet/603 metres)
Distance, one way:	Thunder River Trail, 16 miles (25.6 kilometres). Bill Hall Trail, 12 miles (19.2 kilometres)
Times, one way:	8–10 hours down, 13–15 hours up
Maps:	Tapeats Amphitheatre, Fishtail Mesa, Powell Plateau (United States Geological Survey 7.5'); Grand Canyon National Park (TI), Kaibab National Forest, North Kaibab Ranger District (United States Forest Service)
Season:	spring and autumn
Water:	Thunder River, Tapeats Creek, Colorado River, Deer Creek, Deer Spring
Difficulty:	extremely strenuous

The upper portions of the Thunder River Trail were built by gold miners in 1876 and the final sections into Tapeats Creek were completed in 1926. The Bill Hall Trail was named after a ranger who was killed in an automobile accident while on the way to assist in another accident. Thunder River, one of the world's shortest rivers at 0.5 mile long and the world's only river to flow into a creek, terminates when it flows into Tapeats Creek.

To reach Indian Hollow Campground from Jacob Lake, Arizona take Highway 67 for 26 miles to Forest Road (FR) 422. Drive 18 miles west towards Dry Park to Forest Road (FR) 425, turn west and drive 8 miles south to Forest Road (FR) 232. Turn west and drive 5 miles to the end of the road to Indian Hollow. Forest Road (FR) 422 and 425 are gravel all-weather roads. You may be able to negotiate Forest Road (FR) 232 in a car, although high clearance four-wheel drive vehicles may be necessary in the spring.

Forest Road (FR) 422 can also be accessed from Fredonia, Arizona. Drive 1 mile east on Highway 89A and turn south onto Forest Road (FR) 422. Continue south on Forest Road (FR) 422 past Big Springs, turning west on Forest Road (FR) 425 and west on Forest Road (FR) 232. You'll find Indian Hollow Campground 50 miles south of Fredonia and 17 miles south-west of the Big Springs Ranger Station.

To reach the Bill Hall trailhead, take Forest Road (FR) 425 for 10 miles from Forest Road (FR) 422 to FR 292 at Crazy Jug Point. Continue west along the rim on Forest Road (FR) 292A to the Bill Hall trailhead. Crazy Jug Point is accessible to passenger vehicles. Follow signs to Crazy Jug Point by turning right after 0.25 mile. At the four-way junction, 1.5 miles from Forest Road (FR) 425, take the middle fork onto 292A and proceed 1.5 miles to the trailhead.

The North Kaibab National Forest (USFS) map is indispensable in helping you reach these trailheads. Driving time from Jacob Lake or Fredonia is approximately 1.5 hours. Check with the North Kaibab Ranger District in Jacob Lake or Fredonia to see if the roads are open. Alternative roads may be used if winter snows block Forest Road (FR) 422. Roads close for the winter after the first snows in late October or November.

Directions
From the car park at Indian Hollow, the Thunder River Trail heads west for 0.5 mile on a long sweeping traverse along the rim to Little Saddle. The trail then descends abruptly through the Toroweap, Hermit and Coconino formations to reach the rolling Esplanade. You will see occasional signs for Forest Service (FS) Trail 23. Once the Esplanade is reached, the trail fades as it turns east. First you are in shrub but as you continue east the trail winds through red

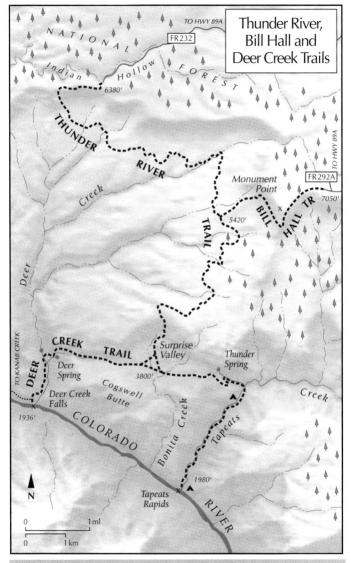

Thunder River,
Bill Hall and
Deer Creek Trails

N A T I O N A L

Indian Hollow

FR232

TO HWY 89A

F O R E S T

6380'

THUNDER

RIVER

Creek

TRAIL

Monument
Point

BILL

HALL TR

FR292A

TO HWY 89A

5420'

7050'

Deer

DEER

CREEK

TRAIL

Surprise
Valley

Thunder
Spring

TO KANAB CREEK

Deer
Spring

3800'

Cogswell
Butte

Creek

Deer Creek
Falls

1936'

COLORADO

Bonita Creek

Tapeats

1980'

Tapeats
Rapids

RIVER

N

0   1ml

0   1km

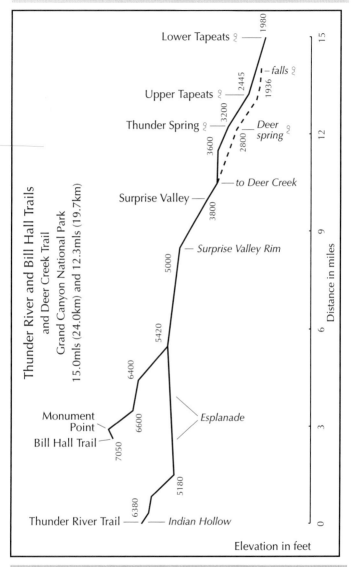

Thunder River and Bill Hall Trails
and Deer Creek Trail
Grand Canyon National Park
15.0mls (24.0km) and 12.3mls (19.7km)

Lower Tapeats — 1980

– falls

Upper Tapeats — 2445

2445

1936

Thunder Spring — 3200

3600

Deer spring

2800

to Deer Creek

Surprise Valley —

3800

Surprise Valley Rim

5000

5420

6400

Monument
Point

6600

Esplanade

Bill Hall Trail —

7050

5180

Thunder River Trail — 6380 — *Indian Hollow*

Distance in miles

Elevation in feet

rock terraces, along the northern fingers of Deer Creek. Terraces just north of the trail provide rain protection if you are caught in a storm.

Approximately 4 miles from Indian Hollow, you reach the junction with the Bill Hall Trail as it descends from Monument Point. Collect water here for your return trip. Longer than the Bill Hall Trail, the Thunder River Trail descends into the canyon on a more gradual course and Indian Hollow Trailhead lies almost 700 feet lower than the Bill Hall trailhead.

The Bill Hall Trail, Forest Service (FS) Trail 95, drops 12 miles from Monument Point to the Colorado River. From the Monument Point car park, the trail ascends south-west to Millet Point and then descends to Monument Point. Heading directly south, it drops steeply through the Kaibab and Toroweap to a break in the ridge between Monument Point and Bridger's Knoll. Scrambling may be required in the initial exposed section. Turning west the trail undulates for 0.5 mile below Monument Point as fantastic canyon views open up. Then it turns and heads straight downhill 0.75 mile through the Hermit to meet the Thunder River Trail.

From the junction with the Bill Hall Trail, the Thunder River Trail heads east across the Esplanade. Cairns mark your route to the rim of the Esplanade where there are sweeping views of Surprise Valley and the South Rim. Next you descend through a break in the Redwall to Surprise Valley. Thunder River Trail heads east as it crosses through the rolling terrain of Surprise Valley to a viewpoint above Thunder River.

Now the trail descends via switchbacks to the east side of Thunder River, a dramatic sight as the powerful torrent drops steeply into the creek. Spray provides a cold shower for anyone who wishes one. Camping is not allowed from the rim of Surprise Valley down the Thunder River drainage to Tapeats Creek. Continue descending via several switchbacks to Upper Tapeats Campground, just below the junction of Tapeats Creek and Thunder River. A 2 mile trail descends on the eastern side or true left of the creek to Lower Tapeats; the trail crosses the creek twice. Though it is possible to descend on the western side, a deep gorge blocks your passage and numerous scrambles and detours are necessary. Crossing Tapeats Creek may be impossible in the spring.

Back in Surprise Valley, another trail veers west to Deer Creek Valley. Dropping off the Surprise Valley Rim, the trail switchbacks down into Deer Valley, soon passing Deer Spring. At the valley bottom, the trail descends following the true left of the creek, passing several campsites before entering the narrows. A few cottonwood trees offer welcome shade. This exquisite location, an oasis in this desert environment, makes a superb spot for a layover day. Layovers can be spent visiting the narrows, swimming, exploring the springs, traversing over to above Bonita Creek or visiting the Colorado River and the waterfall at Deer Creek.

Entering the narrows, you traverse high above the gorge past some white Indian hand prints and then descend a trail to meet the Colorado River at Deer Creek Falls. One of the most photographed spots in the canyon, the pool at the base of the waterfall invites swimming from boaters and backpackers alike.

After your drop off the rim, Deer Spring and Thunder River offer your first perennial water. Though this descent is often made in one long day, plan on collecting water for your climb out or carry extra water on the two-day ascent.

NORTH BASS TRAIL

Start:	North Bass Trailhead at Swamp Point (7,500 feet/2,236 metres)
End:	Colorado River (2,200 feet/670 metres)
Distance, one way:	14 miles (22.5 kilometres)
Times, one way:	9–11 hours down, 15–18 hours up
Maps:	King Arthur Castle, Havasupai Point (United States Geological Survey 7.5′); Grand Canyon National Park (TI); Kaibab National Forest, North Kaibab Ranger District (United States Forest Service)
Season:	late spring and autumn
Water:	Muav Saddle, Colorado River
Difficulty:	extremely strenuous

The North Bass Trail or Shinumo Trail, built by Wallace Bass, helped assist with transporting tourists from his South Bass Trail across the river via a

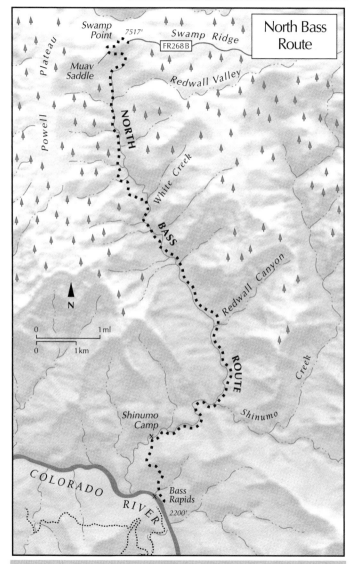

North Bass
Route

Swamp
Point   7517'   Swamp   Ridge
FR268B

Muav
Saddle   Redwall Valley

Plateau

NORTH

Powell

White Creek

BASS

Redwall Canyon

N

0   1 ml

0   1 km

ROUTE

Creek

Shinumo
Camp   Shinumo

COLORADO

RIVER

Bass
Rapids
2200'

cable and up to the North Rim. Today walkers wanting to complete the strenuous cross-canyon trip have the difficult chore of hitching a ride across the river. Problems include making transportation arrangements to two very remote road heads, not to mention descending or ascending the obscure and extremely difficult North Bass Trail. Do not consider attempting this route unless you are accompanied by at least one member of your party who has walked the route previously. All walkers should have extensive experience in the Grand Canyon.

The North Bass, one of the canyon's most strenuous descents, is really a Route. Due to its indistinct nature, hiking this trail requires extensive Grand Canyon hiking experience to follow its challenging brushy course. Only small segments of the original trail exist. If you choose to try, you'll be route finding, talus and boulder hopping and needling your way through brush for the entire time. If you plan to do a round trip, stop to look uphill and visualize your route out.

High clearance vehicles are recommended for the trip to the North Bass (Swamp Point) road head. From Jacob Lake, take Highway 67 26.5 miles to Forest Road (FR) 22 toward Dry Park. In 2 miles at Forest Road (FR) 270, turn west on Forest Road (FR) 223. Proceed 7 miles and turn left on Forest Road (FR) 268 towards Swamp Point and left on Forest Road (FR) 268B. Continue 1.4 miles to the park boundary to road W4. From the park boundary on the deteriorating road, proceed 0.3 mile and bear west passing a campground 8 miles from the boundary. In 0.1 miles you reach the Swamp Point trailhead, 16.5 miles from Highway 67. Snow or fallen trees may block this road into June.

Directions
From the Swamp Point trailhead, descend west on switchbacks to a trail junction on Muav Saddle. From the Muav Saddle to the river, you'll follow White and Shinumo creeks. At the first junction, take the left branch south-east through thickets and brush along the Coconino Sandstone. The right branches to the Muav Saddle cabin; the middle to Powell Plateau. You'll find a spring and another abandoned cabin 1.4 miles from the road head at White Creek on the eastern side trail before the trail turns south.

Heading south at a cairn, descend extremely steeply on rocky sandstone through the Coconino and Hermit past your first pour-off. Switchback through the Esplanade. The route next descends the

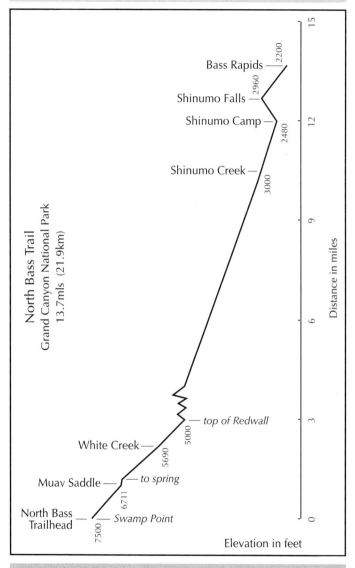

North Bass Trail
Grand Canyon National Park
13.7mls (21.9km)

Elevation in feet

Distance in miles

Bass Rapids — 2200

Shinumo Falls — 2960

Shinumo Camp — 2480

Shinumo Creek — 3000

top of Redwall — 5000

White Creek — 5690

Muav Saddle — *to spring* — 6711

North Bass Trailhead — *Swamp Point* — 7500

talus into the dry White Creek as you boulder hop or bushwhack through the Supai. Continuing your creek descent, follow the wash as best you can over rocks and boulders and around obstacles until around 2 miles from Muav Saddle you reach the top of the Redwall. Before you proceed farther, locate the huge cairn marking the Redwall descent.

The trail now climbs east out of the drainage, descends briefly into another drainage, rises up again and drops into a second and finally a third drainage. Switchbacks drop through the Redwall to reach White Creek. Water flows intermittently now all the way to the Tapeats Narrows. Views spread out to the south into Muav Canyon and Shinumo Amphitheatre.

The route continues on the west side of the creek through the Muav sandstone. At the bench marker BM 4001 on the King Arthur Quadrangle you cross the east side of the creek and descend through the shale to bench marker BM 3480 and a cairned junction.

From here most walkers choose to descend the wash in and out of the drainage through the Tapeats Narrows to below the junction of White and Shinumo Creeks. You will encounter several pour-offs and down climbs. Reaching Shinumo Creek, you find several campsites.

Continuing downstream, you'll cross Shinumo Creek many times, pass by Bass's old cabin and camp and then join the well trodden trail. From Shinumo Camp the trail actually ascends Shinumo Creek to a wide saddle where there are views of the Colorado River and Bass Rapids. At bench marker BM 2917 the now obvious trail descends to the river above Bass Rapids, a popular camping spot for river-runners and walkers. You'll want to rest for at least a day before returning to the rim, a task usually spread out over two days.

NORTH KAIBAB TRAIL

Start:	North Kaibab Trailhead (8,241 feet/ 2,515 metres)
End:	Bright Angel Campground (2,480 feet/ 747 metres)
Distance, one way:	14.2 miles (22.9 kilometres)

Times, one way:	8–9 hours down, 7–9 hours up
Maps:	Bright Angel Point, Phantom Ranch (United States Geological Survey 7.5'); Grand Canyon National Park (TI); Grand Canyon National Park (EP); Bright Angel Trail (EP)
Season:	summer through to autumn
Water:	Supai Tunnel, Roaring Springs, Cottonwood Camp, Phantom Ranch, Bright Angel Campground, Colorado River
Difficulty:	moderate

Francois Matthes, a surveyor who pioneered the North Kaibab Route in 1902, one year later constructed a tourist camp at the mouth of Bright Angel Creek. His original route descended the shorter north arm of Bright Angel Creek. Today the North Kaibab Trail drops through Roaring Springs Canyon. The entire cross-canyon trail system, consisting of the North and South Kaibab trails and the Bright Angel Trail, was completed in 1928.

The North Kaibab Trail begins at the east end of the North Kaibab car park, 2 miles north of Grand Canyon Village and 11 miles south of the North Rim Entrance Station.

Directions
The well-maintained North Kaibab Trail descends from the North Rim dropping all the way to the Colorado River. Mules share the hot, dusty and crowded trail for the first 4.7 miles to Roaring Springs. Following a creek bed rather than a ridge line, canyon walls and trees limit your views. The trail first switchbacks through the Toroweap and Coconino Sandstone, passing through the upper reaches of Roaring Springs Canyon. You reach the Coconino Overlook after 0.5 miles. Looking west you can make out the intersection of Bright Angel and Roaring Springs Canyon. Just below the Coconino Overlook the trail switchbacks through the Hermit Formation until it reaches the Supai Tunnel. (The tunnel, built in the 1930s to replace the Old Bright Angel Trail, was blasted out of the rock in the 1930s by the California Conservation Corps.)

In 0.5 miles you reach the Redwall Bridge built after a 1966 flood wiped out this section of the trail. Crossing to the south side of the

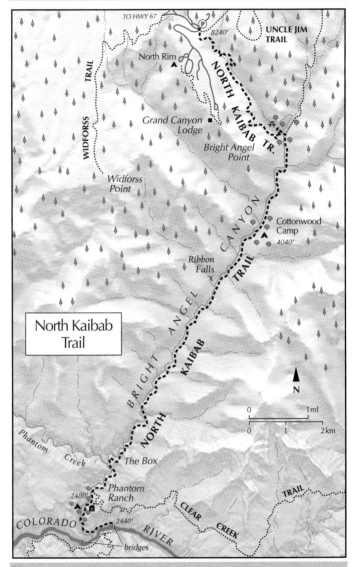

TO HWY 67

P

8240'

UNCLE JIM
TRAIL

North Rim

NORTH KAIBAB TR.

WIDFORSS TRAIL

Grand Canyon
Lodge

Bright Angel
Point

Widforss
Point

BRIGHT ANGEL CANYON

Cottonwood
Camp
4040'

Ribbon
Falls

TRAIL

North Kaibab
Trail

KAIBAB

NORTH

N

0   1 ml
0   1   2 km

Phantom
Creek

The Box

Phantom
Ranch

2480'

TRAIL

COLORADO

2440'

RIVER

CLEAR

CREEK

bridges

Mules ascending the South Kaibab Trail, Grand Canyon National Park

Surprise Valley from Thunder River Trail, Grand Canyon National Park

Bright Angel Trail, Grand Canyon National Park

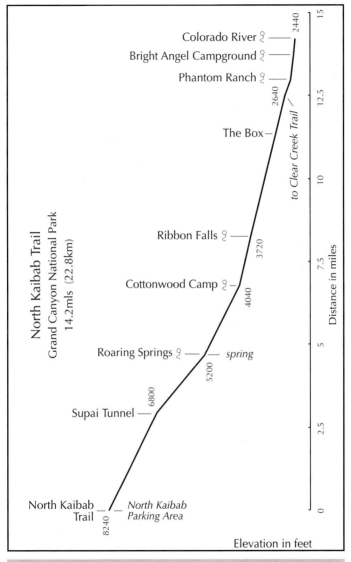

Colorado River — 2440

Bright Angel Campground —

Phantom Ranch —

2640

The Box —

to Clear Creek Trail

Ribbon Falls — 3720

Cottonwood Camp — 4040

Roaring Springs — — *spring*

5200

6800

Supai Tunnel —

North Kaibab Trail — — *North Kaibab Parking Area*

8240

North Kaibab Trail
Grand Canyon National Park
14.2mls (22.8km)

Distance in miles

Elevation in feet

creek, the trail descends another 1.5 miles before it reaches the mouth of Bright Angel Canyon. From here the old overgrown Bright Angel Trail heads west back to the North Rim. A 0.25 mile side trail leads to Roaring Springs, a popular day-hike destination. Cottonwood trees offer welcome shade above several picnic tables.

The trail follows Bright Angel Creek all the way to the Colorado River. The trail turns south on a moderate to easy grade 0.5 mile beyond the junction of the North Kaibab and Bright Angel Creek and across the bridge. The building here houses the caretaker who maintains the water supply for the North Rim. After 2 miles you come to Cottonwood Campground, the first designated campsite on the North Kaibab Trail. In summer you'll find purified water and a ranger in residence. Water taken from Bright Angel Creek should be purified.

After Cottonwood Camp the trail descends gradually 7 miles and 1,500 feet to the Colorado River. Your first 1.8 miles brings you to the turn-off to Ribbon Falls, a spectacular 100 foot high waterfall. The waterfall creates a perfect spot for a shower, an oasis in the otherwise dry and dusty descent. Continuing from Ribbon Falls, the canyon walls slowly narrow. Here several cacti and one non-native palm tree grow while the overall vegetation appears typical of a desert. Passing next through the narrow canyon walls of the Box, you'll soon pass the Clear Creek trailhead veering east. Finally, you arrive at Phantom Ranch and, soon, Bright Angel Campground.

For most times of the year, Phantom Ranch must be reserved almost a year in advance; meals are available to walkers by reservation only. Reserve Bright Angel Campground several months ahead through the BRO. From the campground a short stroll brings you to both the Kaibab and Silver suspension bridges. Crossing the Colorado River, these two bridges link up with the South Kaibab and Bright Angel (River) trails. After a 4,500 foot climb you arrive at Grand Canyon Village on the South Rim. See section 7 for more detailed information on the Corridor trails, backcountry reservation procedures, Phantom Ranch, and specifics on hiking regulations.

NANKOWEAP TRAIL

Start:	Nankoweap Trailhead at FS 610 (8,800 feet/1,365 metres) Nankoweap Trailhead at

	FS 445 at Saddle Mountain (6,455 feet/ 1,967 metres)
End:	Colorado River (2,802 feet/841 metres)
Distance, one way:	14.5 miles (23.2 kilometres) from FR 610 or FR 445
Times, one way:	10–12 hours down, 15–17 hours up
Map:	Point Imperial, Nankoweap Mesa (United States Geological Survey 7.5'); Grand Canyon National Park (TI); Kaibab National Forest (United States Forest Service)
Season:	late spring and autumn
Water:	Nankoweap Creek, Colorado River
Difficulty:	extremely strenuous

Take Arizona Highway 67 south from Jacob Lake, 26 miles to westbound Forest Road (FR) 22 at DeMotte Park, 1 mile south of Kaibab Lodge. Turn east and go 200 yards to Forest Road (FR) 611. Proceed 1.2 miles to Forest Road 610. Bear right 13.5 miles to the Saddle Mountain trailhead. If accessed via Forest Road (FR) 610, the Nankoweap Trail follows brushy Forest Service Trail 57 for 3.4 miles to the National Park Service trailhead. From this trailhead you negotiate 11 rocky, exposed and slippery miles as you descend 5,000 vertical feet to the Colorado River.

Another way to access the Nankoweap Trail is via Highway 89A east of Jacob Lake to Forest Road (FR) 810. Go south on FR 810 to Forest Road 445, which takes you to the other Saddle Mountain trailhead. If you join from the north via Forest Road (FR) 445 follow Forest Service Trail 57 for 3 miles heading south to the National Park Service trailhead.

Directions
From the rim, the Nankoweap drops below Saddle Mountain through the Supai and contours to the east a little over 3 miles to Tilted Mesa. Not for the faint-hearted, the exposed trail narrows to several feet with drop-offs of 100 feet. The Redwall is reached west of Tilted Mesa on a narrow flat promenade above Nankoweap and Little Nankoweap Canyons.

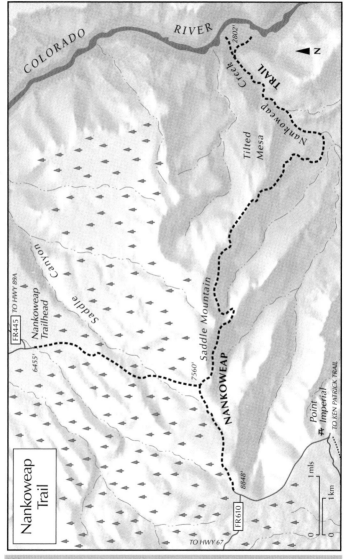

Nankoweap Trail

COLORADO RIVER

Nankoweap Creek

2802'

Tilted Mesa

TRAIL

Nankoweap

Saddle Canyon

FR445 TO HWY 89A

Nankoweap Trailhead

6455'

Saddle Mountain

7560'

NANKOWEAP

Point Imperial

TO KEN PATRICK TRAIL

8848'

FR610

TO HWY 67

1 mls

1 km

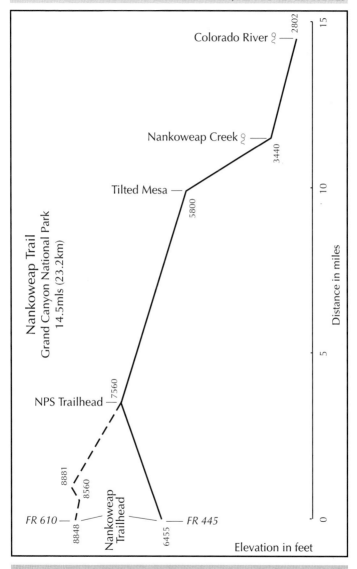

Colorado River — 2802

Nankoweap Creek — 3440

Tilted Mesa — 5800

Nankoweap Trail
Grand Canyon National Park
14.5mls (23.2km)

NPS Trailhead — 7560

8881
8560

FR 610 — 8848

Nankoweap
Trailhead

FR 445
6455

Distance in miles

Elevation in feet

Descending through the steep Redwall you needle your way through layers of scree and talus as you descend farther through the limestone and shale formations. Pick your way through the rubble all the way to the perennial water of Nankoweap Creek. Follow the creek bed downstream for 3 miles, all the way to the Colorado River.

CHAPTER 8

GRAND CANYON NATIONAL PARK: TRANS-CANYON TRAILS, NORTH AND SOUTH RIM

...if you are pleased to see a stream running pure, glorifying a natural pavement;
if you are content to enjoy a river shore, leaving its design undisturbed;
if you think a wilderness river should be left dancing, alive and bringing life;
if you have come, even a little, under the spell of this place,
then this canyon we have seen only a little of
this Grand Canyon, is your Grand Canyon.
Roderick Nash and Ernest Braun

Introduction

The Tonto Trail, the major east-west artery on the southern side of the Colorado River sweeps some 85 or more miles between Red Canyon at Hance Rapids and Bass Canyon. Although not officially part of the Tonto Trail, the 15 mile Escalante Route between Tanner Canyon and Red Canyon adds additional miles to the walker's trans-canyon options.

Not usually walked in its entirety, the Tonto Trail opens up miles of canyon-walking between several convenient access points. Although appearing flat initially, walking the Tonto Trail involves crossing in and out of numerous drainages that indent into the Tonto Platform from the Colorado River. This creates some steep sections as you dip into creek beds and ascend the opposite side. The Tonto Trail supports gorgeous views from all of its sections.

The Tonto Trail between Red Canyon and Bass Canyon is described here along with the Escalante Route in the east to west direction. The section of the Tonto Trail between Garnet Canyon and Bass Canyon is not described here. The Clear Creek Trail, north of the Colorado River, is described from west to east.

Since both the Tonto and Clear Creek trails undulate with little change in elevation, travel on these trails rates as moderate. However, remember that many of the access rim to river trails that are connected together by the Tonto Trail merit strenuous or extremely strenuous ratings. The meandering of the Escalante Route is sometimes less than obvious; cairns mark the way in several places. However, use of the route over recent years has shaped it into more of an obvious trail.

SOUTH RIM, TRANS-CANYON TRAILS

Trail	Distance Miles One way	Distance Kilometres One Way	Rating	Difficulty
Escalante Route: Tanner Canyon to New Hance Trail at Red Canyon	12.0	19.2	Route	Ex. Strenuous
Tonto Trail: New Hance Trail at Red Canyon to Hance Creek	6.4	10.2	Wilderness	Moderate
Tonto Trail: Hance Creek to Cottonwood Creek	5.0	8.0	Wilderness	Moderate
Tonto Trail: Cottonwood Creek to South Kaibab Trail	20.2	32.3	Wilderness	Strenuous
Tonto Trail: South Kaibab Trail to Indian Garden	4.1	6.6	Wilderness	Moderate
Tonto Trail: Indian Garden toHermit Creek	14.5	23.2	Wilderness	Moderate
Tonto Trail: Hermit Creek to Boucher Creek	6.3	10.1	Wilderness	Moderate
Tonto Trail: Boucher Creek to Bass Canyon	30.0	48.0	Wilderness	Strenuous

ESCALANTE ROUTE: TANNER CANYON TO NEW HANCE TRAIL AT RED CANYON

Start:	Tanner Rapids (2,680 feet/817 metres)
End:	New Hance Trail at Red Canyon (2,608 feet/ 795 metres)

Distance, one way:	12 miles (19.2 kilometres)
Times, one way:	10–12 hours
Maps:	Cape Royal, Desert View (United States Geological Survey 7.5'); Grand Canyon National Park (TI)
Season:	spring and autumn
Water:	Tanner Rapids, Unkar Delta, Escalante Creek, Seventyfive Mile Creek, Papago Creek, Hance Rapids
Rating:	extremely strenuous

Directions

Head west from Tanner Rapids along the Colorado River on the sandy river-runners trail that initially veers south, away from the river. Your path undulates over some buttes and up some wooden steps. In less than 1 hour, your route crosses Cardenas Creek. Reaching the Unkar Peninsula, you'll want to refill your water bottles; this is your last water until Escalante Creek. Cross Unkar Peninsula and contour around the north and then west side of the butte that overlooks Unkar Delta. A short detour brings you to the top of the butte that affords excellent views of the delta. Another detour farther west to the canyon edge brings you to a thrilling overlook of Unkar Rapids.

Turn south and head upwards. Gaining elevation gradually over the next 1.5 miles, you rise to the end of an unnamed drainage west of Cardenas Creek. Cairns mark your route. Cross the drainage and turn north-west, gaining a steep 400 feet of elevation as you cross around the east side of Butchart's Ridge. Gorgeous eastern views of the Colorado River, Unkar Delta and Tanner Rapids fill the skyline. You'll find a wonderful lunch stop with sweeping views at the point where the trail circles around the north end of the ridge. After your rest stop, the trail turns south and contours around the west side of the notch.

The National Park Service description of this route presents an alternative that passes directly west through Butchart's Notch. From the west side, the Butchart's Notch Route looks like quite a rocky scramble down back to the trail. Though I have passed through here twice, I've stayed low both times. This straight forward route presents no unusual challenges.

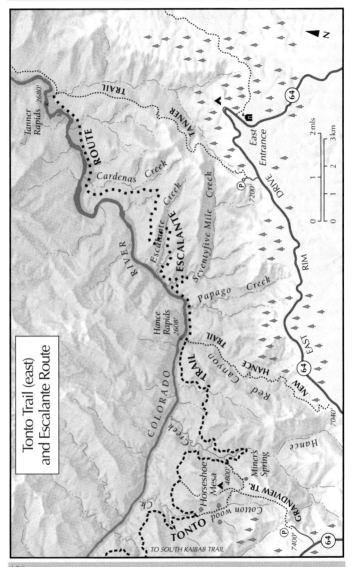

Tonto Trail (east) and Escalante Route

Back on the trail on the west of the Notch, you're now travelling south-west towards Escalante Creek. Cross over the east arm of Escalante Creek and continue west up the hill and descend into the west arm of Escalante Creek. Follow the rocky trail into the creek bed and head north down the creek. When you get to the 20 foot drop-off, backtrack 20 feet and follow the cairns west and north above the drainage. Descend into the drainage and, in 20 minutes, reach a fine camping spot at the Colorado River.

Follow the cairns south-west and along the river until you are above Seventyfive Mile Creek. Turn south and traverse above the creek for about 15 minutes until the cairns lead into the creek bed. Descend into the creek. A 20 foot slide down a rocky ledge drops you into the drainage; you may want to lower your packs. If a pool of water lurks in the creek. This short climb may be difficult to negotiate in the west to east direction. Proceed down the drainage, lowering your packs in several spots if necessary, to Nevills Rapids at Seventyfive Mile Creek.

Next, you may proceed west along the river if the water level is low. A rocky trail leads above the river west for 1 mile to Papago Creek. A chute that requires some scrambling goes down to the beach. Papago Creek offers poor camping choices.

West of Papago Creek, a steep 50 foot high outcrop requires both hands to negotiate. You may wish to raise your packs up with some rope. Follow the cairns that mark the trail south and up another steep 300 feet section, which winds in and out around large rocks. Finally, pass through a break in the rocks. Turn north and descend a steep and loose talus slope to the river; take care not to dislodge rocks onto walkers below. Another 30 minutes along the river through the brush brings you to the New Hance Trail at Red Canyon. You'll find a fine camping spot located west of Red Canyon Wash under some trees a bit back from the river.

TONTO TRAIL: NEW HANCE TRAIL AT RED CANYON TO HANCE CREEK

Start:	New Hance Trail at Red Canyon (2,608 feet/ 795 metres)
End:	Hance Creek (3,670/1,119 metres)

Distance:	6.4 miles (10.2 kilometres)
Times, one way:	3–4 hours
Map:	Cape Royal (United States Geological Survey 7.5′); Grand Canyon National Park (TI)
Season:	spring, winter and autumn
Water:	Hance Rapids, Hance Creek
Rating:	moderate

Directions

From Hance Rapids, at the foot of Red Canyon and the New Hance Trail, proceed west along the river for 20 minutes. The rocky trail takes off above the river and heads east before it turns south. Follow the cairns next as you turn south along the edge of Mineral Canyon. After 30 minutes, turn west and cross Mineral Canyon at Shady Overhang. This aptly named spot provides some shade for a rest stop or lunch. Climb up to the Tonto Platform and continue south to the head of Hance Creek where you'll find perennial water. Miner's (Page) Spring, 30 minutes west, another perennial water source, provides a handy water source if you are ascending to the dry Horseshoe Mesa.

TONTO TRAIL: HANCE CREEK TO COTTONWOOD CREEK

Start:	Hance Creek (3,670/1,119 metres)
End:	Cottonwood Canyon (3,680 feet/ 1,122 metres)
Distance:	5 miles (8 kilometres)
Times, one way:	2–3 hours
Maps:	Cape Royal (United States Geological Survey 7.5′); Grand Canyon National Park (TI)
Season:	spring, winter and autumn
Water:	Hance Creek
Rating:	moderate

Directions
Continue north on the west side of Hance Creek along the Tonto
Trail. In 0.5 mile you pass the turn-off, east, up to Horseshoe Mesa
and Miner's Spring. The Tonto Trail contours north around the base
of Horseshoe Mesa. About 2 miles along, the Cave of the Domes
Trail switchbacks south up the north side of the Mesa and links up
with the Grandview Trail. One mile farther on you come to
Cottonwood Canyon where the Tonto Trail continues west towards
Grapevine Canyon and the South Kaibab Trail. Camp here in the
spring time at Cottonwood Creek or along the creek bed. Another
trail heads south up the west arm of Horseshoe Mesa.

TONTO TRAIL: COTTONWOOD CREEK TO SOUTH KAIBAB TRAIL

Start:	Cottonwood Creek (3,680 feet/ 1,122 metres)
End:	South Kaibab Trail at the Tipoff (3,840 feet/ 1,170 metres)
Distance, one way:	20.2 miles (32.3 kilometres)
Times, one way:	10–13 hours
Maps:	Phantom Ranch, Cape Royal (United States Geological Survey 7.5′); Grand Canyon National Park (TI)
Season:	spring, winter and autumn
Water:	Grapevine Canyon
Rating:	moderate

Directions
From Cottonwood Creek, the Tonto Trail winds 3.5 miles to
Grapevine Creek. From the junction of the Cottonwood Creek Trail
and the Tonto Trail, turn west and head north above Cottonwood
Creek. Some fine campsites line the creek bed. Traverse around Mesa
3928 until you meet the imposing Grapevine Canyon. Stupendous
views of the chasm greet you. Grapevine Canyon holds the
distinction of being the longest tributary drainage along the Tonto
Plateau. Thus, the walk from one side to the other can be long and
tedious in the heat. The trail skirts the south-east arm of Grapevine

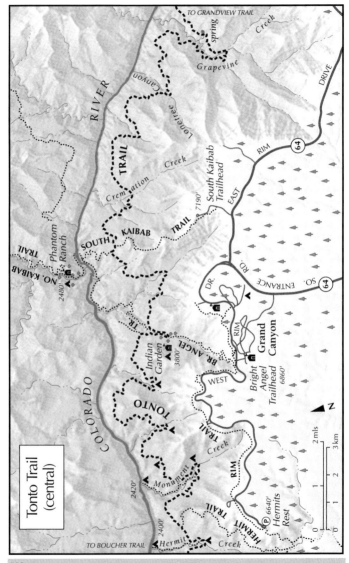

Tonto Trail
(central)

TO GRANDVIEW TRAIL

spring

Creek

Grapevine

DRIVE

RIVER

Canyon

Lonetree Canyon

Cremation Creek

TRAIL

KAIBAB TRAIL

7190'
South Kaibab
Trailhead

EAST RIM

64

SOUTH

NO. KAIBAB TRAIL

Phantom Ranch

2480'

TR

Indian Garden

3800'

BR. ANGEL

WEST

SO. ENTRANCE RD.

DR.

RIM

Grand Canyon

Bright Angel Trailhead
6860'

64

COLORADO

TONTO

TRAIL

Creek

2420'

Monument

RIM

HERMIT TRAIL

N

2 mls

3 km

2400'

TO BOUCHER TRAIL

Hermit Creek

P 6640'
Hermits Rest

Creek before crossing the creek and heading north-west up the opposite side.

Grapevine Creek, supporting the only perennial water source along this section of the Tonto Trail, makes a great spot for a layover day. In spring, large pools of water invite swimmers and cottonwood trees offer well deserved shade.

From Grapevine Creek, now on the west side of the long arm of the creek, head north around the north side of Lyell Butte 5.8 miles to Boulder Creek, your next seasonal water source, often dry in early spring.

Lonetree Canyon, 2.8 miles further, and marking your next seasonal water source, offers a wee bit of shade. Three miles farther on the Tonto Trail you'll reach the south arm of Cremation Canyon. The first and third arms of Cremation Canyon offer the best dry camping spots. From the west arm of Cremation Canyon, it's 1.5 miles along to the South Kaibab Trail at the Tipoff. One half-mile from the west arm, a large rock offers your only shade and protected camping spot. Spectacular views to the north grace this long section of the Tonto Trail. You can see Clear Creek Canyon, Zoroaster Temple, Sumner Butte, Bradley Point and, in the far distance, Bright Angel Canyon. Your next perennial water flows from Pipe Spring, 1.5 miles west of the Tipoff.

TONTO TRAIL: SOUTH KAIBAB TRAIL TO INDIAN GARDEN

Start:	South Kaibab Trail at the Tipoff (3,840 feet/1,170 metres)
End:	Indian Garden (3,800 feet/1,158 metres)
Distance, one way:	4.1 miles (6.6 kilometres)
Times, one way:	2 hours
Maps:	Grand Canyon, Phantom Ranch (United States Geological Survey 7.5'); Grand Canyon National Park (TI)
Season:	all year
Water:	Pipe Spring, Indian Garden
Rating:	moderate

Directions

A small sign at the Tipoff, where there is an emergency telephone and a toilet, marks the intersection of the Tonto Trail with the South Kaibab Trail. Fifteen minutes from the Tipoff, you get an overhead look at Phantom Ranch and Bright Angel Creek. Burro Spring, located 30 minutes further along, may be heard gurgling from the reeds just south of the trail. At about the halfway point, you cross Pipe Creek and its perennial spring. Winding your way west, you pass several small springs, which may be dry in autumn. Plateau Point juts out into your view farther west. Soon you greet civilization at Indian Garden with its buildings, campground, picnic tables, corral, toilets, and water.

TONTO TRAIL: INDIAN GARDEN TO HERMIT CREEK

Start:	Bright Angel Trail at Indian Garden (3,800 feet/1,158 metres)
End:	Hermit Creek (2,960 feet/902 metres)
Distance, one way:	14.5 miles (23.2 kilometres)
Times, one way:	7 hours
Maps:	Grand Canyon (United States Geological Survey 7.5'); Grand Canyon National Park (TI)
Season:	all year
Water:	Hermit Creek, Monument Creek, Indian Garden
Rating:	moderate

Directions

From Indian Garden continue west on the Tonto Trail. Passing the turn-off to Plateau Point, circle north of the Battleship to reach Horn Creek. Plan on carrying water if you've reserved a camping spot at Horn Creek, Salt Creek or Cedar Camp. Cross north around Dana Butte to reach the campsite at Salt Creek. Continuing west crossing around Point 3461 through The Inferno you come to Cedar Spring, just north of the Alligator. One mile farther on you reach Monument Creek. At the head of Monument Creek rises the magnificent spire of Tapeats Sandstone after which the creek bed is named.

A trail, not on the United States Geological Survey maps, leads downhill 1 mile to Granite Rapids where there are fine campsites all along the beach. On the eastern edge of the beach splindly mesquites shield a splendid camp spot. Fine swimming can be found in the upper east wing of Monument Creek.

From Monument Creek, cross north of Cope Butte through two saddles to reach the junction of the Tonto Trail with the Hermit Trail. The Hermit Trail heads south and up to the rim past Cathedral Stairs and Santa Maria Spring.

One mile farther west on the Tonto Trail brings you to the campsites at Hermit Creek. Food should be protected from rodents by hanging packs from the overhead bars. The entire creek bed, especially south, makes for fine exploration with its sculptured walls, rushing water and swimming pools. From here a 1 hour, 600 foot descent north down the rocky creek bed brings you to Hermit Rapids, a highly recommended overnight destination; more scenic than Hermit Camp.

TONTO TRAIL: HERMIT CREEK TO BOUCHER CREEK

Start:	Hermit Creek (2,980 feet/908 metres)
End:	Boucher Creek at Boucher Canyon (2,760 feet/841 metres)
Distance, one way:	6.3 miles (10.1 kilometres)
Times, one way:	3–4 hours
Maps:	Grand Canyon (United States Geological Survey 7.5'); Grand Canyon National Park (TI)
Season:	all year
Water:	Boucher Creek, Hermit Creek
Rating:	moderate

Directions

Heading west again you pass on the west slope of Hermit Creek curving around the point that separates Travertine Canyon and Hermit Creek. Here you gain fine views of the Inner Gorge and back to Hermit Creek. Above you lurk the points of Hermits' Rest, Pima Point and Mojave Point. Next you enter the dry Travertine Canyon as you enter and exit via several rocky ledges.

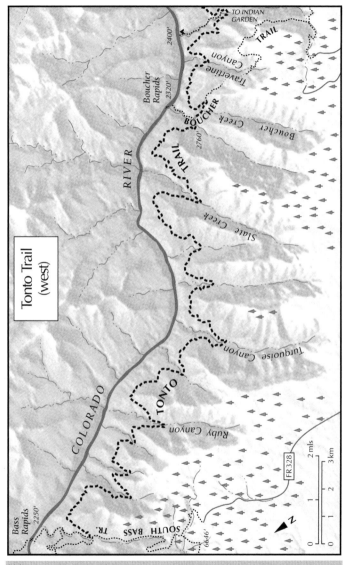

Tonto Trail (west)

TO INDIAN GARDEN

TRAIL

2400'

Boucher Rapids

2320'

Travertine Canyon

BOUCHER

2760'

Boucher Creek

RIVER

TRAIL

Slate Creek

COLORADO

Turquoise Canyon

TONTO

Ruby Canyon

Bass Rapids

2250'

SOUTH BASS TR.

2646'

FR 328

N

2 mls

3 km

The Tonto Trail undulates across the rolling plateau and pleasant walking predominates. Traverse around the north side of Whites Butte. Looking back, you are rewarded with fine views of Hermit Rapids as well as the Hermit Trail. You come now to the junction of the Tonto Trail with the Boucher Trail. Continue for 20 minutes heading west on the Tonto Trail to Boucher Creek where there are several campsites and year-round water. A rocky 30 minute descent from here down Boucher Creek brings you to Boucher Rapids.

TONTO TRAIL: BOUCHER CREEK TO BASS CANYON

Start:	Boucher Canyon (2,760 feet/841 metres)
End:	Bass Canyon (3,200 feet/975 metres)
Distance, one way:	30 miles (41.6 kilometres)
Times, one way:	15–20 hours
Maps:	Grand Canyon, Havasupai Point, Shiva Temple, (United States Geological Survey 7.5'); Grand Canyon National Park (TI)
Season:	spring
Water:	Bass Rapids, Boucher Creek
Rating:	strenuous

If you use good judgement and care, this remote section of the Tonto Trail poses no special difficulties. However, only seasoned canyoneers should attempt this section. Like many sections of the Tonto Trail, spring offers the best chance to take advantage of seasonal water sources. Be sure to check with the BRO before you start on your trip.

The Tonto Trails remains up on the platform across this remote section except when short cutting drainages. There are some steep rocky descents into the creek beds, usually marked by cairns, followed by short steep ascents out of the beds to reach the Tonto Platform again.

Directions
Heading west from your perennial water source at Boucher Creek, your first stop should be Slate Canyon, 5 miles away. Leaving Slate

Canyon, contour around through Agate and Sapphire Canyons. Twelve miles from Boucher Creek you find your next seasonal water source at Turquoise Canyon, a good choice for an overnight stop.

Continuing west, you greet your next seasonal water source at Ruby Canyon after passing through Shaler and Le Conte plateaux. River-runners have named these numerous side canyons "the gems". You'll pass Jasper and then Jade canyons before reaching Ruby Canyon. Next you'll greet Quartz Canyon and then Emerald Canyon and two unnamed drainages before coming to Serpentine Canyon. Four more miles brings you to Bass Canyon. One mile north on the South Bass Trail brings you to Bass Rapids.

If you are planning to join these two rim to river trails it is prudent to descend the South Bass Trail and ascend the steep Boucher Trail or more gradual Hermit Trail. The South Bass trailhead is located 29 miles from Grand Canyon Village on Rowe Well Road and 4 miles north of Pasture Wash Ranger Station on Forest Service Road 328. This unmaintained, rutted road floods any time of year; high clearance four-wheel drive vehicles are recommended. The Hermit's Rest car park, located 8 miles west of Grand Canyon Village on West Rim Road, provides convenient access to the Boucher Trail.

The Tonto Trail terminates 15 miles west of Bass Canyon at Garnet Canyon. Very experienced canyon walkers with rock-climbing skills will want to explore the Royal Arch Route and Apache Trail and visit Elves Chasm.

NORTH RIM TRAILS

Trail	Distance Miles One way	Distance Kilometres One Way	Rating	Difficulty
Clear Creek Trail	8.8	14.0	Wilderness	Moderate

CLEAR CREEK TRAIL

Start:	Clear Creek Trailhead at North Kaibab Trail (2,649 feet/805 metres)
End:	Clear Creek (3,420 feet/1042 metres)

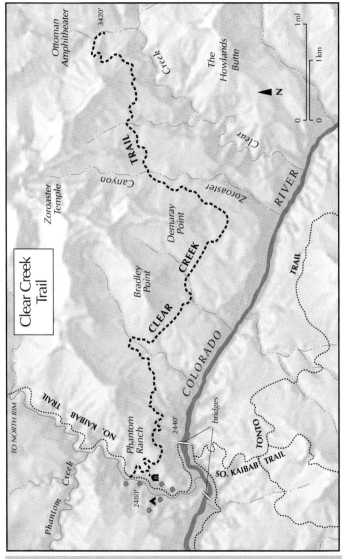

Clear Creek
Trail

Ottoman
Amphitheater

3420'

Creek

The
Howlands
Butte

1 ml

1 km

N

0

0

TRAIL

Clear

Zoroaster
Temple

Canyon

Zoroaster

RIVER

Demaray
Point

CREEK

Bradley
Point

CLEAR

COLORADO

TRAIL

TO NORTH RIM

NO. KAIBAB TRAIL

Phantom
Ranch

bridges

2440'

TONTO

SO. KAIBAB TRAIL

Phantom Creek

2480'

Distance, one way:	8.8 miles (14 kilometres)
Maps:	Phantom Ranch (United States Geological Survey 7.5'); Grand Canyon National Park (TI)
Season:	all year
Water:	Bright Angel Creek, Clear Creek
Rating:	moderate

Directions

The Clear Creek Trail leaves the North Kaibab Trail 0.3 mile north-east of Phantom Ranch. The first 1.5 miles brings you to Phantom Overlook where you can rest on a bench and enjoy the views to Phantom Ranch below. For the first 2 miles the trail criss-crosses steeply on a well-formed path 1,500 feet up above the river to the base of Sumner Butte. Great river views back to the Colorado River suspension bridges and Phantom Ranch compliment the walk once you have reached the plateau.

Camp only after you reach the rim and remember to carry water. If you've been unable to get a campsite at Bright Angel Campground, this makes a great if not better alternative to the crowds at the canyon bottom.

Now begin your 6 mile, level traverse to the east side of Clear Creek. You cross in and out of several drainages as you pass to the south of Bradley and Demaray Points. In the last mile you drop 500 feet to the Clear Creek drainage. Pleasant campsites dot the side of the creek among the cottonwoods. In all, you've walked almost 9 miles from Phantom Ranch. Popular day-hikes from this point include a trip to the Colorado River to the south or north to Cheyava Falls.

CHAPTER 9

GRAND CANYON NATIONAL PARK:
SOUTH AND NORTH RIM TRAILS

I am part of all that I have met;
Yet all experience is an arch wherethro'
Gleams that untravell'd world, whose margin fades
For even and for ever when I move.
Alfred Lord Tennyson

SOUTH RIM TRAILS

Trail	Distance Miles One way	Distance Kilometres One Way	Rating	Difficulty
Rim Trail	9.0	14.4	Rim	Easy
Shoshone Point Trail	1.0	1.6	Rim	Easy

RIM TRAIL

Start:	Hermit Trailhead at Hermits' Rest (6,640 feet/2,023 metres)
End:	Yavapai Point (6,640 feet/2,024 metres)
Distance, one way:	9 miles (14.4 kilometres)
Times, one way:	4 hours
Maps:	Grand Canyon, Phantom Ranch (United States Geological Survey 7.5'); Grand Canyon National Park (TI); Grand Canyon National Park (EP)
Season:	all year
Water:	Hermits' Rest
Rating:	easy

Winding its way along the South Rim from Hermits' Rest to Mather Point, the 9 mile Rim Trail can be reached from any of its major South

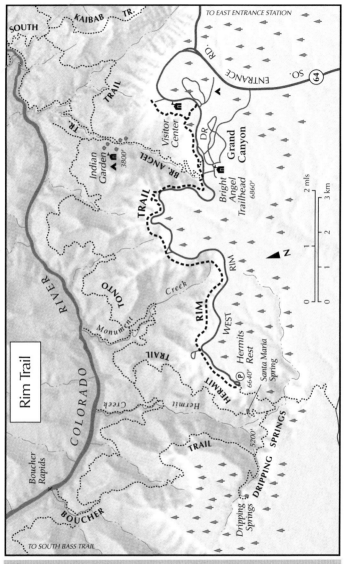

Rim Trail

Rim viewpoints. Some consider it one of the finest of the Grand Canyon walks with its splendid and dramatic views of different parts of the canyon. During the spring and summer, you must take the shuttle bus to points along the trail. Cars are not allowed along the West Rim Road between mid-March and September. Try taking the bus to Hermits' Rest and walking east on the trail toward Grand Canyon Village. The Rim Trail makes a fine short trip, using the bus to access the different viewpoints, or a longer day-walk.

Paved and wheelchair accessible for 3.5 miles between Yavapai and Maricopa points, the rest of the trail alternates between rocky sections, groomed trail and broken pavement. Lightweight shoes will suffice for its entire length. Children should keep clear from the canyon's precipitous edge.

Directions
The Rim Trail heads east from Hermits' Rest passing first by Pima Point. From here you can see sections of the Hermit Trail as it winds its way down Cathedral Stairs. Hermit and Boucher Rapids are also visible. From Hermits' Rest to Maricopa Point the Rim Trail passes close to the rim with dangerous drop-offs. The section between Hermits' Rest and Maricopa Point is much less used than the Trail's eastern section.

The 4 mile section between Pima Point to Mohave Point boasts spectacular views. From Pima Point, continue along the rim southeast and you soon pass above the Abyss, a deep chasm which indents into the rim at the south end of Monument Creek. This impressive amphitheatre cuts a deep void into the layers of rock. From this section of the Trail you can see the Tonto Trail as it undulates east to west along the Tonto Platform. East of the Abyss, the Trail turns north towards Mohave Point. The Tonto Trail is visible traversing the Tonto Platform and you can see Hermit and Granite Rapids.

Between Mohave and Maricopa Point you pass the Powell Memorial, built to honour the early Grand Canyon explorer, J. Wesley Powell. Views are now to the east where you can see the Bright Angel Trail snaking its way from Indian Garden to the rim. Pass the Rim Trail Overlook which gives you a bird's eye view of Bright Angel Trail. Soon the numbers of visitors increase as you descend to reach the bus stop at the end of West Rim Road.

Next, heading into the main and busiest section of the village, you pass the Bright Angel trailhead, the busy Bright Angel and El Tovar Hotels, and Vercamp's Curios. Views are across the wide canyon and, at your feet, cottonwoods shade the verdant Indian Garden. The final part of the Trail heads to Yavapai Point, overlooking Garden Creek, as it follows the wooded edge of the South Rim. A turn-off south heads to the visitor centre.

SHOSHONE POINT TRAIL

Start:	East Rim Drive (7,200 feet/2,195 kilometres)
End:	Shoshone Point (7,300 feet/2,225 metres)
Distance, one way:	1 mile (1.6 kilometres)
Time, one way:	20 minutes
Maps:	Phantom Ranch (United States Geological Survey 7.5'; Grand Canyon National Park (TI); Grand Canyon National Park (EP)
Season:	all year
Water:	none
Difficulty:	easy

Directions

The Shoshone Point Trail starts from an unmarked turnout 1.75 miles east of Yaki Point along East Rim Drive. From the car park walk through the locked gate on to the dirt road. One mile through the pine forest brings you to picnic tables and the canyon's edge. The area can be rented from the park service for special occasions. Shoshone Point juts out from the rim and offers excellent views down to Grapevine and Cremation Creeks. To the west, the South Kaibab Trail switchbacks down the east side of O'Neill Butte. It is possible to visually follow much of the South Kaibab to Grandview Loop.

NORTH RIM TRAILS: INTRODUCTION

The main North Rim of the Grand Canyon lures visitors with several fine walks starting from near the main visitor centre. The lofty North Rim provides a cool alternative to the soaring temperatures of the lower canyon. In recent years the number of visitors to this far away haven has increased, especially after glowing reports in numerous travel magazines. Cape Royal, Point Imperial and Bright Angel Point boast some of the most outstanding and unusual canyon views. Be sure not to miss them.

From the main North Rim, only the North Kaibab Trail drops below the rim. As it winds its way down Roaring Springs Canyon, rising walls block views from the trail. This Corridor Trail (see section 7) makes up part of the major artery for walkers wanting to walk across the canyon.

To reach the North Rim, follow Arizona Highway 67 south from Jacob Lake, Arizona for 31 miles to the North Rim Entrance Station. The Cape Royal Road/Point Imperial Road veers east 9.5 miles from the Entrance Station. The park road heads 2.5 miles farther south to Grand Canyon Lodge and the visitor centre.

NORTH RIM TRAILS

Trail	Distance Miles One way	Distance Kilometres One Way	Rating	Difficulty
Cape Royal Trail	0.3	0.5	Rim	Easy
Cliff Springs Trail	0.5	0.8	Rim	Easy
Cape Final Trail	2.0	3.2	Rim	Easy
Ken Patrick Trail	10.0	8.0	Rim	Moderate
Bright Angel Point Trail	0.5	0.4	Rim	Easy
Transept Trail	1.5	2.4	Rim	Easy
Widforss Trail	5.0	8.0	Rim	Easy
Uncle Jim Trail	2.5	4.0	Rim	Easy

CAPE ROYAL TRAIL

Start:	Cape Royal car park (7,800 feet/ 2,377 metres)
End:	Cape Royal (7,865 feet/2,397 metres)
Distance, one way:	0.6 mile (1 kilometre)
Time, one way:	10 minutes
Maps:	Cape Royal (United States Geological Survey 7.5'); Grand Canyon National Park (TI)
Season:	mid-May to mid-October
Water:	none
Difficulty:	easy

From the Cape Royal/Point Imperial Road junction with the park road, turn east and proceed 14.3 miles to the end of the road at Cape Royal.

From the car park at the end of the Cape Royal Road, this short trail passes Angel's Window to the end of Cape Royal. A short detour guides you to a viewpoint above this large eroded gap in the canyon's limestone layer.

Directions
Continuing on to Cape Royal, the stunning view extends almost 360° to include Vishnu Temple, Freya Caste, Wotans Throne, Coronado Buttes and the Colorado River, 70 miles below Lee's Ferry. From this point, the Colorado River winds 18 more miles to Phantom Ranch and 207 miles west to Lake Mead. On the far southern rim, you can see the Desert View Lookout and Horseshoe Mesa at the base of the Grandview Trail. In the far distance, the San Francisco peaks line the horizon.

CLIFF SPRINGS TRAIL

Start:	Cape Royal Road (7,700 feet/2,347 metres)
End:	Cliff Springs (7,500 feet/2,286 metres)
Distance, one way:	1 mile (1.6 kilometres)
Time, one way:	20 minutes
Maps:	Walhalla Plateau (United States Geological Survey 7.5'); Grand Canyon National Park (TI)
Season:	mid-May to mid-October
Water:	none
Difficulty:	easy

From the Cape Royal/Point Imperial Road Y-junction with the park road, turn east and proceed 13.7 miles to the Cliff Springs trailhead on the east side of the road. You will be 0.6 miles north of the end of the road at Cape Royal. This trail starts from the east side of the Cape Royal Road.

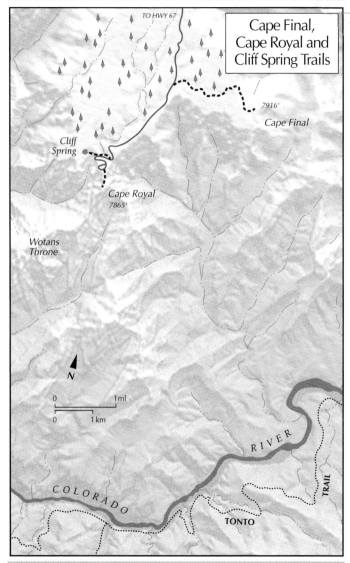

Cape Final,
Cape Royal and
Cliff Spring Trails

TO HWY 67

7916'

Cape Final

Cliff
Spring

Cape Royal
7865'

Wotans
Throne

N

0   1 ml
0   1 km

RIVER

TRAIL

COLORADO

TONTO

Directions
Cross the road and begin your descent. In 100 yards you'll pass the old Anasazi granary. Continue to drop through pine trees to meet a rocky draw and reach a series of Kaibab cliffs. Here numerous seeps converge and drip into pools. Contour around the ledges and boulders until you arrive at an obvious end point with fine views of Cape Royal. Retrace your steps back to the car.

CAPE FINAL TRAIL

Start:	Cape Royal Road (7,800 feet/2,377 metres)
End:	Cape Final (8,000 feet/2,438 metres)
Distance, one way:	2 miles
Time, one way:	1 hour
Maps:	Walhalla Plateau (United States Geological Survey 7.5'); Grand Canyon National Park (TI)
Season:	mid-May to mid-October
Water:	none
Difficulty:	easy

This pleasant day or overnight walk starts from a small turnout off the Cape Royal Road 11.7 miles north of the Y-junction with the Point Imperial Road and 2.5 miles south of the end of the road at Cape Royal. If you wish to spend the night, don't forget to pick up a backcountry permit and carry water.

Directions
From the car park, follow the Cape Final Trail east through the pine trees - the road undulates through the forest. After 1 mile, at the clearing, your first canyon views include the Little Colorado River, Lava Creek and the towered Siegfried Pyre. Turning south in the trees you amble along this level trail to the south side of Cape Final. Your views from here include Unkar Creek and Delta along the Escalante Route. In the distance the Painted Desert, the South Rim and the Coconino Plateau mark the horizon. Retrace your steps back to the road.

KEN PATRICK TRAIL

Start:	Point Imperial (8,803 feet/2,683 metres)
End:	Cape Royal Road (8,440 feet/2,572 metres)
Distance, one way:	3 miles (4.8 kilometres)
Time, one way:	1.5 hours
Maps:	Point Imperial (United States Geological Survey 7.5'); Grand Canyon National Park (TI)
Season:	mid-May to mid-October
Water:	none
Difficulty:	moderate

From the Cape Royal Road/Point Imperial Road junction with the park road, turn east and go 5.4 miles to the Y-junction. Continue north for 2.7 miles to Point Imperial.

Point Imperial, the highest point on either rim, marks one of the finest views in all of the Grand Canyon. Flat topped Mt. Hayden adorns the foreground views. In the distance you can make out the mouth of the Little Colorado, Marble Platform, Cedar Mountain and Humphrey's Peak 12,633 feet (3,851 metres), the highest point in Arizona. The 10 mile long Ken Patrick Trail connects the North Kaibab trailhead with Point Imperial. Its most scenic 3 mile section, described here, follows the canyon rim.

Directions
From the west end of the Point Imperial car park, walk down the stairs and enjoy the fine views of Mt. Hayden. In the distance you can see the Little Colorado River, the Painted Desert and the San Francisco Peaks. The trail, with its ups and downs, passes through the forest and then descends 100 feet on switchbacks below the road. Then the trail ascends away from the road into the forest. Continuing south-west, the trail continues with its undulations just west of the rim. You can see Nankoweap Creek and the general path of the Nankoweap Trail. In a bit over 2 miles the trail curves east and continues up and down to reach the Cape Royal Road. Continue south-west for 7 miles to the North Kaibab trailhead or retrace your steps back to your car at Point Imperial.

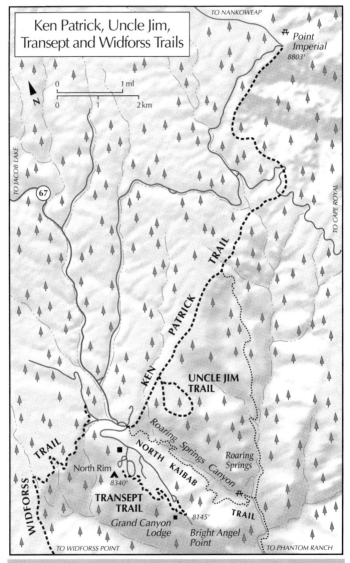

Ken Patrick, Uncle Jim,
Transept and Widforss Trails

TO NANKOWEAP

Point
Imperial
8803'

TO JACOB LAKE

67

TO CAPE ROYAL

KEN PATRICK TRAIL

UNCLE JIM
TRAIL

WIDFORSS TRAIL

TRAIL

Roaring Springs Canyon

NORTH KAIBAB

Roaring
Springs

North Rim
8340'

TRANSEPT
TRAIL

8145'

Grand Canyon
Lodge

Bright Angel
Point

TRAIL

TO WIDFORSS POINT

TO PHANTOM RANCH

0   1 ml

0   1   2 km

N

Tanner Trail, Grand Canyon National Park

BRIGHT ANGEL POINT TRAIL

Start:	Grand Canyon Lodge (8,161 feet/ 2,487 metres)
End:	Bright Angel Point (8,250 feet/2,515 metres)
Distance, one way:	0.5 miles (0.8 kilometres)
Time, one way:	10 minutes
Maps:	Bright Angel Point (United States Geological Survey 7.5'); Grand Canyon National Park (TI); Grand Canyon National Park (EP)
Season:	mid-May to mid-October
Water:	none
Difficulty:	easy

Beginning at Grand Canyon Lodge at the north end of Highway 67 and the park road, this short trail straddles a ridge across Roaring Springs Canyon and Transept Canyon and ends at Bright Angel Point. Bright Angel Point presents one of the finest Grand Canyon views with Deva, Brama, Angel's Gate and Zoroaster Temples prominently displayed in the foreground.

Directions
From this point, you can follow the course of the North Kaibab Trail down Roaring Springs Canyon until it connects with Bright Angel Canyon at Roaring Springs and then continues to the Colorado River. On the distant South Rim you can identify Yaki Point at the start of the South Kaibab Trail and some of the hotels.

TRANSEPT TRAIL

Start:	North Rim Campground (8,000 feet/ 2,438 metres)
End:	Grand Canyon Lodge (8,161 feet/ 2,487 metres)
Distance, one way:	1.5 miles (2.4 kilometres)
Time, one way:	40 minutes
Maps:	Bright Angel Point (United States Geological Survey 7.5'); Grand Canyon National Park (TI); Grand Canyon National

	Park (EP)
Season:	mid-May to mid-October
Water:	none
Difficulty:	easy

From Jacob Lake, Arizona drive along Arizona Highway 67, south, for 31 miles to the North Rim Entrance Station. Continue south on the park road for 21 miles to the turn-off to the campground and the general store.

This popular 1.5 mile trail links Campsite 15 at the North Rim Campground with the Bright Angel Lodge. Although views are partially blocked by pine trees and shrubs, its undulating course overlooks Transept Canyon for its entire length.

WIDFORSS TRAIL

Start:	Widforss Trailhead (8,000 feet/2,438 metres)
End:	Widforss Point (8,250 feet/2,515 metres)
Distance, one way:	5 miles (8 kilometres)
Time, one way:	2 hours
Maps:	Bright Angel Point (United States Geological Survey 7.5'); Grand Canyon National Park (TI); Grand Canyon National Park (EP)
Season:	mid-May to mid-October
Water:	none
Difficulty:	easy

Drive 4 miles north of Grand Canyon Lodge to the turn-off for the Widforss trailhead. Turn west and follow the dirt road 1 mile to the car park. From the Cape Royal Road/Point Imperial Road junction with the park road, proceed 0.25 miles south to the turn-off to the Widforss trailhead.

Apart from a short climb at the beginning of the walk, the mostly level trail makes a fine, easy day trip. Overnight camping is allowed; be sure to pick up a backcountry permit and carry water. A self-guiding brochure describes the first half of the walk.

Directions
The first 0.5 mile winds through typical North Rim forests of pine, fir and aspen trees. Views open up along the first half of the trail as it passes the edge of Transept Canyon. From some of the viewpoints, you get glimpses of Grand Canyon Lodge on the far side of the Canyon. At 2.5 miles, the halfway point, the route passes through heavy forest and then, surprisingly, opens up to panoramic vistas. The trail stops 0.5 mile south-east of Widforss Point itself and overlooks Haunted Canyon.

UNCLE JIM TRAIL

Start:	North Kaibab Trailhead (8,241 feet/2,515 metres)
End:	Uncle Jim Point (8,031 feet/2,448 kilometres)
Distance, one way:	2.5 miles (4 kilometres)
Time, one way:	1.5 hours
Maps:	Bright Angel Point (United States Geological Survey 7.5'); Grand Canyon National Park (TI); Grand Canyon National Park (EP)
Season:	mid-May to mid-October
Water:	none
Difficulty:	easy

The North Kaibab trailhead is 0.9 miles south of the Cape Royal Road/Point Imperial Road junction on the park highway and 2 miles north of Grand Canyon Lodge.

Directions
Starting from the North Kaibab trailhead, this trail overlaps for its first 2 miles with the Ken Patrick Trail. At first traversing along the rim of Roaring Springs Canyon, the trail turns south soon reaching the junction with a 1.5 mile loop. Joining the loop in either direction you cross level terrain and then greet a viewpoint above the North Kaibab Trail and Roaring Springs Canyon. Continue around to complete the loop and return to the car park on the first section of the trail. Walkers share this waterless trail with mules.

CHAPTER 10

GRAND CANYON NATIONAL PARK: LONG DISTANCE ROUTES

I am glad I shall never be young without wild country to be young in.
Of what avail are forty freedoms without a blank spot on the map!
Aldo Leopold

Introduction

Once you've a few miles of Grand Canyon hiking under your boots, perhaps on the Corridor trails or the Grandview Trail, you'll want to explore more of the park by connecting several of the rim to river trails. I give some information and personal ideas about the trips below. See section 6 (South Rim, River to River trails and section 8, Trans-canyon trails) for descriptions of the individual trails that make up the loops. The Kanab Canyon – Thunder River Loop is described in detail at the end of this section.

LONG DISTANCE ROUTES

Trail	Distance Miles One way	Distance Kilometres One Way	Rating	Difficulty
Boucher Trail to Hermit Trail Loop	23.0	36.8	Wilderness	Ex. strenuous
Hermit Trail to Bright Angel Trail Loop	22.9	36.6	Wild/Corr	Strenuous
North to South Rim: North Kaibab Trail to Bright Angel Trail	23.3	37.2	Corridor	Moderate
South Kaibab Trail to Bright Angel Trail	16.3	26.1	Corridor	Moderate
Grandview Trail to South Kaibab Trail	27.8	44.4	Wild/Corr.	Strenuous
Escalante Route: Tanner Trail to Grandview Trail	33.0	52.8	Wilderness	Ex. strenuous
Kanab Canyon to Thunder River Route	50.5	80.8	Route	Ex. strenuous

The suggested routes and trails below give you an idea for several overnight trips in Grand Canyon National Park. Walkers with no previous experience in the Grand Canyon should try the Corridor trails, South Kaibab to Bright Angel Loop and the trans-canyon North Kaibab to Bright Angel trip.

Combining the rim to river trails with sections of the Tonto Trail and Escalante Route make splendid overnight trips. Experienced beginners can consider the Hermit to Bright Angel Loop. A step up from these trips is an overnight trip on Horseshoe Mesa on the Grandview Trail or the Grandview Trail to South Kaibab Trail trip. More experience is recommended for the Boucher to Hermit Loop or Escalante Route, Tanner Trail to Grandview Trail or New Hance Trail. Only experienced canyoneers should attempt the Kanab Canyon to Thunder River Loop.

BOUCHER TRAIL TO HERMIT TRAIL LOOP

Start:	Hermits' Rest (6,640 feet/2,023 metres)
End:	Hermits' Rest (6,640 feet/2,023 metres)
Distance, one way:	23 miles (36.8 kilometres)
Times:	3–4 days
Maps:	Grand Canyon (United States Geological Survey 7.5');
	Grand Canyon National Park (TI); Grand Canyon National Park (EP)
Season:	all year
Water:	Boucher Creek, Boucher Rapids, Hermit Creek
Rating:	extremely strenuous

This loop takes advantage of Hermits' Rest as a convenient trailhead for the 3–4 day-walk. In summer, take the shuttle bus to the end of the West Rim Drive from Grand Canyon Village at the South Rim. Other times of the year you can drive yourself to the car park at the end of the road.

The Boucher Trail, one of the more difficult rim to river trails, has become more popular in recent years. Sections are exposed and one short part requires down climbing.

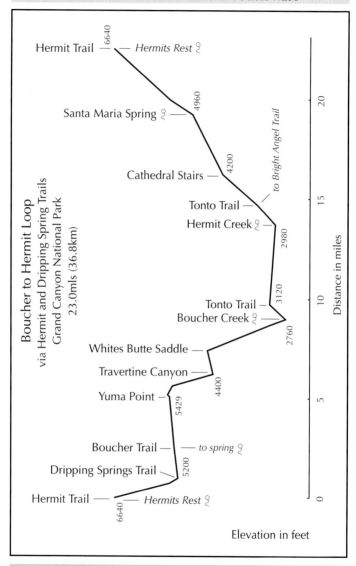

Boucher to Hermit Loop
via Hermit and Dripping Spring Trails
Grand Canyon National Park
23.0mls (36.8km)

Hermit Trail — | 6640 — *Hermits Rest* ♀

Santa Maria Spring ♀ — 4960

Cathedral Stairs — 4200

Tonto Trail —
Hermit Creek ♀ — 2980

Tonto Trail — 3120
Boucher Creek ♀ — 2760

Whites Butte Saddle —
Travertine Canyon — 4400
Yuma Point — 5429

Boucher Trail — — *to spring* ♀
Dripping Springs Trail — 5200
Hermit Trail — 6640 — *Hermits Rest* ♀

to Bright Angel Trail

Distance in miles

Elevation in feet

Directions

Descend the Boucher Trail, walk west to east on the Tonto Trail and ascend the Hermit Trail. The section of the Tonto Trail that connects Boucher Canyon with Hermit Creek undulates across the Tonto Trail on a straightforward course and presents no difficulties. The popular Hermit Trail, trodden upon by hikers as much as a Corridor trail, resembles a maintained trail. You'll find the Hermit Trail takes a more gradual ascent than the steep Boucher Trail. Extra days can be spent at Boucher Creek, Hermit Creek or Hermit Rapids.

HERMIT TRAIL TO BRIGHT ANGEL TRAIL LOOP

Start:	Hermits' Rest (6,640 feet/2,023 metres)
End:	Bright Angel Trailhead (6,860 feet/ 2,091 metres)
Distance, one way:	22.9 miles (36.6 kilometres)
Backpacking times:	3–4 days
Maps:	Grand Canyon, Phantom Ranch (United States Geological Survey 7.5'); Grand Canyon National Park (TI); Grand Canyon National Park (EP)
Season:	all year
Water:	Hermit Creek, Hermit Rapids, Monument Creek, Indian Garden
Rating:	moderate

The Hermit to Bright Angel Loop has become one of the Canyon's most popular overnight trips. This popular trip is not a true loop at all but start's at Hermits' Rest and ends at the Bright Angel trailhead near Kolb Studio. A bus or taxi will connect you back to your car. You must camp in one of the several designated sites along the way. A good step up from the Corridor trails, this long distance trail can be easily handled by first-time canyon walkers with some backpacking experience. Most walkers choose to descend the Hermit Trail. Pleasant layover days can be spent at Hermit Rapids or Granite Rapids.

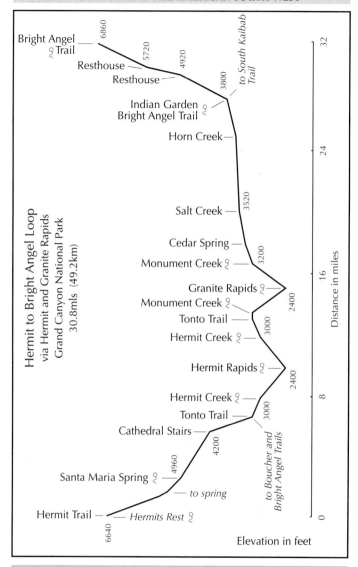

Hermit to Bright Angel Loop
via Hermit and Granite Rapids
Grand Canyon National Park
30.8mls (49.2km)

Bright Angel Trail — 6860

Resthouse — 5720

Resthouse — 4920

to South Kaibab Trail

Indian Garden
Bright Angel Trail — 3800

Horn Creek —

Salt Creek — 3520

Cedar Spring —

Monument Creek — 3200

Granite Rapids —

Monument Creek — 2400

Tonto Trail — 3000

Hermit Creek —

Hermit Rapids — 2400

Hermit Creek —

Tonto Trail — 3000

Cathedral Stairs —

to Boucher and Bright Angel Trails

Santa Maria Spring — 4960

to spring — 4200

Hermit Trail — 6640

Hermits Rest —

Distance in miles

32

24

16

8

0

Elevation in feet

136

CROSS-CANYON: NORTH KAIBAB TRAIL TO BRIGHT ANGEL TRAIL

Start:	North Kaibab Trailhead (8,241 feet/ 2,515 metres)
End:	Bright Angel Trailhead (6,860 feet/ 2,091 metres)
Distance, one way:	23.3 miles (37.2 kilometres)
Backpacking times	3–4 days
Maps:	Grand Canyon, Phantom Ranch, Bright Angel Point (United States Geological Survey 7.5′); Grand Canyon National Park (TI); Grand Canyon National Park (EP)
Season:	mid-May to mid-October
Water:	Supai Tunnel, Roaring Springs, Cottonwood Camp, Phantom Ranch, Bright Angel Campground, Colorado River, Indian Garden
Difficulty:	moderate

This popular trip links the North Rim with the South Rim. It utilizes the only bridges that cross the Colorado River near Phantom Ranch and Bright Angel Campground. You must make the long, although pleasant, 5 hour drive between the South Rim and North Rim. Contact Transcanyon Shuttle (Appendix B) for information on bus services between the two points.

Trans-canyon hikers are allowed to use North Rim Campground, located near the general store, without a prior reservation. Check at the campground entrance for information and location of your site. You must obtain the usual backcountry permit for your walk.

Though many people feel this is a "must-do" and then can claim they have "walked the Grand Canyon", I found it disappointing. This trail is partially paved and dotted with buildings. The trails are heavily used by day-walkers, backpackers, runners, and mules alike. I have logged many many miles in other more scenic, less crowded, true wilderness areas of the Grand Canyon.

Walkers on The North Kaibab and the Bright Angel trails following creek bed depressions, rather than ridge lines, are deprived of spectacular canyon views. The three Corridor

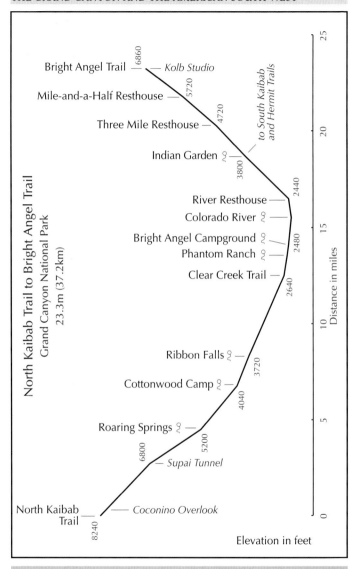

North Kaibab Trail to Bright Angel Trail
Grand Canyon National Park
23.3m (37.2km)

Bright Angel Trail — 6860 — *Kolb Studio*

Mile-and-a-Half Resthouse — 5720

Three Mile Resthouse — 4720

Indian Garden ⚲ — 3800

to South Kaibab and Hermit Trails

River Resthouse — 2440

Colorado River ⚲ —

Bright Angel Campground ⚲ — 2480

Phantom Ranch ⚲ —

Clear Creek Trail — 2640

Ribbon Falls ⚲ — 3720

Cottonwood Camp ⚲ — 4040

Roaring Springs ⚲ — 5200

6800 — *Supai Tunnel*

North Kaibab Trail — 8240 — *Coconino Overlook*

Distance in miles
0   5   10   15   20   25

Elevation in feet

campsites, Cottonwood, Bright Angel and Indian Garden, are overcrowded and heavily used. If you wish to get away from it all, look elsewhere. Try any of the other long distance walks described here.

SOUTH KAIBAB TRAIL TO BRIGHT ANGEL TRAIL

Start:	South Kaibab Trailhead near Yaki Point (7,190 feet/2,192 metres)
End:	Bright Angel Trailhead (6,860 feet/ 2,091 metres) at Kolb Studio
Distance, one way:	16.3.miles (26.1 kilometres)
Backpacking time:	2 days
Maps:	Phantom Ranch (United States Geological Survey 7.5'); Grand Canyon National Park (TI); Grand Canyon National Park (EP)
Season:	all year
Water:	Bright Angel Campground, Indian Garden
Rating:	moderate

This extremely popular 2–3 days walk makes up the park's most popular overnight trip. Accessible all year around, water is available on the ascent at Indian Garden all year and at Three Mile and One-and-a-Half Mile rest houses during the summer. Extra days may be spend exploring the North Kaibab Trail or Clear Creek. This route can be walked as a backpack trip staying at Bright Angel Campground or at Indian Garden on the walk out. Lighten your load by staying in the cabins or dormitories at Phantom Ranch. An additional night may be spent at Indian Garden on the ascent if you are backpacking.

Although this is the most popular overnight trip in the park and the South Kaibab is a spectacular trail, the Bright Angel is disappointing. The National Park Service does recommend that all first-time canyon hikers keep to the Corridor trails. If not hiking in the heat of summer, you may want to consider returning to the rim on the more scenic South Kaibab Trail.

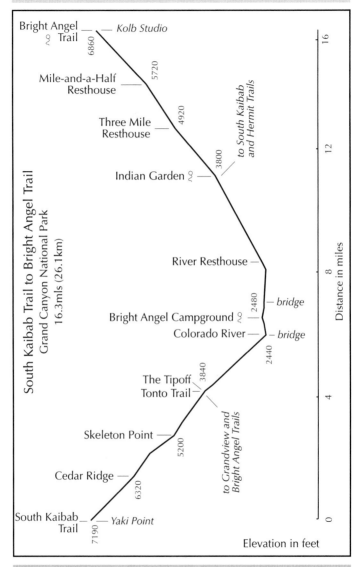

Bright Angel ___ — *Kolb Studio*
 ⚲ Trail   6860   5720

Mile-and-a-Half ___
Resthouse   4920

Three Mile ___
Resthouse   3800   — *to South Kaibab
and Hermit Trails*

Indian Garden ⚲ ___

River Resthouse ___

                                        2480 — *bridge*
Bright Angel Campground ⚲ ___
Colorado River ___ — *bridge*
                                        2440

The Tipoff   3840
Tonto Trail ___   — *to Grandview and
Bright Angel Trails*

Skeleton Point ___   5200

Cedar Ridge ___   6320

South Kaibab ___ — *Yaki Point*
Trail   7190

South Kaibab Trail to Bright Angel Trail
Grand Canyon National Park
16.3mls (26.1km)

Distance in miles
16   12   8   4   0

Elevation in feet

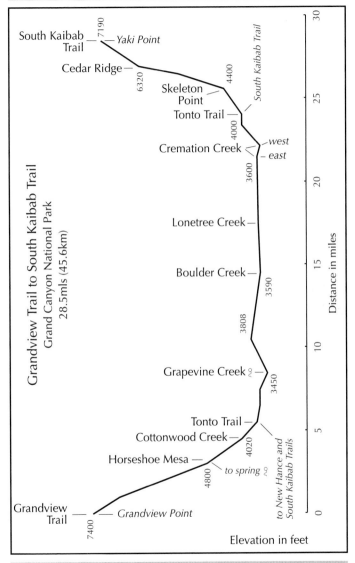

Grandview Trail to South Kaibab Trail
Grand Canyon National Park
28.5mls (45.6km)

South Kaibab Trail — *Yaki Point* — 7190

Cedar Ridge — 6320

Skeleton Point

Tonto Trail — 4400

South Kaibab Trail

Cremation Creek — 4000 — *west* — *east* — 3600

Lonetree Creek —

Boulder Creek — 3590

3808

Grapevine Creek ∞ — 3450

Tonto Trail —

Cottonwood Creek —

Horseshoe Mesa — 4020

to spring ∞ — 4800

to New Hance and South Kaibab Trails

Grandview Trail — *Grandview Point* — 7400

Distance in miles

30 — 25 — 20 — 15 — 10 — 5 — 0

Elevation in feet

GRANDVIEW TRAIL TO SOUTH KAIBAB TRAIL

Start:	Grandview Trailhead at Grandview Point (7,400 feet/2,256 metres)
End:	South Kaibab Trailhead near Yaki Point (7,190 feet/2,192 metres)
Distance:	27.8 miles (44.4 kilometres)
Backpacking times:	4 days
Maps:	Grandview Point, Cape Royal, Phantom Ranch (United States Geological Survey 7.5'); Grand Canyon National Park (TI); Grand Canyon National Park (EP)
Season:	autumn, winter and spring
Water:	Grapevine Creek
Rating:	strenuous

This walk offers a fine introduction to canyon-walking without the challenges and steep descents of either the Boucher, Tanner, or New Hance trails. It is possible to continue this trip by heading further west on the Tonto Trail to the Hermit Trail or at the South Kaibab Trail descending to Indian Garden. This walk is best attempted in the spring. Although Grapevine Creek has perennial water, the spring offers the best chance of water in Cottonwood and Lonetree creeks. Otherwise, water will have to be carried after Grapevine Creek.

ESCALANTE ROUTE: TANNER TRAIL TO GRANDVIEW TRAIL

Start:	Tanner Trailhead at Lipan Point (7,349 feet/2,240 metres)
End:	Grandview Trailhead at Grandview Point (7,400 feet/2,256 metres)
Distance:	33.3 miles (52.8 kilometres)
Backpacking times:	4–6 days
Maps:	Cape Royal, Desert View (United States Geological Survey 7.5'); Grand Canyon National Park (TI); Grand Canyon National Park (EP)

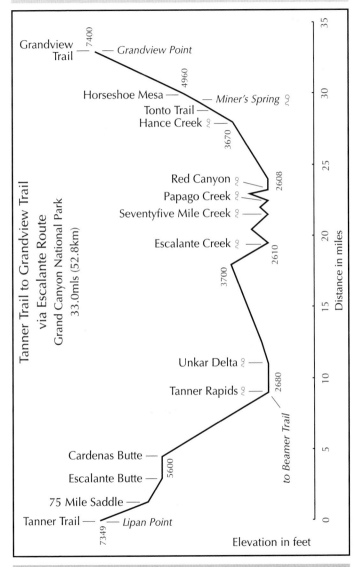

Tanner Trail to Grandview Trail
via Escalante Route
Grand Canyon National Park
33.0mls (52.8km)

Grandview
Trail ── 7400 ── *Grandview Point*

Horseshoe Mesa ── 4960

Tonto Trail ──
Hance Creek ⚇ ── *Miner's Spring* ⚇

3670

Red Canyon ⚇ ── 2608
Papago Creek ⚇ ──
Seventyfive Mile Creek ⚇ ──

Escalante Creek ⚇ ── 2610

3700

Unkar Delta ⚇ ──
Tanner Rapids ⚇ ── 2680 *to Beamer Trail*

Cardenas Butte ── 5600
Escalante Butte ──
75 Mile Saddle ──
Tanner Trail ── *Lipan Point*
7349

Distance in miles

Elevation in feet

Season:	spring and late autumn
Water:	Colorado River at Tanner Rapids, Escalante Creek, Papago Creek, Red Canyon; Hance Creek, Miner's Spring
Rating:	extremely strenuous

This splendid multi-day-walk provides a challenging trip for those walkers who are not adverse to some scrambling, together with steep descents and talus hopping. The Escalante Route (see section 8) is less travelled than the Tonto Trail and provides the walker with a wilderness experience using convenient South Rim access points.

KANAB CANYON TO THUNDER RIVER ROUTE

Start:	Sowats Point (6,200 feet/1,890 metres) to Colorado River (2,000 feet/609 metres)
End:	Indian Hollow (6,380 feet/1945 metres)
Distance:	50.5 miles (80.8 kilometres)
Times:	7–9 days
Maps:	Tapeats Amphitheatre, Powell Plateau, Grama Spring, Kanab Point, Jumpup Point, Fishtail Mesa (United States Geological Survey 7.5')
Season:	spring and late autumn
Water:	Kanab Creek, Colorado River, Fishtail Rapids, Deer Creek, Deer Creek Spring, Tapeats Creek, Thunder River
Rating:	extremely strenuous

This splendid multi-day trip for experienced canyon backpackers is one of the most spectacular routes in the park. According to the author and well-known canyon explorer George Steck, you pass by many of the canyon "must see" points. In dry conditions passenger cars can navigate the road to Sowats Point although in the spring there may be mud and deep ruts; four-wheel drive may be necessary. A car shuttle between Indian Hollow and Sowats Point makes your trip easier. The trip will be described in a counter-clockwise direction, the easiest and most practical way to walk the loop.

Although Kanab Creek is marked with a trail on the Grand Canyon National Park Trails Illustrated Map (TI), I have never seen a trail here and "route" is a much more accurate classification. Only serious canyoneers should travel here. You should know how to swim and be comfortable with bouldering, scrambling and route finding. Seasonal water may be available in Kwagunt Hollow, Jumpup Canyon, west up Indian Hollow from Jumpup Canyon and in upper Kanab Canyon. Water flows year round in Kanab Creek.

To reach Sowats Point, take Highway 67 for 26 miles to FR 422. Drive 18 miles west towards Dry Park to FR 425. Turn west and drive for 6.5 miles south to FR 233. Turn west again and drive another 8.5 miles to the car park for entrance into the Kaibab National Forest.

Forest Road 422 can also be accessed from Fredonia, Arizona. Drive 1 mile east on Highway 89A and then turn south onto FR 422. Continue south on FR 422, past Big Springs, turning west on FR 425 and west again on FR 233 to Sowats Point.

Directions
About 200 yards before Sowats Point on FR 233, the trail descends west at a sign into the Kaibab National Forest. Pass the Kaibab National Forest entrance sign-in register and head west around the south-west side of Sowats Point. The steep slippery trail descends through the Kaibab, Toroweap, and Coconino Formations and, in 2 miles, reaches a group of cottonwood trees. The easiest and most scenic access into Jumpup Canyon heads straight west, cross-country from the trees descending into the drainage of Kwagunt Hollow. The trail, however, continues north to Sowats Canyon, an alternative access into Jumpup Canyon.

Kwagunt Hollow, easily negotiated with some scrambling and boulder-clambering, joins Jumpup Canyon after 3 miles. After reaching Jumpup Canyon, turn south on flat terrain as you pass through the several miles of narrows. Early in the season there may be water in Kwagunt Hollow, Jumpup Canyon or at the junction of Kanab Creek and Jumpup Canyon. In dry years, or later in the season, water may not be found until you have descended into Kanab Creek for several miles. Jumpup Canyon rises 1,000 feet up

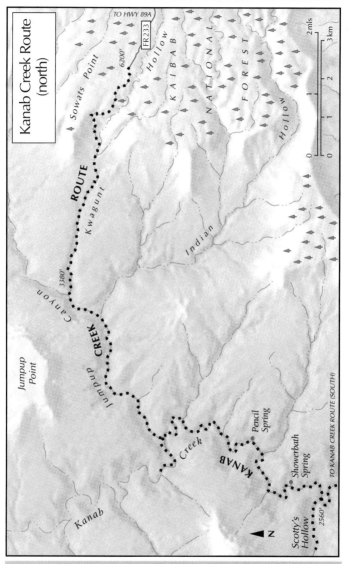

Kanab Creek Route
(north)

TO HWY 89A

FR 233

Sowats Point

6200'

Hollow

KAIBAB

NATIONAL

FOREST

Hollow

2 mls

3 km

ROUTE

Kwagunt

Indian

3380'

Canyon

Jumpup Point

Jumpup CREEK

Jumpup

Kanab

Creek

Pencil
Spring

KANAB

Showerbath
Spring

TO KANAB CREEK ROUTE (SOUTH)

Kanab

Scotty's
Hollow

2560'

N

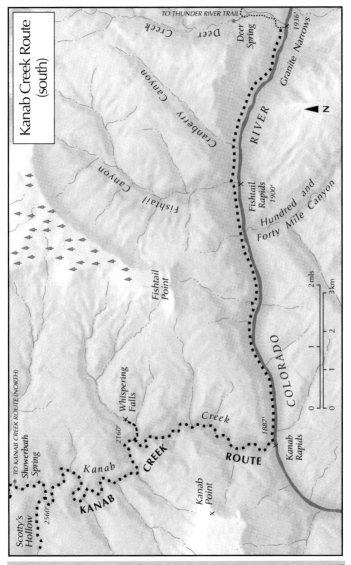

Kanab Creek Route (south)

TO THUNDER RIVER TRAIL

Deer Creek

Deer Spring

Granite Narrows 1936'

Cranberry Canyon

RIVER

N

Fishtail Canyon

Fishtail Rapids 1900'

Hundred and Forty Mile Canyon

Fishtail Point

2 mls

3km

COLORADO

Whispering Falls

2160'

Creek

1887'

TO KANAB CREEK ROUTE (NORTH)

Showerbath Spring

Kanab

CREEK

ROUTE

Kanab Rapids

Kanab Point

Scotty's Hollow

2560'

KANAB

147

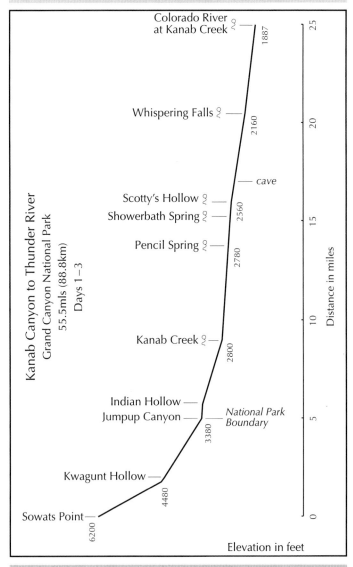

Kanab Canyon to Thunder River
Grand Canyon National Park
55.5mls (88.8km)
Days 1–3

Colorado River at Kanab Creek ⌇ — 1887

Whispering Falls ⌇ — 2160

— *cave*

Scotty's Hollow ⌇ — 2560
Showerbath Spring ⌇ —

Pencil Spring ⌇ — 2780

Kanab Creek ⌇ — 2800

Indian Hollow —
Jumpup Canyon — 3380   *National Park Boundary*

Kwagunt Hollow — 4480

Sowats Point — 6200

Distance in miles
25
20
15
10
5
0

Elevation in feet

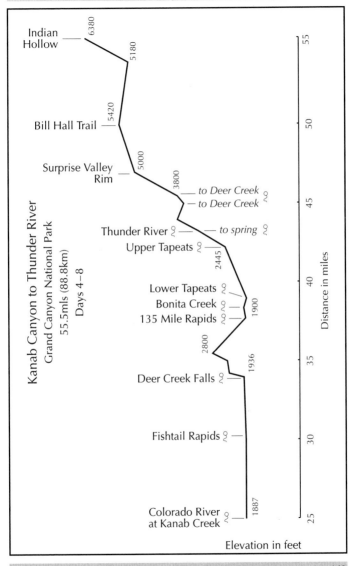

Kanab Canyon to Thunder River
Grand Canyon National Park
55.5mls (88.8km)
Days 4–8

Indian Hollow — 6380
5180
Bill Hall Trail — 5420
Surprise Valley Rim — 5000
3800
— to Deer Creek ⌇
— to Deer Creek ⌇
Thunder River ⌇ — — to spring ⌇
Upper Tapeats ⌇ 2445
Lower Tapeats ⌇
Bonita Creek ⌇ 1900
135 Mile Rapids ⌇ —
2800
Deer Creek Falls ⌇ — 1936
Fishtail Rapids ⌇ —
Colorado River ⌇ 1887
at Kanab Creek ⌇

Distance in miles
55
50
45
40
35
30
25

Elevation in feet

from the creek bottom; at the narrowest point, the walls are 20 feet apart. Indian Hollow joins from the west after a mile. When Jumpup Canyon is dry, there is often water 30 minutes up Indian Hollow. The Jumpup Narrows, dangerous during flash flood season, present one of many outstanding sights on this route.

Your route continues down Jumpup Canyon through the splendid narrows to Kanab Creek. Here you enter Grand Canyon National Park and overnight permits are required. In rainy years, water may be available in upper Kanab Creek. The first perennial water is Pencil Spring, clearly marked on the Kanab Point 7.5 minute quad, around 3 miles from the Jumpup/Kanab junction. This horizontal display of dripping ferns juts out from overhanging rocks. Around 1.5 miles farther on you reach overhanging Showerbath Spring where the creek has undercut the bank to support a green and red array of plants. One mile farther on, the terrain becomes more difficult as larger boulders, swimming pools, and rushing water block easy passage and provides challenging walking. At Scotty's Hollow, where the canyon makes a 180° turn, you'll find a convenient camping spot. Scotty's Castle is the name given to the tower that adorns the 180° turn. If you have excess energy you can hike up Scotty's Hollow. Just a few minutes up the canyon a waterfall cuts through the rocks and creates a splendid series of small bathing pools.

Continuing down the canyon your route is slowed by tedious negotiation around large boulders and pools of water. Canyon walls rise steeply from the sides of the creek. Less than a mile from Scotty's Hollow a large cave, providing shelter from the rain, juts into the canyon walls on the east side of the creek. Four hours down the canyon from Scotty's Hollow, be sure to stop at the next major drainage that joins from the east. Long remembered by any visitor, a 10 minute walk up this major drainage brings you to the Whispering Falls. Here water has carved a passage through a rock slide adorned with flowers and falling into a deep clear pool. Though the water is definitely "whispering", it is clearly not a "falls". In *Grand Canyon Loop Hikes I*, Steck calls it the Slide of Susurrus, perhaps a more accurate description.

Continuing down the creek your passage soon eases and in 1 hour you pass some interesting Muav ledges on the true left of the creek. In another couple of hours the difficulties lighten even more as you reach the Colorado River. Fine camping spots can be found 10 minutes before reaching the river just before the creek's final swing east. At the river, the east side of the creek supports additional camping spots. Take care crossing over to them; if the mud is deep or the river is high, backtrack north up the creek and cross to the other side of the creek first before continuing south to the river.

To continue to Deer Creek, Thunder River, and Tapeats Creek your route bears east along the Colorado River to Fishtail Rapids. From the mouth of Kanab Creek, it is two days of boulder hopping to reach Deer Creek. The shadeless, hot and tedious section between Kanab Creek and Fishtail Rapids tests even the most rugged canyoneer. The rocks are blisteringly hot and jagged so, despite the heat, you may consider wearing lightweight gloves and long pants. Give strong consideration to walking this section in the cool morning. The route, taking anywhere from 4–7 hours, follows just above the river for the entire day. I have been through this section three times and each time it is challenging. Difficulty depends on where the boulders have fallen and been placed as a result of the previous winter and the fluctuating water levels of the Colorado River. After the struggle, you will be glad to find a sandy and somewhat shaded stopping point at Fishtail Rapids.

After a night at Fishtail Rapids, continue east along the river, for another 4 hour trip, although considerably easier than your previous day's toils. There is a trail for much of the way, often veering several hundred feet above the Colorado River as it avoids cliffs and outcropping that make staying close to the river impassable. Within 1.5 hours, you come to Steck's "Siesta Spring", a flow of water coming from one of the Cranberry Canyon drainages. It was a mere trickle when I last passed by, even in a heavy wet year. Just after the drainage, you head high, away from the river. The trail drops back to the river east of a wash on a crumbling rocky slope. The last mile ends easily as you walk on rocks next to the river to Deer Creek Falls, no doubt a welcome sight.

Join the trail to Deer Creek up into Surprise Valley where you can continue on to the Thunder River Trail and Tapeats Creek, described in section 7. An alternate route traverses from Deer Creek above the river, high above the rapids to Bonita Creek and the Lower

Tapeats campsite. It may be difficult to ascend Tapeats Creek in the spring; crossing may be extremely dangerous until the winter water levels lessen into the summer.

CHAPTER 11

VISITING ZION NATIONAL PARK

*Nothing can exceed the wondrous beauty of Zion ... in the nobility
and beauty of the sculptures there is no comparison*
Clarence E. Dutton, 1880

Introduction

Close to the metropolitan areas of Las Vegas and Salt Lake City, Zion
is the busiest of Utah's National Parks. Most of the park's three
million visitors a year spend their time in the Zion Canyon, often
enjoying a short day-walk. The park, however, encompasses 229
square miles, complete with hiking trails, springs for water,
sweeping views and deep canyons. Visits to its high, cool plateaux
guide the walker far away from the valley crowds.

History

The original inhabitants of Zion, the Anasazi Indians, lived in the
Zion Valley from AD 500 to AD 1200. The tribes are better known for
their habitation of the Four Corners area of the United States, where
the states of Colorado, Arizona, New Mexico, and Utah meet.
Following the Anasazi, other tribes, sub-tribes of the Paiute,
occupied the Zion area. Eventually the Mormon settlers displaced
them, although some of their descendants still live in surrounding
communities.

In 1861 Joseph Black began farming the Zion Valley. Another
Mormon, Isaac Behunin, moved to Utah in 1863 and settled in
Springdale. He built his home in the red-walled canyon just north
of the town, the area occupied today by Zion Lodge. He farmed the
fertile Zion Valley and grazed sheep in the upper plateaux. It was
he who conferred the name Zion, or the promised land, on the area.
The Great White Throne, Court of the Patriarchs, and Angels'
Landing, are names given to the surrounding canyon walls, which
reflect the religious devotion of its settlers. Many of the place names
in Zion are taken directly from Mormon theology.

Although travel was hampered by poor roads, the area always

inspired writers and artists. Slowly knowledge of the red-walled vertical canyons with its sculptured walls spread. Originally known as Mukuntuweap, the area acquired the status of a National Monument in 1909. Ten years later it became Zion National Park. Plans soon followed for new roads and development that markedly improved access to the park. Construction of the Zion-Mt. Carmel tunnel began in 1927 and completion of the road through the tunnel integrated several sections of the park. In 1920 approximately 3,500 people visited Zion National Park. In 1998, visitors numbered around 4 million.

Getting there

Zion National Park makes a 3 hour, 158 mile car trip from Las Vegas, Nevada, a 6 hour, 325 mile trip from Salt Lake City, Nevada and a 1 hour, 42 mile trip from St. George, Utah. In addition, Zion is a 2 hour, 86 mile drive from Bryce Canyon National Park, a 5 hour, 253 mile drive from the South Rim of the Grand Canyon, and a 3 hour, 120 mile ride from the North Rim of the Grand Canyon and a 6 hour, 284 mile ride from Death Valley, California.

You reach Zion by proceeding north from Las Vegas or south from Salt Lake City on Interstate 15 towards St. George. Just north of St. George, take the Hurricane exit to Utah Route 9. Proceed through the small towns of Hurricane, Virgin and Rockville and continue 37 miles to Springdale, just south of the park entrance. East of Zion from US 89 turn west at Mt. Carmel junction on Utah Route 9 to reach the park's East Entrance.

Getting around

Public transportation is not available into Zion National Park. Salt Lake City, Utah or Las Vegas, Nevada offer the closest major airports and numerous car rental options. Rental cars are also available in St. George and Cedar City, Utah but it is more practical to obtain cars from the larger cities of Salt Lake City or Las Vegas. From the Zion Canyon Visitor Centre, it is 6 miles to the end of the Zion Canyon Scenic Drive, 13 miles through the Checkerboard Mesa to the East Entrance, 40 miles to Lava Point, and 45 miles to the Kolob Canyons Visitor Centre on the west side of the park.

Zion Valley transportation

Zion National Park has inaugurated a new bus transportation

system. Scheduled to operate during the busy months of March to October and at other peak periods, all visitors, except those staying at the Zion Lodge, will be required to use shuttle bus access into Zion Valley. The shuttle system will decrease congestion, traffic and smog in Zion Canyon. A new visitor centre and car park are being constructed near the Watchman Campground.

An open air tram, practical to use if day-walking from Weeping Rock or the Temple of Sinawava, departs from Zion Lodge and serves the area between the Lodge and the Temple of Sinawava. Use it to reach your car after ending the East Rim Trail at Weeping Rock or the overnight Narrows trip at the Temple of Sinawava.

Weather and seasons

The park, lodge and campgrounds remain open all year, although many park services such as ranger talks, hikers' shuttle and tram rides, run only between April and October. Spring or autumn make the best time for a visit when temperatures are ideal and summer visitors have headed home.

Many valley and south-west desert trails are usable all year. In winter, when the higher elevations can only be accessed using snowshoes or skis, the Chinle Trail makes a fine outing. Valley trails such as the Riverside Trail, Emerald Pools and Weeping Rock are open all year. Those trails that connect the valley floor with the rim, such as the East and West Rim trails and Observation Point Trail, may be blocked by snow during the winter and early spring.

Moderate temperatures prevail in spring and autumn, the most comfortable seasons for walking. Wildflowers dot the high country from late April into early June. Be aware, however, that the rivers and streams overflow in spring and narrow canyon-walking may be dangerous.

Temperatures in Zion vary tremendously between the higher and lower valley elevations. Summer temperatures soar in the valley, often exceeding 100 °F, with the high country averaging around 75 °F. The high plateaux stay cooler and remain pleasant for walking when the lower elevations broil. Autumn brings cool clear temperatures and brilliant colours highlight the high country trees in late September and in the valley in late October.

The most unpredictable wet weather occurs in the spring. March is the rainiest month, yet it can snow into April. Thunderstorms,

Average Valley Temperatures and Precipitation
Zion National Park

	Max °F (°C)		Min °F (°C)		Precp ins (cm)	
January	52	(11)	29	(-2)	1.6	(4.1)
February	57	(13)	31	(-1)	1.6	(4.1)
March	63	(18)	36	(2)	1.7	(4.3)
April	73	(22)	43	(6)	1.3	(3.3)
May	83	(28)	52	(11)	0.7	(1.8)
June	93	(34)	60	(16)	0.6	(1.5)
July	100	(38)	68	(20)	0.8	(2.0)
August	97	(36)	66	(19)	1.6	(4.1)
September	91	(33)	60	(16)	1.4	(3.6)
October	78	(26)	49	(9)	1.0	(2.5)
November	63	(17)	39	(3)	1.2	(3.1)
December	53	(12)	30	(1)	1.5	(3.8)

which can produce flash floods and limit canyon-walking, peak in July and August. Winter snows close high country trails and bring a dusting of snow to the valley.

Lodging

The Zion Lodge, the only accommodation inside the park, offers year-round motel-style rooms and cabins. Here the Virgin River peacefully flows near your footsteps; you can almost touch the red canyon walls outside your door. A restaurant, gift shop, dining room, snack bar, and Post Office offer limited visitor services. Reservations, made through AmFac Parks and Resorts (see Appendix B), should be made several months in advance, especially for the busy spring and summer seasons. AmFac Parks and Resorts maintains a full selection of available rooms and cabins through their telephone reservation service. Limited Zion Lodge reservations are available on the internet. You will find other lodging in nearby Springdale. Zion Lodge also co-ordinates a hikers' shuttle to many of the park's trailheads.

Camping

Zion's South and Watchman campgrounds lie near the park's south entrance. Reservations are accepted for the Watchman Campground; the South Campground operates on a first-come first-served basis (see Appendix B). Lava Point, on the Kolob Terrace Road, has a 6 space primitive campground without water. Campgrounds fill early in summer. Nearby Springdale offers a small private campground with showers.

Visitor services

Zion Canyon Visitor Centre provides information, a museum, books, weather reports and a slide show. The Zion Canyon Visitor Centre and the Kolob Canyons Visitor Centre issue backcountry permits.

Zion Natural History Association

The Zion Natural History Association, a non-profit-making organization, helps to maintain park land and preserve its resources. Members are entitled to discounts on purchases at visitor centres at all national parks and monuments.

Interpretative programmes

Ranger led activities feature various topics ranging from geology, plant and animal life to human history. Programmes, which run from May to October, vary from walks, talks at the centre, and campfire programmes at the campgrounds. Schedules are posted at the visitor centre and campgrounds.

Other facilities

Limited supplies are most readily available on Utah Route 9 in Springdale, just outside the south entrance to the park. You will find motels, a Post Office, a laundromat, showers, a bank, restaurants, small grocery stores, petrol stations and limited backpacking and camping supplies. Nearby St. George and Cedar City, Utah offer full services.

Time zones

The state of Utah, including Zion National Park and Bryce Canyon National Park, operates on Mountain Standard Time (MST). Daylight Savings Time (MDT or Mountain Daylight Time) when the clocks are pushed ahead 1 hour, stays in effect between early April and late October. Utah runs 1 hour ahead of Nevada, which operates on Pacific Standard time (PST) and Pacific Daylight Time (PDT).

CHAPTER 12

WALKING IN ZION NATIONAL PARK

We are the pilgrims master, we shall go
Always a little further; it may be
Beyond the last blue mountain barred with snow
James Elroy Flecker

Overnight permits and fees

Overnight camping permits can be obtained for a small fee from the Zion Canyon and Kolob Canyons visitor centres. The National Park Service limits the number of permits for camping in Timber Creek and La Verkin Creek, Hop Valley, Potato Hollow, the West Rim and The Narrows.

Day-walking

Permits are not required for most day-walking. You will need a permit, however, if you wish to complete The Narrows walk downstream from Chamberlain's Ranch to the Temple of Sinawava in one day. Permits must be obtained at the visitor centre the day before your hike. You will not need a permit to do the day-walk, Up The Narrows, upstream from the Temple of Sinawava.

Permits are also required for day-hikes in any of the canyons requiring artificial aid such as the Left Fork of North Creek (the Subway), Kolob Creek, or Orderville Canyon. Check with the visitor centre for up-to-date requirements on travel in these areas. Descriptions of these off-trail canyon routes, beyond the scope of this guide, can be found in books available at the visitor centres. Overnight camping is prohibited in many of Zion's canyons.

Hiking The Narrows

People come from all over the world to hike the Zion Narrows (section 18). This unique experience presents its own risks and rewards. No trail exists and you must walk in the river bed through deep water. Flash floods and hypothermia present constant dangers. A sample of narrows-walking can be obtained by walking Up The Narrows to Orderville Canyon (section 15).

An overnight trip in The Narrows offers time to enjoy its astounding scenery in its unique environment. Day-walks for the entire 16 mile Narrows trip are permitted only during the long light days of summer. The most practical and enjoyable time to walk The Narrows is from July through to early October when the water temperature rises, the flow of water lessens and speed slows. If walking between July and August be sure to check on the weather forecast and be wary of the chance of flash floods.

Shuttle services
From mid-April through to mid-October, the Zion Lodge provides a shuttle service to many of the walks in this book. You may ride from Zion Lodge to the western Kolob Canyons area of the park to Lee Pass, to all road heads off the Kolob Terrace Road (eg. Hop Valley, Wildcat Canyon and Lava Point road heads), to the East Entrance on Utah State Highway 9 and to Chamberlain's Ranch at the start of The Narrows walk. Contact the Zion Lodge travel desk for information. Especially during the busy summer season, reservations should be made several weeks in advance.

Groups
The National Park Service encourages groups of less than six people. To minimize environmental impact, groups of twelve or more must divide into smaller groups.

Maps
All trails in Zion appear on the plastic coated *Trails Illustrated* (TI) Zion National Park 1:37700 map with contour intervals of 50 feet. This may be all you will need. United States Geological Survey (USGS) 7.5 minute maps provide excellent additional detail. You may buy the 7.5 minute series at the Zion Canyon Visitor Centre or obtain them by mail either from the Zion Natural History Association or from the United States Geological Survey (USGS) (see Appendix B).

Weather and seasons
The South-West Desert trails and most Zion Canyon trails remain open all year. Both bake in the scorching summer heat. High country trails are accessible usually from mid-to-late April through October. Spring and autumn are the most pleasant times for walking; valley summer heat can be unbearable. The higher elevations maintain cooler temperatures during the summer.

West Rim Trail, Zion National Park

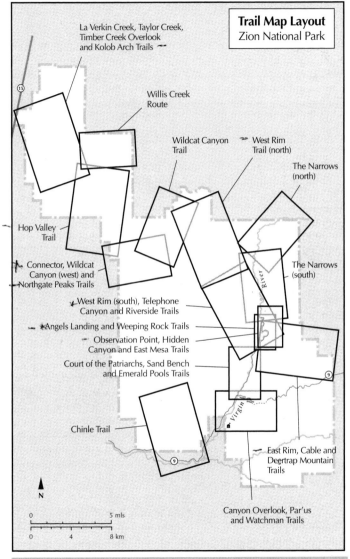

Trail Map Layout
Zion National Park

La Verkin Creek, Taylor Creek,
Timber Creek Overlook
and Kolob Arch Trails

Willis Creek
Route

Wildcat Canyon
Trail

West Rim
Trail (north)

The Narrows
(north)

Hop Valley
Trail

Connector, Wildcat
Canyon (west) and
Northgate Peaks Trails

The Narrows
(south)

West Rim (south), Telephone
Canyon and Riverside Trails

Angels Landing and Weeping Rock Trails

Observation Point, Hidden
Canyon and East Mesa Trails

Court of the Patriarchs, Sand Bench
and Emerald Pools Trails

Chinle Trail

East Rim, Cable and
Deertrap Mountain
Trails

N

0   5 mls

0   4   8 km

Canyon Overlook, Par'us
and Watchman Trails

Each year the amount of winter snow determines the exact beginning and end of the high country walking season. Snow blocks the upper sections of the East Rim, West Rim and Observation Point trails in winter. Upper sections of these trails may be icy and dangerous to traverse.

Minimum impact

If you are not using designated sites, you should camp 100 feet away from any water source and 0.5 mile from springs. Camp in previously used sites and refrain from making site improvements. Since fires are not allowed in the backcountry, you must carry a backpacking stove. Stay on trails; cutting corners destroys vegetation and leads to erosion. For all litter, "pack it in, pack it out". Leave the backcountry cleaner than when you passed through.

Water sources

Backcountry water must be treated, boiled or purified. All washing, either of dishes, clothing or yourself, should take place 100 feet from the water source. Zion springs, the most reliable water sources, are found throughout the backcountry. Year-round water sources appear on this book's maps, fact panels, and route profiles.

Waymarking

Signs stand at almost all trail junctions in the park. Though some of the backcountry receives limited use, all trails are distinct and easy to follow.

Flash floods

Thunderstorms many miles upstream cause huge torrents of water to rush down creek beds, washes and canyon bottoms. Especially during the peak flash flood season from July through to August, any threat of rain should warn you against walking in narrow canyons. Heed the flash flood warnings as well if you are day-walking upstream from the Temple of Sinawava to Orderville Canyon (section 15).

Insects, reptiles and mammals

Deerflies proliferate along creeks in summer. Tiny, irritating, insects abound in the mid-to-late spring. Both can persist into autumn. Mosquitoes predominate during the summer months. Repellent, long sleeves and long pants provide protection.

Non-poisonous are snakes sometimes seen in Zion including the garter, gopher, and whip snakes. The western rattlesnake, Zion's only poisonous reptile, strikes only when frightened or provoked. Leave them alone and they will slither away.

CHAPTER 13

ZION NATIONAL PARK: KOLOB CANYONS TRAILS

Only a fool can predict the weather.
Unknown

Introduction

The Kolob Canyons section of Zion National Park, making up its north-west border, hosts many fewer visitors than the busy eastern Zion Canyon. To reach this area from the Zion National Park South Entrance, take Utah Highway 9 west through Virgin and Rockville for 22 miles to Highway 17 and turn north. Proceed 6 miles to Interstate 15, turn north and, in 13 miles, take Exit 40 to Kolob Canyons. Allow 1 hour driving time from Zion Canyon.

KOLOB CANYONS TRAILS

Trail	Distance Miles One way	Distance Kilometres One Way	Rating
(Timber Creek Overlook	0.5	0.8	Easy
Middle Fork of Taylor Creek	2.5	4.0	Moderate
La Verkin Creek	7.0	11.2	Moderate
Kolob Arch	0.3	0.5	Moderate
Willis Creek Route	4.5	7.2	Moderate
Hop Valley	6.7	10.7	Moderate

TIMBER CREEK OVERLOOK

Start:	End of Kolob Canyons Road (6,250 feet/1,905 metres)
End:	Timber Creek Overlook (6,369 feet/ 1,941 metres)
Distance, one way:	0.5 miles (0.8 kilometres)
Time, one way:	20 minutes

Maps:	Kolob Arch (United States Geological Survey 7.5'); Zion National Park (TI)
Season:	April through to November
Water:	none
Rating:	easy

From the car park, 5.3 miles east of the Kolob Canyons Visitor Centre at the end of Kolob Canyons Road, the trail heads south across a knoll. In 0.5 mile it reaches a lookout over the Timber Creek drainage. Splendid views east to Shuntavi Butte and Timber Top Mountain greet you.

You can see the path of the La Verkin Creek Trail as it rounds Gregory Butte. Retrace your steps back to your car.

MIDDLE FORK OF TAYLOR CREEK TRAIL

Start:	Taylor Creek parking area (5,480 feet/1,670 metres)
End:	Double Arch Alcove (6,050 feet/1,844 metres)
Distance, one way:	2.5 miles (4 kilometres)
Time, one way:	1 hour
Maps:	Kolob Arch (United States Geological Survey 7.5'); Zion National Park (TI)
Season:	April through to October
Water:	none
Rating:	moderate

Starting from the Taylor Creek car park, 2 miles east of the Kolob Canyons Visitor Centre on Kolob Canyons Road, this walk visits the less popular, but no less scenic, western section of the Park. The Middle Fork of Taylor Creek is limited to day use only. Camp only in the North Fork of Taylor Creek.

Directions
From the Taylor Creek car park the trail heads east and descends 80 feet down steps to reach Taylor Creek. Follow the creek east and upstream as you continually cross the creek in and out of the water. In another 0.75 mile, you pass the rundown Larsen Cabin, used for

logging settlements at the turn of the century. From the cabin, dramatic views to Tucupit Point tower 1,500 feet above the creek. In 0.25 mile the North Fork of Taylor Creek branches north; camping is allowed 0.5 mile north of the confluence.

Continuing along the Middle Fork, the trail roughens as the canyon narrows. Now you ascend gradually as you enter the canyon between Tucupit Point and Paria Point. Next the red-walled canyons rise above the deteriorated 1930 Fife Cabin. The canyon bends south, ending at Double Arch Alcove. Here, a recess in the rock forms an overhanging cliff and an alcove; water drips from its interior. Retrace your steps back to the car park.

LA VERKIN CREEK TRAIL

Start:	Lee Pass (6,060 feet/1,847 metres)
End:	Hop Valley Trail (5,360 feet/1,634 metres)
Distance, one way:	7 miles (11.2 kilometres)
Time, one way:	3–4 hours
Maps:	Kolob Arch (United States Geological Survey 7.5′); Zion National Park (TI)
Season:	April through to November
Water:	La Verkin Creek, Beatty Spring
Rating:	moderate

This popular 14 mile round trip, often completed in one day, begins from Lee Pass, 3.8 miles east of the Kolob Canyons Visitor Centre on Kolob Canyons Road. Some walkers make a short trip to the small waterfall and pools located near the Corral, 4.8 miles from Lee Pass. Bearcat Canyon and Hop Valley, father down La Verkin Creek, merit an overnight stay. If you plan to camp, you must pick up a backcountry permit at the Zion Canyon Visitor Centre or at the Kolob Canyons Visitor Centre. Camp only in designated sites along Timber and La Verkin Creeks and in Hop Valley.

Directions
From the car park at Lee Pass, the trail heads south and descends 500 feet steeply through sage brush. In 1 mile you meet the cottonwood-lined Timber Creek drainage where you'll see the first of the area's designated campsites. As you follow the creek, splendid

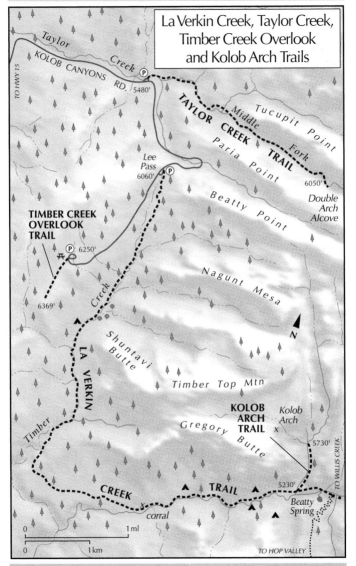

La Verkin Creek, Taylor Creek,
Timber Creek Overlook
and Kolob Arch Trails

Taylor

KOLOB CANYONS RD.

Creek

TO HWY 15

5480'

TAYLOR

CREEK

TRAIL

Tucupit Point

Middle Fork

Lee
Pass
6060'

Paria Point

Beatty Point

6050'

Double
Arch
Alcove

**TIMBER CREEK
OVERLOOK
TRAIL**

6250'

Creek

Nagunt Mesa

N

6369'

Shuntavi
Butte

Timber Top Mtn

LA

VERKIN

**KOLOB
ARCH
TRAIL**

Kolob
Arch
x

5730'

Timber

Gregory Butte

TO WILLIS CREEK

5230'

CREEK

TRAIL

corral

Beatty
Spring

0   1 ml

0   1 km

TO HOP VALLEY

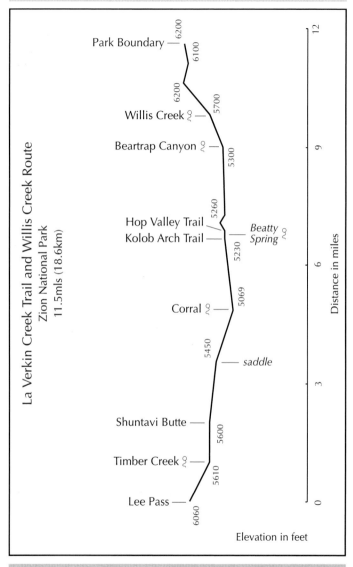

La Verkin Creek Trail and Willis Creek Route
Zion National Park
11.5mls (18.6km)

Park Boundary — 6200
6100

6200
Willis Creek — 5700

Beartrap Canyon — 5300

5260
Hop Valley Trail —
Kolob Arch Trail — *Beatty Spring*
5230

5069
Corral —

5450
— *saddle*

Shuntavi Butte —
5600

Timber Creek —
5610

Lee Pass —
6060

Distance in miles

Elevation in feet

eastern views to Shuntavi and Gregory Buttes mark the horizon. Your route descends gradually as you round the edge of Shuntavi Butte and approach a low saddle. Now there are views to the east and south down the La Verkin Creek drainage. From the saddle, you soon approach a fine lunch stop at a small waterfall and slick-rock pools carved from the bedrock known as the Corral. Continuing up the drainage on the creek's true left and north side past several designated campsites, the walls of Gregory Butte to the north and Neagle Ridge to the south rise from the drainage. One hour farther through grassy meadows along the sandy creek bed brings you to the Kolob Arch Trail.

From the Kolob Arch Junction, the La Verkin Creek Trail continues upstream and in 0.2 mile fords to the true right or south side of the creek. Just after crossing the creek, Beatty Spring, a perennial water source, drips down a rock wall. Pass several more campsites and ascend 50 feet up a hill, and in 5 minutes you'll reach a trail junction and the end of the La Verkin Creek Trail. The Willis Creek Route continues straight ahead and the Hop Valley Trail ascends to the east.

KOLOB ARCH TRAIL

Start:	Kolob Arch Trail (5,230 feet/1,594 metres)
End:	Under Kolob Arch (5,730 feet/1,747 metres)
Distance, one way:	0.3 miles (0.5 kilometres)
Time, one way:	20 minutes
Maps:	Kolob Arch (United States Geological Survey 7.5′); Zion National Park (TI)
Season:	April through to November
Water:	La Verkin Creek
Rating:	moderate

Directions

Turning north from the La Verkin Creek Trail, ascend along the true left of a small stream among numerous boulders. One half mile from the main trail, three small drainages intersect below a flat bench. A sign marks the end of the trail at a viewpoint; travel beyond this point is not allowed. Far up and to the west spans the sprawling 292 foot Kolob Arch, rivalling 291 foot Landscape Arch in Arches National Park for the title of the world's largest free standing arch. From this point, the arch appears quite small; many visitors leave disappointed with this view.

WILLIS CREEK ROUTE

Start:	Junction of Hop Valley Trail and La Verkin Creek Trail (5,360 feet/1,633 metres)
End:	Park Boundary (6,200 feet/1,890 metres)
Distance, one way:	4.5 miles (7.2 kilometres)
Time, one way:	3 hours
Maps:	Kolob Arch, Kolob Reservoir (United States Geological Survey 7.5'); Zion National Park (TI)
Season:	April through to October
Water:	Willis Creek
Rating:	moderate

Willis Creek can be explored as an extra day from the Kolob Arch area when backpacking across Zion National Park. Access Willis Creek only from the western La Verkin Creek. Some older maps show a now closed trail crossing private land west of Kolob Reservoir and then joining the Willis Creek Trail from its eastern park boundary. Eastern access through the private land west of Kolob Reservoir requires special written permission.

Directions
From the Hop Valley Trail junction east of Beatty Spring, continue north up La Verkin Creek. Even in the spring the water levels are usually low and you should have no difficulty fording the creek. Several pleasant designated campsites line the creek bed. After a bit over 1 mile Herb's Point dominates to the north and in 2 miles you reach Beartrap Canyon. Continuing up the canyon you come to the junction of La Verkin and Willis Creek where your route turns east. Massive cliff walls rise above the creek. Water seeps through into the previously dry creek bed as you rise higher and higher up the drainage. A gate marks the park boundary and your turn around point. You must retrace your steps back to La Verkin Creek.

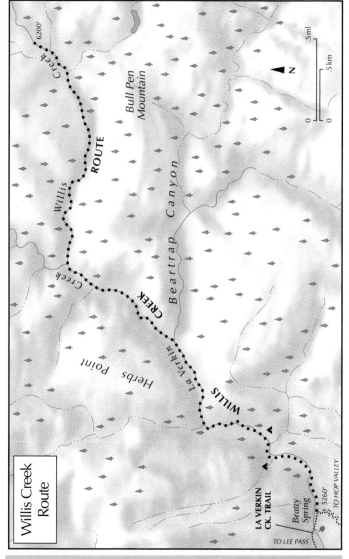

Willis Creek
Route

The 30 minute walk to the waterfall up Beartrap Canyon makes a worthwhile detour. The walls of the canyon slowly close in above you as the canyon narrows. A waterfall blocks your passage father up the canyon.

HOP VALLEY TRAIL

Start:	Junction of Hop Valley Trail at La Verkin Creek (5,360 feet/1,634 metres)
End:	Kolob Terrace Road (6,350 feet/ 1,935 metres)
Distance, one way:	6.7 miles (10.7 kilometres)
Time, one way:	4 hours
Maps:	Kolob Arch, The Guardian Angels (United States Geological Survey 7.5'); Zion National Park (TI)
Season:	mid-April through to October
Water:	Hop Valley
Rating:	moderate

The Hop Valley trailhead can be accessed from its western end at La Verkin Creek as described above or from the east from the Hop Valley trailhead on the Kolob Terrace Road. To reach its eastern end, drive 13 miles north of Virgin, Utah on the Kolob Terrace Road. If you are walking my Across Zion route (see section 18), you will be walking from La Verkin Creek to the Hop Valley trailhead from west to east as described here. If you are planning a day-walk to Kolob Arch, the most scenic route connects La Verkin Creek with the Kolob Terrace Road.

Directions
From the junction of the La Verkin Creek Trail, just up the hill from Beatty Spring, and at the start of the Willis Creek Route, turn uphill and east on the Hop Valley Trail. Climb 500 feet up switchbacks to an overlook of Hop Valley where you can see Gregory Butte and Timber Top Mountain behind you.

From here there are fine views to Hop Valley as you descend through the trees to the bottom of the hill and to the valley bottom. You'll soon see some designated campsites on the north side of the

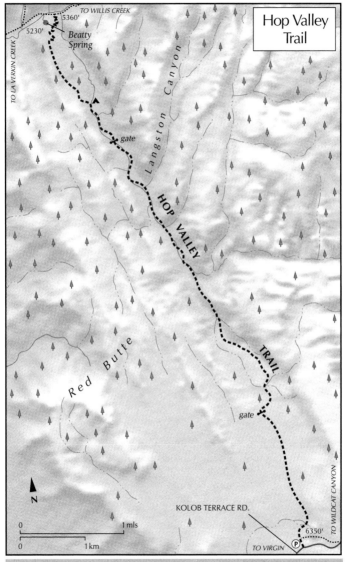

Hop Valley
Trail

TO WILLIS CREEK

5360'

5230'

*Beatty
Spring*

TO LA VERKIN CREEK

Langston Canyon

gate

HOP

VALLEY

TRAIL

R e d   *B u t t e*

gate

6350'

TO WILDCAT CANYON

N

0   1 mls

0   1 km

KOLOB TERRACE RD.

TO VIRGIN   Ⓟ

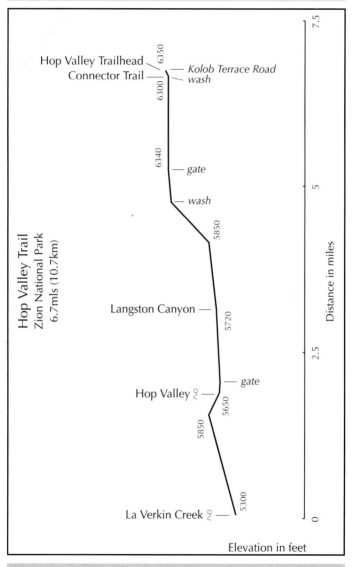

Hop Valley Trailhead
Connector Trail
6350
6300
Kolob Terrace Road
wash

6340
— *gate*
— *wash*
5850

Hop Valley Trail
Zion National Park
6.7mls (10.7km)

Langston Canyon —
5720

— *gate*
Hop Valley ⚲ —
5650
5850

5300
La Verkin Creek ⚲ —

Distance in miles
7.5
5
2.5
0

Elevation in feet

creek. At this section of the valley you will notice that the creek water disappears as it flows underground to form Beatty Spring in La Verkin Creek. When you reach the valley floor, follow one of the cattle trails south across the grassy, sometimes muddy bottom, along the sides of the creek. Pass through the gate into private property. Criss-cross the creek several times. As you wander down the pleasant sandy valley you soon see Langston Canyon joining from the east. As you reach the end of the valley you then begin a gradual ascent 500 feet between the towering cliffs and two creeks' beds until you reach the upper plateau.

Cross the arid plateau with its chaparral (dense brushwood) and other low-lying vegetation. Behind you are the red walls of La Verkin Creek. Red Butte rises to the west. In 1 mile another gate and fence mark your exit from private land. The vague road now winds south through the vegetation as Firepit Knoll forms a helpful landmark to the east. Soon you cross a wash and a sign leading east to the Connector Trail. In 0.1 mile you reach the Hop Valley trailhead and Kolob Terrace Road.

CHAPTER 14

ZION NATIONAL PARK: WEST RIM TRAILS

Adventure is not in the guidebook
And Beauty is not on the map.
Jerry and Renny Russell

Introduction

This stunning section of Zion National Park, most easily reached from Virgin, Utah along the Kolob Terrace Road, provides a variety of walking trails. From Zion National Park South Entrance, take Utah Highway 9 south through Springdale and Rockville to the town of Virgin. Turn north on the Kolob Terrace Road to reach all the road heads. Even if you aren't planning to walk, take a few hours to drive this scenic road, far away from the valley crowds.

WEST RIM TRAILS

Trail	Distance Miles One way	Distance Kilometres One Way	Rating
Connector Trail	4.0	6.4	Moderate
Wildcat Canyon	5.8	9.3	Moderate
Northgate Peaks	2.2	3.5	Easy
West Rim Trail	14.2	22.7	Strenuous

CONNECTOR TRAIL

Start:	Hop Valley Trailhead (6,350 feet/ 1,935 metres)
End:	Wildcat Canyon Trail (6,950 feet/ 2,118 metres)
Distance, one way:	4 miles (6.4 kilometres)
Time, one way:	2 hours
Maps:	The Guardian Angels (United States Geological Survey 7.5') (trail not marked on map); Zion National Park (TI)

Season:	mid-April through to October
Water:	none
Rating:	moderate

The Hop Valley Trail takes off from the car park 13 miles north from Virgin, Utah off the Kolob Terrace Road. The Connector Trail, allowing walkers to cross Zion on foot without having to walk along the Kolob Terrace Road, provides a convenient, albeit hot and dry, link between the Kolob Terrace Road and the Wildcat Canyon Trail.

Directions
From the Hop Valley car park, walk north 0.1 mile on the trail that heads to Hop Valley. Turn east when you reach the old creek bed and the signpost. In 0.25 mile the trail crosses the Kolob Terrace Road to enter the north end of Lee Valley. Spendlove Knoll juts up to the south and Firepit Knoll to the north. After 45 minutes and 1.5 miles, the trail passes through Pine Spring Wash. In another 1.3 miles, you reach a pine-tree-laden saddle north of Pine Valley Peak where you are rewarded with a fine view of North Guardian Angel. Continue east 1 mile until the Connector Trail joins the Wildcat Canyon Trail about 1 mile from the Wildcat Canyon Parking Area and 0.1 mile west of the Northgate Peaks Trail, where there is fine camping among its pine forest.

Water along the Connector Trail may be sparse to non-existent. In spring Pine Springs Wash may harbour several unexpected water pockets. Ask the park service if anyone has reported them. The closest perennial water flows from Wildcat Canyon Spring several miles ahead. If you are walking across the park on my "Across Zion" trip, you may wish to collect water either near the Hop Valley trailhead or, better yet, off the trail at the Wildcat Canyon and Northgate Peaks Trail junction.

WILDCAT CANYON TRAIL

Start:	Wildcat Canyon Trailhead (7,000 feet/2,134 metres)
End:	Lava Point Trailhead (7,460 feet/2,274 metres)

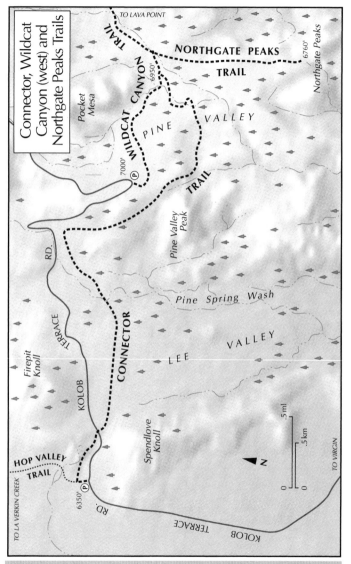

Connector, Wildcat Canyon (west) and Northgate Peaks Trails

TO LAVA POINT

NORTHGATE PEAKS

TRAIL

6760'

Northgate Peaks

TRAIL

WILDCAT CANYON

6950'

Pocket Mesa

PINE VALLEY

7000'

Ⓟ

TRAIL

Pine Valley Peak

Pine Spring Wash

CONNECTOR

LEE VALLEY

RD.

TERRACE

KOLOB

Firepit Knoll

Spendlove Knoll

.5 ml

.5 km

N

0

0

HOP VALLEY TRAIL

6350'

Ⓟ

TO LA VERKIN CREEK

RD.

KOLOB TERRACE

TO VIRGIN

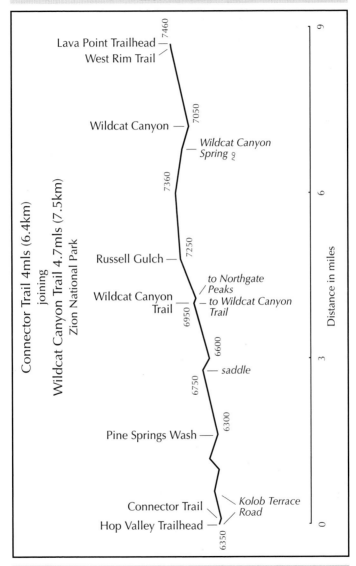

Lava Point Trailhead — 7460
West Rim Trail

Wildcat Canyon — 7050

Wildcat Canyon Spring ⌇

7360

7250

Russell Gulch —

Wildcat Canyon Trail — 6950

to Northgate Peaks
to Wildcat Canyon Trail

6600

— *saddle*

6750

Pine Springs Wash — 6300

Connector Trail 4mls (6.4km)
joining
Wildcat Canyon Trail 4.7mls (7.5km)
Zion National Park

Connector Trail —

Kolob Terrace Road

Hop Valley Trailhead — 6350

Distance in miles

9

6

3

0

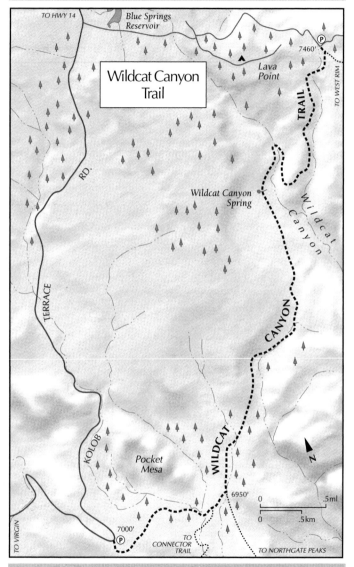

TO HWY 14

Blue Springs
Reservoir

7460'

TO WEST RIM

Lava
Point

Wildcat Canyon
Trail

TRAIL

RD.

Wildcat Canyon
Spring

Wildcat Canyon

TERRACE

CANYON

N

KOLOB

Pocket
Mesa

WILDCAT

6950'

0   .5ml

0   .5km

7000'

TO VIRGIN

TO
CONNECTOR
TRAIL

TO NORTHGATE PEAKS

Distance, one way:	5.8 miles (9.3 kilometres)
Time, one way:	3 hours
Maps:	Kolob Reservoir, The Guardian Angels (United States Geological Survey 7.5'); Zion National Park (TI)
Season:	mid-April through to October
Water:	Wildcat Canyon Spring
Rating:	moderate

The Wildcat Canyon car park is located 16 miles north of Virgin on Kolob Terrace Road.

Directions

From the car park walk east on the old road through the pine forest. In 0.5 mile, the Connector Trail to Hop Valley joins from the south-west. In another 0.1 mile, the Northgate Peaks Trail turns south. Bear north-east and head steadily uphill past Russell Gulch. You reach your high point around 1.5 miles from the trail junction and begin your descent into Wildcat Canyon. From the high point in another 0.5 mile, you come to Wildcat Canyon Spring, clearly visible on the west side of the trail, where a sign reads "Purify Water". Wildcat Canyon offers poor camping. One half mile farther on the trail you cross dry Wildcat Creek and begin a 1 mile ascent to the West Rim Trail. At the trail junction at the top of the hill you join the West Rim Trail. Turn south towards Zion Canyon or walk north 0.1 mile to the Lava Point car park.

NORTHGATE PEAKS TRAIL

Start:	Wildcat Canyon Trailhead (7,000 feet/ 2,134 metres)
End:	Lookout to North Guardian Angel (6,760 feet/2,060 metres)
Distance, one way:	2.2 miles (3.5 kilometres)
Time, one way:	1 hour
Maps:	The Guardian Angels (United States Geological Survey 7.5') (trail not on map); Zion National Park (TI)
Season:	mid-April through to October

Water:	none
Rating:	easy

The Wildcat Canyon car park off Kolob Terrace Road, 16 miles north from Virgin, Utah off Kolob Terrace Road, provides the easiest access to this pleasant trail. This remote, little used trail offers many fine, dry camping spots on its level pine studded plateau.

Directions

From the Wildcat Canyon trailhead proceed east for 1 mile to the junction with the Connector Trail. Continue straight ahead and go 0.1 mile to the Northgate Peaks Trail Junction and turn south. The Wildcat Canyon Trail heads north-east.

Heading south from the trail junction, you notice immediately a well-worn path dropping to the west. This path leads into Russell Gulch to the popular off-trail route descending the Left Fork and passing through the Subway. Remaining on the main trail, continue straight ahead through the pine forest. Eventually the trees thicken and block your view. Later the vistas open up as the trail ends at a lava formed viewpoint. Northgate Peaks line either side of your gaze and North Guardian Angel stands directly in front of you. Numerous canyons and gorges of the central park area make up the rest of the landscape. Checker boarding adorns many of the stone faces and domes. In the far distance you can identify The Bishopric and Inclined Temple and the drainages of the Right and Left Fork.

WEST RIM TRAIL

Start:	Lava Point Trailhead (7,460 feet/ 2,274 metres)
End:	Grotto picnic area (4,298 feet/1,310 metres)
Distance, one way:	14.2 miles (22.7 kilometres)
Time, one way:	7 hours
Maps:	Kolob Reservoir, Temple of Sinawava, The Guardian Angels (United States Geological Survey 7.5'); Zion National Park (TI)
Season:	mid-April through to October
Water:	West Rim (Cabin) Spring
Rating:	strenuous

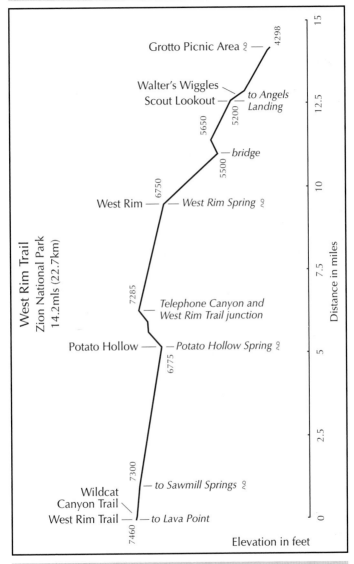

West Rim Trail
Zion National Park
14.2mls (22.7km)

Grotto Picnic Area — 4298

Walter's Wiggles
Scout Lookout — 5200 — *to Angels Landing*

5650

— *bridge*
5500

6750
West Rim — — *West Rim Spring*

7285
— *Telephone Canyon and West Rim Trail junction*

Potato Hollow — — *Potato Hollow Spring*
6775

7300
— *to Sawmill Springs*

Wildcat
Canyon Trail
West Rim Trail — — *to Lava Point*
7460

Distance in miles

Elevation in feet

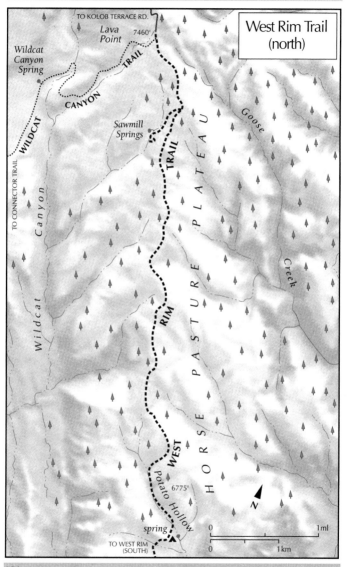

West Rim Trail
(north)

TO KOLOB TERRACE RD.

*Lava
Point* 7460'

*Wildcat
Canyon
Spring*

WILDCAT

CANYON   TRAIL

TO CONNECTOR TRAIL

Canyon

Wildcat

*Sawmill
Springs*

TRAIL

PLATEAU

Goose

Creek

RIM

PASTURE

HORSE

WEST

Potato Hollow

6775'

spring

TO WEST RIM
(SOUTH)

N

0   1ml

0   1km

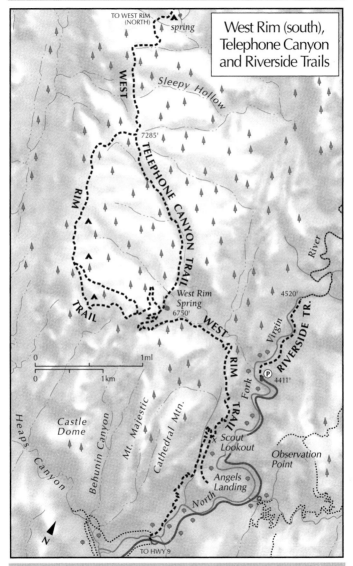

TO WEST RIM
(NORTH)

spring

West Rim (south), Telephone Canyon and Riverside Trails

WEST

Sleepy Hollow

7285'

RIM

TELEPHONE CANYON TRAIL

River

TRAIL

4520'

West Rim
Spring
6750'

WEST

Virgin

RIVERSIDE TR.

RIM

0   1ml

0   1km

Fork

TRAIL

P
4411'

Castle
Dome

Behunin Canyon

Mt. Majestic

Cathedral Mtn.

x Scout
Lookout

Observation
Point

Heaps Canyon

Angels
Landing

North

N

TO HWY 9

One of Zion's most spectacular walks and its most popular backpacking route, the West Rim Trail can be walked as an overnight trip or a long day-walk. Three springs at Potato Hollow, Sawmill Springs and West Rim (Cabin) Spring provide water. Camp only in designated sites dotting the West Rim and Potato Hollow area. The overnight trip, included in my Across Zion itinerary (see section 18), allows more time to admire the first class views of many distant parts of the park. The least strenuous and most scenic trip starts from the Lava Point trailhead and descends to the valley floor. The hardy can start from the Grotto picnic area and ascend 3,000 feet to the West Rim. This second alternative misses some of the finest park views from the West Rim Trail and south from Potato Hollow.

To reach the trailhead from Virgin, Utah take the Kolob Terrace Road for 21 miles to the Lava Point turn-off and turn east. Proceed 1 mile to where three roads intersect. Take the middle road directly east and to the north of the road to Lava Point. The West Rim Trail begins 1.25 miles down this road at the trail register and vehicle barrier. Contact the Zion Lodge for a convenient shuttle service to Lava Point.

Directions

From the West Rim trailhead, follow the flat jeep road south, soon crossing the junction with the Wildcat Canyon Trail. One mile from the start a trail branches west to Sawmill Springs. A short detour down a small hill brings you to the spring in a lovely meadow.

The main trail continues on top of the plateau unfortunately marred by many lightening strikes and fires. The sandstone finger of Horse Plateau juts out over the North Fork of the Virgin River and the cliffs of Goose Creek. Views of North and South Guardian Angel open up on the west. After 4 miles the trail descends a gully to grassy Potato Hollow where you'll admire fine views towards The Narrows and the Virgin River. You may want to reserve a designated campsite here in the vicinity of Potato Hollow Spring and leave the scenic West Rim Trail for the morning.

Leaving grassy Potato Hollow you climb steeply south enjoying splendid views north to Imlay Canyon, Sleepy Hollow and Greatheart Mesa. Reaching the top of a ridge the trail drops a bit as spectacular southern views to the Inclined Temple, Ivins Mountain and the Right Fork become evident. As you descend a narrow ridge, these views grab your attention before finally reaching the bottom of a small saddle. Climbing steeply again 400 feet up the ridge from Potato Hollow, you come to the junction of the Telephone Canyon Trail and West Rim Trail.

The Telephone Canyon Trail, a shorter but much less scenic alternative to the West Rim Trail, branches east to meet the West Rim Spring Junction. The dramatic West Rim Trail turns west and begins its scenic meandering along the edge of the West Rim. The views from this trail are some of the most spectacular in the park. White and red sandstone rock formations mix among finger-like valleys and bald-topped plateaux. The first views take in South Guardian Angel and the Right Fork of North Creek. The trail then veers southeast and crosses southern Horse Plateau. Turning south you gaze down into Heaps Canyon and the Inclined Temple. Three other grand flat-topped mesas ornament your distant views. As you meander east, Behunin Canyon comes into view and you can see Castle Dome to the south and farther east the flat top of Mount Majestic and Cathedral Mountain.

Numbered campsites are scattered along this section of the West Rim. Soon the trail switchbacks down 300 feet to meet the Telephone Canyon Trail and nearby West Rim (Cabin) Spring. This small spring, trickling out of the rock 100 yards east down the edge of a 700 foot cliff, served as a park service cabin until it burned down in the 1970s. Its spring provides your last water source until you reach Zion Valley.

Returning to the junction near the spring, you begin another dramatic section of the trail. Here you skirt the edge of the rim on a wide path next to high Navajo sandstone cliffs. Made of either rock or pavement, the trail winds its way along switchbacks 1.5 miles down to the valley floor. Take care in the spring when ice or snow make this section treacherous. Looking back you can see the high, water-stained West Rim cliffs you have just descended.

Reaching the floor below the West Rim, you descend 0.5 mile into a dry wash and cross a bridge. Continuing north from the bridge, you turn abruptly south and begin a 150 foot climb that soon tops out with fine views north to the Mountain of Mystery and across the valley to The Great White Throne and Red Arch Mountain. The trail winds down to Scout Lookout and reaches the base of Angels' Landing. Hopefully, you will have allowed for the detour to the top of Angels' Landing. Here you feel back at civilization as you will meet many day-walkers ascending from Zion Canyon.

See the description in section 15, Zion Canyon Trails, for the climb of Angels' Landing and for the last section of the West Rim Trail from Scout Lookout to the Grotto picnic area.

CHAPTER 15

ZION NATIONAL PARK: ZION CANYON TRAILS

Silence alone is worthy to be heard.
Henry David Thoreau

ZION CANYON TRAILS

Trail	Distance Miles One way	Distance Kilometres One Way	Rating
Gateway to The Narrows or Riverside Trail	1.0	1.6	Easy
Up The Narrows to Orderville Canyon	3.2	5.1	Strenuous
Weeping Rock	0.2	0.3	Easy
Hidden Canyon	1.0	1.6	Moderate
Observation Point	3.7	5.9	Strenuous
Angels' Landing via Scout Lookout	2.5	4.0	Strenuous
Lower Emerald Pool	0.6	1.0	Easy
Middle Emerald Pool	1.0	1.6	Easy
Upper Emerald Pool	1.3	2.1	Moderate
Court of the Patriarchs	0.1	0.2	Easy
Sand Bench Horse Trail	3.4	5.4	Easy
Par'us	2.0	3.2	Easy
The Watchman	5.8	9.3	Moderate

GATEWAY TO THE NARROWS OR RIVERSIDE TRAIL

Start:	Temple of Sinawava (4,411 feet/ 1,344 metres)
End:	Virgin River (4,490 feet/1,368 metres)
Distance, one way:	1 mile (1.6 kilometres)
Time, one way:	20 minutes
Maps:	Temple of Sinawava (United States

	Geological Survey 7.5′); Zion National Park (TI)
Season:	all year
Water:	Virgin River
Rating:	easy

Zion's most popular walk, Gateway to The Narrows or the Riverside Trail, starts from the northernmost end of the Zion Canyon Scenic Road at the Temple of Sinawava. This paved, wheelchair-accessible trail follows the Virgin River 1 mile up the narrowing canyon. Heading upstream on the true left of the Virgin River below steep cliffs, you are flanked by the towering Pulpit to the west and the red-faced Temple of Sinawava to the east. Hanging gardens of wildflowers line the path in the spring. On a hot summer's day you can cool your feet in the river.

If no flash-flood danger exists, you can continue upstream from the trail's end. The route snakes through the Virgin River to Orderville Canyon, 2.2 miles ahead. This part of the walk overlaps with the last section of The Narrows Route described next under "Up The Narrows to Orderville Canyon."

UP THE NARROWS TO ORDERVILLE CANYON

Start:	Temple of Sinawava (4,418 feet/1,347 metres)
End:	Orderville Canyon (4,610 feet/1,405 metres)
Distance, one way:	3.2 miles (5.1 kilometres)
Time, one way:	3 hours
Maps:	Temple of Sinawava (United States Geological Survey 7.5′); Zion National Park (TI)
Season:	June through to October
Water:	Virgin River
Rating:	strenuous

This trip, starting from The Temple of Sinawava at the end of the Zion Canyon Road and overlapping with the last section of The Narrows Route, offers a splendid example of canyon-walking. If you don't want to backpack or attempt the whole of The Narrows in a single day, this route provides a sneak peak at some narrows-walking. You may be inspired to return later for the complete trip.

Water temperatures chill the hardiest walkers - even in summer - so be sure to carry warm clothing. Protective clothing, available for rent in Springdale, provides extra warmth; special shoes prevent slipping on the rocks. The name "Up The Narrows" may confuse you since this walk does not include the true "narrows" section of the Virgin River located between Deep Creek and Orderville Canyon. (See section 16, Zion National Park, Long Distance Walks, for a more complete description of equipment needed and risks associated with canyon-walking.)

Directions

Starting at the Temple of Sinawava car park, follow the Gateway to The Narrows Trail (Riverside Trail) for 1 mile to the end of the concrete path. Continue straight ahead and enter the Virgin River. Fighting the current, weave back and forth across pebbly side-bars and sandy beaches to find shallow crossing areas.

Carving a 2,000 foot channel down from the Markagunt Plateau, the Virgin River has created grottoes, side canyons, seeps and waterfalls. One mile north of the end of the concrete trail, Mystery Canyon presents itself as a trickle of water from the east side of the canyon. Orderville Canyon, the first major canyon to join the Virgin River, enters from the east, 2.2 miles from the start. Though its upper reaches can only be explored with specialized equipment, you can wander a short way upstream before your passage is blocked.

Returning to the Virgin River at Orderville Canyon, the "Narrows" section begins 0.5 mile north of the junction and continues for 2 miles upstream beyond this point. Do not enter this section during bad weather, thunderstorms or in the event of any risk of flash floods. Return to the parking area by retracing your steps downstream.

WEEPING ROCK

Start:	Weeping Rock car park (4,350 feet/1,326 metres)
End:	Weeping Rock (4,450 feet/1,356 metres)

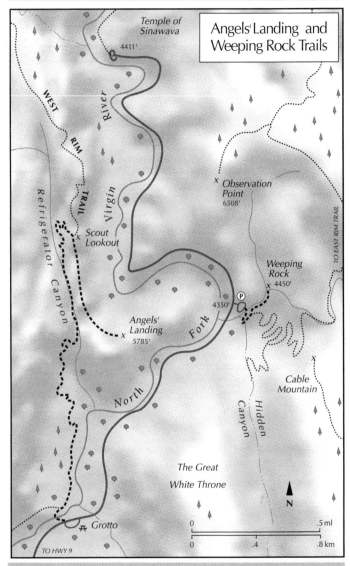

Angels' Landing and
Weeping Rock Trails

Temple of
Sinawava
4411'

WEST

RIM

TRAIL

River

Refrigerator Canyon

Virgin

Scout
Lookout

x Observation
Point
6508'

Weeping
Rock
x 4450'

TO EAST RIM TRAIL

P
4350'

Angels'
Landing
x 5785'

North

Fork

x

Cable
Mountain
x

Hidden
Canyon

The Great
White Throne

N

0   .5 ml

0   .4   .8 km

Grotto

TO HWY 9

Big Springs, The Narrows, Zion National Park

Middle Fork of Taylor Creek, Zion National Park

Distance, one way:	0.2 miles (0.3 kilometres)
Time, one way:	10 minutes
Maps:	Temple of Sinawava (United States Geological Survey 7.5'); Zion National Park (TI)
Season:	all year
Water:	none
Rating:	easy

From the Weeping Rock car park, 4.4 miles up Zion Canyon Scenic Drive, follow the trail south over the creek. Interpretative signs describe the vegetation. In 5 minutes the trail forks and the East Rim Trail continues east and up from here.

Directions
The trail continues north to an overlook under Weeping Rock. Rain "weeps" from a spring in the sandstone roof of the alcove above you. Retrace your steps to the car or turn east at the junction to continue to Observation Point and Hidden Canyon.

HIDDEN CANYON AND OBSERVATION POINT

Start:	Weeping Rock car park (4,350 feet/1,326 metres)
End:	Hidden Canyon (5,100 feet/1,554 metres) or Observation Point (6,508 feet/1,984 metres)
Distance, one way:	to Hidden Canyon 1 miles (1.6 kilometres); to Observation Point 3.7 miles (5.9 kilometres)
Time, one way:	3 hours to Observation Point
Maps:	Temple of Sinawava (United States Geological Survey 7.5'); Zion National Park (TI)
Season:	June through to October
Water:	none
Rating:	moderate

Starting from the Weeping Rock car park, 4.4 miles up Zion Canyon Scenic Drive, these two hikes may be completed separately or

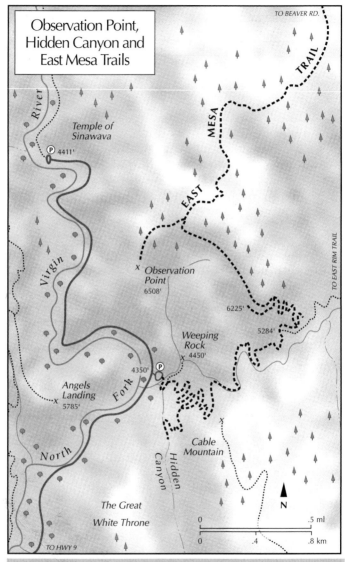

Observation Point,
Hidden Canyon and
East Mesa Trails

TO BEAVER RD.

TRAIL

MESA

EAST

River

Temple of
Sinawava

P 4411'

TO EAST RIM TRAIL

Virgin

x Observation
Point
6508'

6225'

5284'

Weeping
Rock
x 4450'

4350'
P

Angels
Landing
x 5785'

Fork

x

North

Cable
Mountain

Hidden Canyon

The Great
White Throne

N

0   .5 ml

0   .4   .8 km

TO HWY 9

together. The hike to Observation Point offers a wonderful alternative to the crowded hike to Angels' Landing or Scout Lookout. These trails, cut into the sandstone in the 1930s, show off imposing views of the Zion Canyon, just as splendid as their better known cross-canyon counterparts.

Directions
From the car park follow the interpretative trail south and in 5 minutes continue east at the junction that turns to Weeping Rock. Ascend the cliffs below Cable Mountain in a series of switchbacks. In 30 minutes the trail to Hidden Canyon branches south. A traverse along the slick-rock walls leads to the mouth of Hidden Canyon sandwiched between The Great White Throne and the sheer walls of Cable Mountain. Potholes formed by rainwater wear grooves into the canyon walls. Continuing 0.5 mile upstream from the mouth of the canyon brings you to a small arch.

Back on the trail to Observation Point, climb past the turn-off to Hidden Canyon. After several more switchbacks, you enter cool Echo Canyon, weaving amidst the red-walled cliffs and washes until you reach a signed junction. The trail to Observation Point continues west and East Rim Trail branches east. Snow or ice may block the upper sections of this trail in spring. Cutting into the sandstone, the trail rises steeply as it climbs to a high plateau to meet the East Mesa Trail. Turn south and soon reach Observation Point. Outstanding views of The Great White Throne, Cable Mountain, the West Rim, Angels' Landing and the Zion Canyon greet you. Retrace your steps back to the car.

ANGELS' LANDING VIA SCOUT LOOKOUT

Start:	Grotto picnic area (4,290 feet/1,308 metres)
End:	Angels' Landing (5,790 feet/1,765 metres)
Distance, one way:	2.5 miles (4 kilometres)
Time, one way:	2 hours
Maps:	Temple of Sinawava (United States Geological Survey 7.5'); Zion National Park (TI)
Season:	March through to November
Water:	none
Rating:	strenuous

This famous walk to Angels' Landing distinguishes itself as the most popular day-walk in Zion. Begin from the Grotto picnic area, 0.5 mile north of the Zion Lodge on the Zion Canyon Scenic Drive.

Directions
From the picnic tables, cross the road and take the footbridge to the true right of the Virgin River. Just after crossing the river, the trail to Emerald Pools veers south-west. The path to Angels' Landing follows the river north amidst a jumble of boulders.

Ahead you can see the trail as it switchbacks upward through the sandstone. Leaving the switchbacks behind, enter cool Refrigerator Canyon. The famous 21 switchbacks of Walter's Wiggle's follow as you climb the last 1,000 feet to Scout Lookout. This section was blasted into solid rock during construction by the Civilian Conservation Corps (CCC) in 1926. Fine views down the sheer walls into the Zion Canyon greet you. Scout Lookout, a popular turn-around point for many day-walkers, marks the turn-off to Angels' Landing. Three miles farther along this trail along with a steep ascent brings you to West Rim (Cabin) Spring and the West Rim Trail and Telephone Canyon Trail junction.

Angels' Landing, clearly viewed from here, makes a highly recommended and exciting detour. However, if you are afraid of heights or are accompanied by small children, do not attempt it. Forego your ascent also in wet, icy conditions or thunderstorms. From Scout Lookout, the trail appears more treacherous than it truly is and many a frightened walker turns back here. Chains and wide steps protect the entire path.

From Scout Lookout, follow the trail south, first up over a notch and across a narrow spine to the north side of the landing. Next ascend an extremely steep sandstone ridge, equipped with chains, rails and wide steps. Steep drop-offs mark both sides of the trail. Continue upward and hold on tightly. Reaching the upper knife edge of the landing, you are rewarded with views across the Zion Valley to the Great White Throne, Cable Mountain, the South Zion Valley and the Observation Point Trail as it winds its way up to the rim from Weeping Rock. Carefully retrace your steps to Scout Lookout and back to the Grotto picnic area.

EMERALD POOLS

Start:	Zion Lodge (4,276 feet/1,303 metres)
End:	Upper Emerald Pool (4,520 feet/1,378 metres) via Lower and Middle Pools
Distance, one way:	0.6 miles (1 kilometres) to Lower Pool; 1 miles (1.6 kilometres) to Middle Pool; 1.3 miles (2.1 kilometres) to Upper Pool
Time, one way:	10 minutes to Lower Pool; 20 minutes to Middle Pool; 45 minutes to Upper Pool
Maps:	Temple of Sinawava (United States Geological Survey 7.5′); Zion National Park (TI)
Season:	all year
Water:	none
Rating:	moderate

There are three emerald pools to visit; all are accessible by linked trails. From the Emerald Pools car park, across from the Zion Lodge, cross the Virgin River on a bridge to the west and true right of the river. Just across the river, the fork that bears north marks the easiest wheelchair accessible path to the Lower Pool. A turn south accesses a loop trail to the Upper and Middle Pools and the Sand Bench Trail.

Directions

Taking the north fork toward the Lower Pool, you wander among a forest of trees until you reach an overhang. In the spring, Heaps Canyon Creek drips into the Lower Pool and forms the Emerald Pools. From the Lower Pool a steeper, more difficult, trail leads in 0.2 mile to the Middle Pool and, in another 0.3 mile, to the Upper Pool.

Back at the first junction, if you wish to visit the Middle and Upper Pools, follow the southern fork until it turns sharply to the north and in 1 mile leads you to the Middle Pool. As you climb up the trail, you are rewarded with views across the canyon to The Great White Throne and Red Arch Mountain. To the north you see The Spearhead and to the east Lady Mountain. Passing near the Middle Pool, a narrow trail climbs to the Upper Pool. Cross the field of boulders and its many intersecting paths. From here sandstone

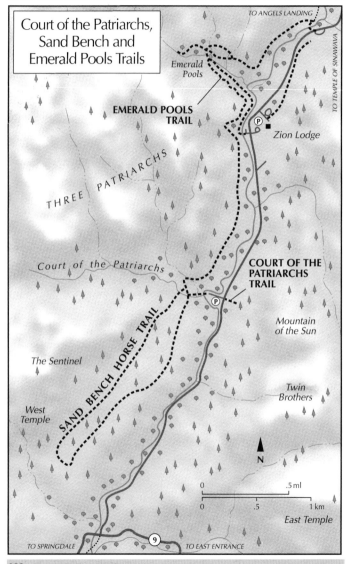

Court of the Patriarchs,
Sand Bench and
Emerald Pools Trails

TO ANGELS LANDING

Emerald
Pools

TO TEMPLE OF SINAWAVA

**EMERALD POOLS
TRAIL**

P

Zion Lodge

THREE PATRIARCHS

Court of the Patriarchs

**COURT OF THE
PATRIARCHS
TRAIL**

P

Mountain
of the Sun

SAND BENCH HORSE TRAIL

The Sentinel

Twin
Brothers

West
Temple

N

0   .5 ml

0   .5   1 km

East Temple

TO SPRINGDALE   (9)   TO EAST ENTRANCE

cliffs rise from three sides and after rain a waterfall drops into the Upper Pool.

From any of the pools, you can retrace your steps back to the car park or head north for 0.8 mile to the Grotto picnic area. Fine views of Observation Point, The Great White Throne and Angels' Landing line this path. A 0.6 mile almost flat trail, paralleling Zion Drive, connects the Zion Lodge and the Grotto picnic area. From the latter, walk east towards the ranger's residence and follow the path south through the trees until it emerges from the forest near Zion Lodge.

COURT OF THE PATRIARCHS

Start:	Court of the Patriarchs car park (4,250 feet/ 1,295 metres)
End:	Court of the Patriarchs viewpoint (4,290 feet/ 1,308 metres)
Distance, one way:	0.1 miles (0.2 kilometres)
Time, one way:	5 minutes
Maps:	Springdale East (United States Geological Survey 7.5'); Zion National Park (TI)
Season:	all year
Water:	none
Rating:	easy

This popular paved trail, open all year, offers fine views of the entire Zion Canyon.

Directions
From the Court of the Patriarchs car park, 2.2 miles up Zion Canyon Scenic Drive from Utah Route 9, the concrete trail ascends east from the road until it ends at a canyon overlook. You see the Sentinel, Court of the Patriarchs, Mt. Moroni and far down the valley to Angels' Landing. Return to the car park by retracing your steps.

SAND BENCH HORSE TRAIL

Start:	Court of the Patriarchs car park (4250 feet/ 1,295 metres)
End:	Corral (4,600 feet/1,402 metres)
Distance, semi-loop:	3.4 miles (5.4 kilometres)

Time, one way:	2 hours
Maps:	Springdale East (United States Geological Survey 7.5'), Zion National Park (TI)
Season:	all year
Water:	none
Rating:	moderate

From the Court of the Patriarchs car park, 2.2 miles up Zion Canyon Scenic Drive, take the road to the west side of the road, pass the water tank and cross the Virgin River. Horses frequent this dusty trail from spring through to autumn.

Directions
On the far side, turn south and climb above the river until you reach the fork in the trail. The north fork brings you to the Emerald Pools and the south fork quickly connects you to the Sand Bench Loop. Before you stand the Court of the Patriarchs with the red cliffs of the Three Patriarchs and Mt. Moroni soars above you.

Begin a 500 foot climb on the south-west fork around the loop. The Streaked Wall dominates the view ahead of you; The Watchman looms across the canyon. At the south end of the loop you come to a picnic table, a rest area and a corral. As you circle north, you are rewarded with views of the Mountain of the Sun, the East Temple and the Twin Brothers. Combine this hike with the Emerald Pool Trail into a half-day hike.

PAR'US TRAIL

Start:	South Campground (4,000 feet/ 1,219 metres)
End:	Zion Canyon Drive at Utah State Highway 9 (4,000 feet/1,219 metres)
Distance, one way:	2 miles (3.2 kilometres)
Time, one way:	1 hour
Maps:	Springdale East (United States Geological Survey 7.5'); Zion National Park (TI)
Season:	all year
Water:	Virgin River
Rating:	easy

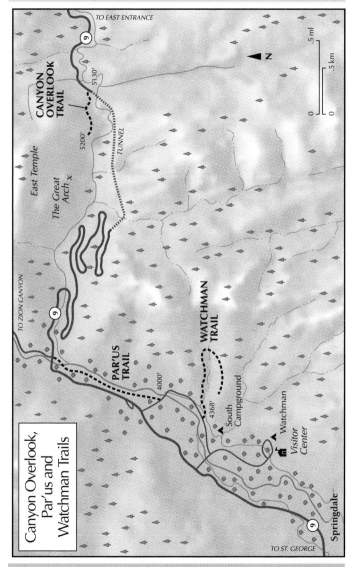

TO EAST ENTRANCE

9

5130'

CANYON
OVERLOOK
TRAIL

5200'

TUNNEL

East Temple

The Great
Arch x

TO ZION CANYON

9

WATCHMAN
TRAIL

PAR'US
TRAIL

4000'

4368'

South
Campground

Watchman

Visitor
Center

9

Springdale

TO ST. GEORGE

N

.5 ml

.5 km

Canyon Overlook,
Par'us and
Watchman Trails

This flat, 2 mile walk on a paved wheelchair-accessible trail, shared with bicycles, starts west of the Virgin River at the South Campground. Fine views north to the Towers of the Virgin, the Streaked Wall, and lower Zion Canyon stretch out before you. The trail ends when it intersects the Zion Canyon Scenic Drive.

THE WATCHMAN

Start:	Watchman car park, east of South Campground (3,900 feet/1,189 metres)
End:	Viewpoint (4,368 feet/1,331 metres)
Distance, around loop:	5.8 miles (9.3 kilometres)
Time, one way:	3 hours
Maps:	Springdale East (United States Geological Survey 7.5′); Zion National Park (TI)
Season:	all year
Water:	none
Rating:	moderate

To reach The Watchman trailhead, drive 0.25 mile from the South Entrance and turn east into the Watchman Campground. Just past the self-pay station, take the service road north-east for 400 yards to the Watchman Trail car park.

Directions

From the car park, the trail ascends a knoll below Bridge Mountain and the Watchman. As you near the base of the Watchman, the trail ascends the mountain via switchbacks. Fine views open up westward across the Virgin River to the Towers of the Virgin and southward to the town of Springdale. Be sure to supervise children near the steep drop-offs. Once on the top, continue around the loop from the viewpoint and retrace your steps to the car park.

CHAPTER 16

ZION NATIONAL PARK: EAST RIM TRAILS

Today looked so easy yesterday.
Gary Ladd

EAST RIM TRAILS

Trail	Distance Miles One way	Distance Kilometres One Way	Rating
Canyon Overlook Trail	0.5	0.8	Easy
East Rim Trail	9.8	15.7	Moderate
East Mesa Trail	2.5	4.0	Easy
East Boundary to Echo Canyon Trail	0.6	1.0	Easy
Stave Spring Junction to Cable Mountain Trail	2.9	4.6	Easy
Stave Spring Junction to Deertrap Mountain Trail	3.2	5.1	Easy

CANYON OVERLOOK TRAIL

Start:	Mt. Carmel Tunnel (5,130 feet/1,563 metres)
End:	Canyon Overlook (5,200 feet/1,584 metres)
Distance, one way:	0.5 mile (0.8 kilometres)
Time, one way:	20 minutes
Maps:	Springdale East (United States Geological Survey 7.5'); Zion National Park (TI)
Season:	all year
Water:	none
Rating:	easy

From the South Entrance of Zion National Park, north of Springdale, Utah take State Highway 9 through the Mt. Carmel Tunnel. The Canyon Overlook Trail begins just east of the tunnel from the north side of the road. There are several lay-bys along the road for parking.

Directions
Ramble up a short series of uneven steps. In 5 minutes you'll reach several walkways with iron railings. Proceed under numerous rock overhangs beside steep drop-offs. Be cautious, especially if accompanied by small children. The trail weaves back and forth among pine trees ending at a lookout with fine views of the West and East Temples, Towers of Virgin and the south Zion Canyon. Retrace your steps back to your car.

EAST RIM TRAIL

Start:	East Entrance (5,740 feet/1,750 metres)
End:	Weeping Rock (4,360 feet/1,329 metres)
Distance, one way:	9.8 miles (15.7 kilometres)
Time, one way:	4 hours
Maps:	The Barracks, Temple of Sinawava, Springdale East (United States Geological Survey 7.5'); Zion National Park (TI)
Season:	May through to October
Water:	Stave Spring
Rating:	moderate

To reach the East Rim Parking Area take Utah State Highway 9 13 miles to the Zion National Park East Entrance. The East Rim Trail starts from the parking area 150 yards west of the East Entrance.

This splendid lightly used Zion trail connects the park's East Entrance with the Zion Valley at Weeping Rock. The walk can be completed as a day trip or as an overnight including side trips to Cable and Deertrap mountains (section 18). Use the Zion Lodge shuttle to reach the East Entrance. Views from the east side of Zion Canyon highlight a different perspective of the valley than views from the popular West Rim walks. Stave Spring, 5.5 miles from the start, provides the only reliable water along the route.

Directions
From the trailhead next to the ranger's residence, pass by the register station to the dusty trail. Following Clear Creek Wash you climb as the trail bends north into Cave Creek. Turning south you pass high above Cave Creek to gain fine views to the Checkerboard

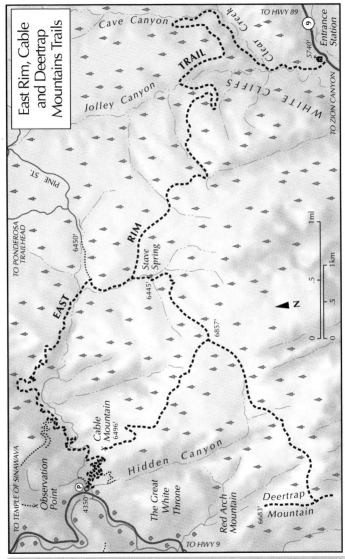

East Rim, Cable and Deertrap Mountains Trails

Cave Canyon

Jolley Canyon

TO HWY 89

Clear Creek

Entrance Station

TRAIL

WHITE CLIFFS

TO ZION CANYON

5740'

9

PINE ST.

TO PONDEROSA TRAILHEAD

EAST RIM

6450'

Stave Spring

6445'

6857'

N

1 ml

1 km

.5

.5

0

0

TO TEMPLE OF SINAWAVA

Cable Mountain
6496'

Observation Point

4350'

Hidden Canyon

The Great White Throne

Red Arch Mountain

Deertrap Mountain

6683'

TO HWY 9

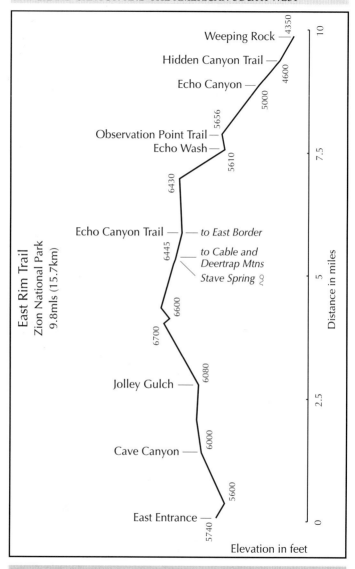

East Rim Trail
Zion National Park
9.8mls (15.7km)

Weeping Rock — 4350
Hidden Canyon Trail —
Echo Canyon —
4600
5000
5656
Observation Point Trail —
Echo Wash —
5610
6430
Echo Canyon Trail — — to East Border
6445
— to Cable and
Deertrap Mtns
Stave Spring ⌇
6600
6700
6080
Jolley Gulch —
6000
Cave Canyon —
5600
East Entrance —
5740

Distance in miles

10

7.5

5

2.5

0

Elevation in feet

Mesa, Jolley Gulch and the White Cliffs of Zion. Next heading westward, the trail crosses dry Jolley Gulch and climbs gradually to a hilltop dotted with pine, juniper and manzanita. A short gradual descent brings you to the small but reliable Stave Spring. One hundred and fifty yards beyond the spring, you come to the trail junction for the Deertrap Mountain Trail leading to Cable and Deertrap mountains. Turn west if you are planning this splendid side trip.

Overnight walkers will want to collect water here; camp at least 0.5 mile from the spring. If continuing on to Deertrap and Cable mountains, some nice camping sites dot the plateau along the Deertrap Mountain Trail. Or, if you are heading directly to the valley, the trees and foliage above Echo Canyon shelter lovely camping spots.

Bear east if you are continuing on the East Rim Trail. In 0.2 mile the trail to the Ponderosa trailhead veers to the east. The East Rim Trail, now signed as the Echo Canyon Trail, continues west from this junction across the flats and through hoards of sagebrush to the head of an unnamed side canyon. Traversing above this canyon past several campsites, you are greeted with splendid views of the West Rim. Then the trail drops precipitously off the East Rim and zigzags on a rock-strewn path into Echo Canyon. Looking upward and south you can make out the cable works on the edge of Cable Mountain.

Follow the cairns across several side canyons until you reach the junction with the trail to Observation Point. The Observation Point Trail ascends west and the route to the valley and the Weeping Rock trailhead continues south downhill. (See the description of the Observation Point Trail (section 15) for an account of the final 2 miles down to the valley.) Upon reaching the Weeping Rock trailhead, catch the open air tram back to the Zion Lodge.

EAST BOUNDARY TO ECHO CANYON TRAIL

Start:	East Boundary from Pine Street (6,450 feet/ 1,966 metres)
End:	Echo Canyon Trail (6,400 feet/1,951 metres)
Distance, one way:	0.6 mile (1 kilometre)
Time, one way:	20 minutes
Maps:	Temple of Sinawava, Springdale East

	(United States Geological Survey 7.5');
	Zion National Park (TI)
Season:	May through to October
Water:	none
Rating:	easy

From the East Entrance to Zion National Park, take Utah State Highway 9 east 2.5 miles and turn north on North Fork Country Road. Follow the road 5.4 miles and turn left into the Zion Ponderosa Ranch and Resort. Pass under the entrance sign and continue straight ahead onto the narrow dirt Twin Knolls Road. Proceed 0.8 mile and turn left onto Buck Road. Take the immediate right fork and drive 0.6 mile turning left at the next fork. Continue on this road to Pine Street and park on the side of the road. Walk 0.5 mile west on Pine Street down the rocky rutted road past several summer homes to the park boundary.

Directions
From the park gate, take the trail west running gradually downhill through a grove of ponderosa pines. A few minutes more will bring you into an open meadow and to a trail junction. Turn south to go to Cable and Deertrap mountains. Turn north to join the East Rim Trail to Weeping Rock and Echo Canyon.

EAST MESA TRAIL

Start:	East Boundary from Beaver Road (6,520 feet/1,987 metres)
End:	Observation Point (6,500 feet/1,981 metres)
Distance, round trip:	2.5 miles (4 kilometres)
Time, one way:	1 hour
Maps:	Temple of Sinawava (United States Geological Survey 7.5'); Zion National Park (TI)
Season:	May through to October
Water:	none
Rating:	easy

Follow the directions to Zion Ponderosa Ranch and Resort (see East Boundary to Echo Canyon Trail above) and pass under the main entrance sign. Continue straight ahead on Twin Knolls Road. Drive 0.8 mile and turn right onto Beaver Road. Proceed as far as you can on the rutted road. Park the car on the shoulder and continue on foot about 0.5 mile to the fenced park entrance.

Directions

From the hiker's gate, the trail, an old dirt road, crosses a high plateau dotted with ponderosa pines. The trail ascends gently with views to the north all the way to the Pink Cliffs of the Virgin Rim. After 1.5 miles, just before a knoll and the trail's high point, a side path heads to an overlook of Mystery Canyon. Back at the main trail you now turn south with commanding views of Zion and Echo Canyons. The trail then skirts the edge of an unnamed canyon that joins the Virgin River in the north.

After traversing a low saddle, the trail descends gradually to reach the Observation Point Trail. Turn south-west and in 0.3 mile you reach Observation Point, with its splendid views of the entire Zion Canyon, Angels' Landing and the West Rim. Though less scenic than the trail from Weeping Rock, this trail offers a much less strenuous way to enjoy Observation Point's splendid views.

The trail map to the East Mesa Trail can be found in section 15, Zion Canyon Trails, along with the map of the trail to Observation Point and Hidden Canyon.

STAVE SPRING JUNCTION TO CABLE MOUNTAIN AND DEERTRAP MOUNTAIN TRAILS

Start:	Stave Spring Junction (6,445 feet/ 1,964 metres)
End:	Cable Mountain (6,496 feet/1,980 metres) and Deertrap Mountain (6,683 feet/ 2,037 metres)
Distance, one way:	2.9 miles (4.6 kilometres) to Cable Mountain; 3.2 miles (5.1kilometres) to Deertrap Mountain
Time, one way:	1 hour to Cable Mountain; 1.5 hours to Deertrap Mountain
Maps:	Temple of Sinawava, Springdale East (United States Geological Survey 7.5'); Zion National Park (TI)

Season:	May through to October
Water:	Stave Spring
Rating:	easy

This trailhead, located just next to Stave Spring, can be reached via the East Rim Trail from the East Entrance, from Weeping Rock on the East Rim Trail or from the East Boundary via the Echo Canyon Trail. A combination of the East Rim Trail with detours to Cable and Deertrap mountains makes a pleasant overnight trip (see section 18, Zion National Park, Long Distance Walks). An 11 mile day-walk to Cable and Deertrap mountains can be completed in the summer from the East Boundary via the Echo Canyon Trail to Stave Spring Junction.

Directions
From the Stave Spring Trail Junction you meet the East Rim Trail connecting from the Park's East Entrance, the trail from Weeping Rock and the Echo Canyon Trail. Stave Springs trickles from a pipe 150 yards south of the junction. Continue south-west through a pine forest for 1.1 miles on the signed Deertrap Mountain Trail to the Y-junction of the trail for Cable and Deertrap mountains.

The left fork, the Deertrap Mountain Trail, heads 2.1 miles south-west across a barren mesa and several draws. A brisk climb leads to the top of the mesa, descends briefly and climbs again to another mesa. The trail soon arrives at the top of Deertrap Mountain. A northern spur ends at a promontory with views of Angels' Landing and the Temple of Sinawava. The southern spur affords fine views of the East Temple and Twin Brothers.

Retrace your steps back to the Y-junction of the trail to Deertrap and Cable mountains. Turning north-west on the right fork towards Cable Mountain you climb gently and are rewarded by northern views to the Pink Cliffs of the Virgin Rim. The trail then descends gradually 1.8 miles to meet the sandstone cliffs and the void of Zion Canyon. (Ruins of the old Zion tramway rest near the cliff's edge. Between 1904 and 1926 it was used to transport logs into the Zion Canyon.) Your view overlooks the Big Bend of the Virgin River, the Organ, Angels' Landing, and the West Rim.

Retrace your steps back to the Y-junction and then to the Stave Spring junction. Continue on to your final destination whether you return to the East Entrance, Weeping Rock or to the East Boundary.

CHAPTER 17

ZION NATIONAL PARK: SOUTH-WEST DESERT TRAILS

There's a long trail a winding into the land of my dreams.
Stoddard King

Introduction

The South-West Desert area of Zion National Park hosts fewer visitors than any other area in the park. In winter, this area makes an excellent alternative to the snowy high country trails. Unbearable heat plagues this area in summer. Several off-trail routes, such as Huber and Coalpits Wash, provide an opportunity for round trip walks, rather than backtracking on the Chinle Trail.

SOUTH-WEST DESERT TRAILS

Trial	Distance Miles One way	Distance Kilometres One Way	Rating
Chinle Trail	8.1	13.0	Moderate
Huber Wash	2.4	4.0	Moderate

CHINLE TRAIL

Start:	Park Boundary on Utah Highway 9 (4,020 feet/1,230 metres)
End:	Coalpits Wash (4,100 feet/1,252 metres)
Distance, one way:	8.1 miles (13 kilometres)
Time, one way:	4–5 hours
Maps:	Springdale West (United States Geological Survey 7.5'); Zion National Park (TI)
Season:	autumn, winter and spring
Water:	Coalpits Wash
Rating:	moderate

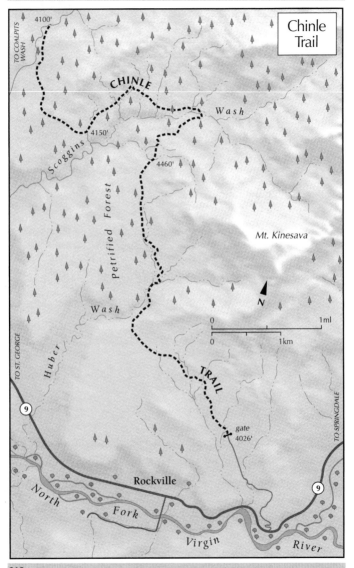

Chinle
Trail

4100'

TO COALPITS WASH

CHINLE

Wash

4150'

Scoggins

4460'

Petrified Forest

Mt. Kinesava

N

Wash

0   1ml
0   1km

Huber

TRAIL

TO ST. GEORGE

gate
4026'

9

TO SPRINGDALE

Rockville

9

North   Fork

Virgin   River

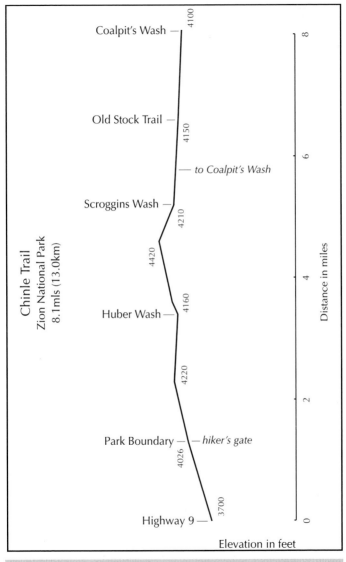

Chinle Trail
Zion National Park
8.1mls (13.0km)

Coalpit's Wash — 4100

Old Stock Trail — 4150

— *to Coalpit's Wash*

Scroggins Wash — 4210

4420

Huber Wash — 4160

4220

Park Boundary — — *hiker's gate*
4026

3700

Highway 9 —

Distance in miles

8   6   4   2   0

Elevation in feet

This remote part of the park provides solitude not found in other parts. An excellent alternative to the Zion Valley during the cool winter months, these trails may be walked as an overnight hike or as a day trip. Elevation gain remains minimal and numerous campsites dot the route.

From the South Entrance to Zion National Park, drive 3.5 miles south on Utah State Highway 9. Between Springdale and Rockville, turn north onto a dirt turnout and park here. The dirt road crosses private land; close all gates behind you. From the highway, a "four-wheel drive" road heads north 1.2 miles to the Chinle trailhead. Walk or drive to the end of the road to the hiker gate and Park boundary.

Directions

From the trailhead, follow the sandy path north-west with fine views of the red cliffs of Mount Kinesava ahead of you. After a little over 1 mile, pass under the power lines and traverse a wash. After 3 miles, descend into the usually dry Huber Wash. You may wish to return to your car by taking Huber Wash south, although you'll have to walk a few miles along Utah Highway 9.

From Huber Wash, ascend 150 feet and traverse the eastern flanks of the Petrified Forest with its age-old wood. Petrified wood dots the landscape. (You may not collect samples in a National Park.) Now Mt. Kinesava rises even closer to the east and to the north-west Cougar Mountain impresses with its surrounding cliffs. Continuing north you now gain views of the east of the West Temple, an unusual view for park visitors. From Huber to Scroggins Wash dry desert landscape characterizes your walk. Now, veering west, we climb above Scroggins Wash, then climb in and out of a gully before descending into the dry Scroggins Wash.

Just west of the wash, a cross-country route to Coalpits Wash follows a wash north through a gap in the ridge and joins another wash that descends into Coalpits Wash. From Coalpits Wash you can turn south-west to the end of the Chinle Trail and then loop back to your car.

Back at the Chinle Trail, ascend gradually through a small saddle. Turning south-west you follow a wash and cross another small saddle and soon pass a sign marking the Old Scoggins Stock Trail. The Chinle Trail continues west and then terminates at

Coalpits Wash. Detours include exploring upstream to the 1908 oil well ruins; you should not camp here. Travel downstream past the small waterfall to the alcove and to the spring and overhanging garden, located just past where the creek turns south.

HUBER WASH

Start:	Hiker's Gate for Huber Wash Route (3,700 feet/1,128 metres)
End:	Chinle Trail at Huber Wash (4,160 feet/ 1,268 metres)
Distance, one way:	2.5 miles (4 kilometres)
Time, one way:	2 hours
Map:	Springdale West (USGS 7.5'); Zion National Park (TI)
Season:	autumn, winter and spring
Water:	none
Rating:	moderate

Drive 6.1 miles west on Utah State Highway 9 from the South Entrance to Zion National Park through Springdale and Rockville. Drive into the pullout on the north side of the road and proceed to the hiker's gate. If you start at the Chinle Trail you can loop these two walks together, walking a short way on Utah Highway 9.

Directions
From the pullout, pass through the hiker's gate. (Take care to close all gates along the route.) Follow the road past the transformer station. When the road forks, take the left fork down into the wash. Turn north and pass through the hiker's gate on the east side of the wash. Stay in the wash; mud may be under your feet after rain. As you proceed north, Mt. Kinesava dominates your far view and the Petrified Forest ornaments the near view.

When the wash branches, proceed north-east. Soon you come to a jam of petrified logs. To bypass the dry fall, backtrack 150 feet and climb up on the western shelf of the canyon. Look for a chimney that leads you up to the mesa. Backpackers may wish to raise their packs with 25 feet of rope. Once on the mesa, follow the paths east to reach the Chinle Trail.

CHAPTER 18

ZION NATIONAL PARK: LONG DISTANCE ROUTES

Prayer of the tired walker:
"If you pick 'em up,
O lord, I'll put 'em down."
Anonymous

LONG DISTANCE ROUTES

Trail	Distance Miles One way	Distance Kilometres One Way	Rating
Across Zion via Hop Valley and the West Rim	37.6	60.2	Moderate
The Zion Narrows	15.5	24.8	Strenuous
East Rim Trail via Cable Mountain and Deertrap Mountain	20.4	32.6	Moderate

ACROSS ZION VIA HOP VALLEY AND THE WEST RIM

Start:	Lee Pass (6,060 feet/1,847 metres)
End:	Grotto picnic area (4,298 feet/1,310 metres)
Distance, one way:	37.6 miles (60.2 kilometres)
Times, one way:	4–5 days
Maps:	Kolob Arch, Kolob Reservoir, Temple of Sinawava, The Guardian Angels (United States Geological Survey 7.5′); Zion National Park, Utah (TI)
Season:	late-April through to October
Water:	Beatty Spring, La Verkin Creek, Hop Valley, Wildcat Canyon Spring, Potato Hollow Spring, West Rim (Cabin) Spring
Rating:	moderate

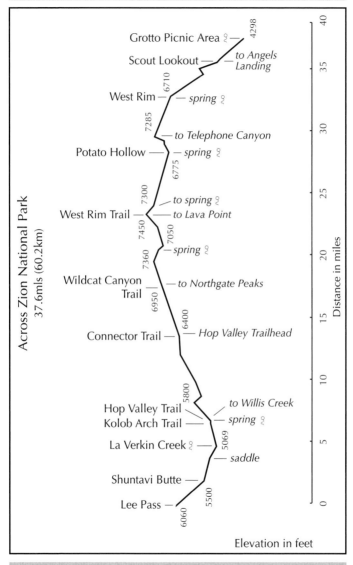

Across Zion National Park
37.6mls (60.2km)

Distance in miles

Grotto Picnic Area — 4298
Scout Lookout — — *to Angels Landing*
West Rim — 6710 — *spring*
7285
— *to Telephone Canyon*
Potato Hollow — 6775 — *spring*
7300
West Rim Trail — 7450 — *to spring*
7050 — *to Lava Point*
7360 — *spring*
Wildcat Canyon Trail — 6950 — *to Northgate Peaks*
Connector Trail — 6400 — *Hop Valley Trailhead*
5800
Hop Valley Trail — — *to Willis Creek*
Kolob Arch Trail — 5069 — *spring*
La Verkin Creek — — *saddle*
Shuntavi Butte — 5500
Lee Pass — 6060

Elevation in feet

The splendid Kolob Arch area of Zion National Park's north-eastern section, much less visited than the busy eastern valley, conceals many of the Park's hidden treasures.

From the Zion National Park South Entrance, take Utah Highway 9, west, through Virgin and Rockville for 22 miles to Hurricane. Turn north on Highway 17. Proceed for 6 miles to Interstate 15. Turn north and, after 13 miles, take Exit 40 to Kolob Canyons. Allow 1 hour driving time from Zion Canyon.

Begin with a visit to the Kolob Canyon Visitor Centre where you will find exhibits on the flora and fauna of the Park. You may pick up backcountry permits here. Next, take Kolob Canyons Road 3.5 miles east to Lee Pass. Call the Zion Lodge for information on their shuttle service to Lee Pass.

If you do not have enough time for the entire Across Zion itinerary, several shorter alternatives are recommended. The Kolob Arch area is a popular overnight trip. The Kolob Arch area can be reached from the west via La Verkin Creek and from the east via the more scenic Hop Valley. You can explore Timber and La Verkin creeks and make a short detour to the arch. Both routes boast diverse scenery. A valuable extra day allows time to explore Willis Creek and Beartrap Canyon.

The Across Zion trip covers the Park's most splendid backcountry area. From Lee Pass you descend the La Verkin Creek Trail as it drops into the La Verkin and Timber Creek drainage and meets the Hop Valley Trail and Kolob Arch Trail. Turning east and crossing Hop Valley, you meet the Kolob Terrace Road. From here the 4 mile Connector Trail links up with the Wildcat Canyon Trail and a short detour south brings you to fine, albeit waterless, camping on the Northgate Peaks Trail. A short spur trail leads you to the Northgate Peaks Overlook.

Directions

Retracing your steps to the Wildcat Canyon Trail you pass Wildcat Canyon Spring. Descend into Wildcat Canyon and ascend out of the canyon to join the West Rim Trail near Lava Point. You next cross Horse Plateau and descend to Potato Hollow, where there are fine views of the Virgin River Canyon and The Narrows. Next, one of the most spectacular trails in the Park takes you along the West Rim with outstanding views of the Right Fork and Phantom Valley.

Meeting the West Rim Trail at the West Rim (Cabin) Spring you drop down to Scout Lookout where another short detour will take you up the famous Angels' Landing. Finally wind your way down Walter's Wiggles to the Zion Valley at the Grotto picnic area.

The above trails - La Verkin Creek Trail, Hop Valley Trail, the Connector Trail, the Northgate Peaks Trail, the Wildcat Canyon Trail and the West Rim Trail - are described individually in sections 14 and 15.

THE ZION NARROWS

Start:	Chamberlain's Ranch (5,830 feet/ 1,777 metres)
End:	Temple of Sinawava car park (4,411 feet/ 1,344 metres)
Distance, one way:	15.5 miles (24.8 kilometres)
Times, one way:	12 hours or 2 days
Maps:	Temple of Sinawava (United States Geological Survey 7.5'); Zion National Park (TI)
Season:	late June to October
Water:	North Fork of Virgin River, Virgin River
Rating:	strenuous

This famous, highly recommended, classic Zion walk, Utah's most renowned hike, can be completed in one long summer day or as an overnight trip. Overnight walkers are only allowed to walk downstream from Chamberlain's Ranch to the Temple of Sinawava. This 16 mile trip wanders through high sandstone cliffs goes past arches and waterfalls. The entire route meanders in the riverbed; there is no trail. Walking from the "bottom up" starting at the Temple of Sinawava and proceeding north up the Virgin River to Orderville Canyon is described in section 15.

Special National Park Service regulations apply for The Narrows walk. Permits are required for your walk from Chamberlain's Ranch to the Temple of Sinawava either for a day-walk or overnight walk. Obtain your permit at the Zion Canyon Visitor Centre. Camping spots are pre-assigned by the park service. The best time of year to walk The Narrows is late June to early October. Flash floods peak late July into August. Frigid water temperatures and swift currents

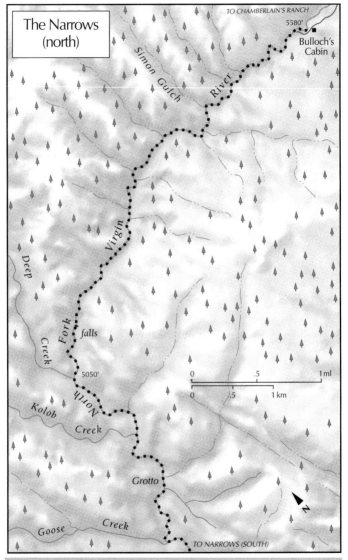

The Narrows (north)

TO CHAMBERLAIN'S RANCH
5580'
Bulloch's Cabin

Simon Gulch

River

Virgin

Deep

Fork

Creek

falls

5050'

North

Kolob

Creek

Grotto

Goose Creek

0 .5 1 ml
0 .5 1 km

N

TO NARROWS (SOUTH)

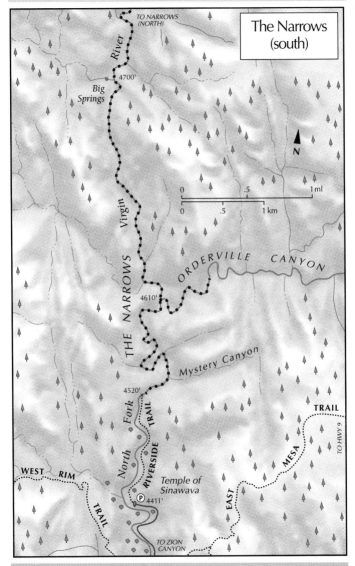

The Narrows
(south)

TO NARROWS
(NORTH)

River

4700'

Big
Springs

N

0   .5   1 ml

0   .5   1 km

Virgin

ORDERVILLE   CANYON

THE NARROWS

4610'

Mystery Canyon

4520'

North Fork

RIVERSIDE   TRAIL

TRAIL

TO HWY 9

WEST   RIM

MESA

Temple of
Sinawava

EAST

TRAIL

P 4411'

TO ZION
CANYON

limit canyon-walking during the colder months of the year. Protective gear and shoes are available for rent in Springdale.

Signs of possible flash floods include: changes in the water from clear to muddy; rising water; thunderstorms or sounds of thunder; a roar of water upstream. Seek higher ground immediately and do not try to out run the flood. Stay on high ground until the high water subsides, sometimes up to 72 hours.

Danger lurks in the swift strong currents and deep pools of water. Take care when crossing the river and choose your wading spots with caution. Look for the shallow spots; wide areas are often shallower than narrow crossings. A walking stick aids in providing stability and helps check the depth of the water. Be prepared to swim. Chest deep holes exist. Wrap all your clothes in double stuff sacks or plastic bags. Bring warm clothing for chilly nights.

The Zion Lodge provides a shuttle to the start of the walk at Chamberlain's Ranch. Seating is limited; especially during the busy summer season, you should reserve your space several weeks ahead. Take the early shuttle to allow the maximum amount of time in this unique setting. If you have two vehicles you can shuttle one car to Chamberlain's Ranch. Overnight parking is not allowed at the Temple of Sinawava. Check with the National Park Service for other parking regulations. Use the open air tram to return to your car if you've left it at the Zion Lodge.

See the Zion Adventure Company in Springdale, Utah for information on flash flood risk, equipment rental and current data on water depth, flow, and temperature. Rentals are available for walking sticks, "water tennies" and neoprene booties, waterproof backpacks and canyon dry suits.

To reach Chamberlain's Ranch take Utah State Highway 9, 2.5 miles east from the Park's East Entrance. Turn left on North Fork Road and continue for 18 miles to the bridge over the North Fork River. Turn left after the bridge and drive 0.25 mile to the gate to Chamberlain's Ranch. Drive 0.5 mile to the river where you can park; no camping is allowed. Please respect private property. Allow 1.5 hours for the drive from Zion Canyon to Chamberlain's Ranch.

Directions
Cross the river and begin your walk on the road along the river for the next 3 miles. The Chamberlains have requested that you do not

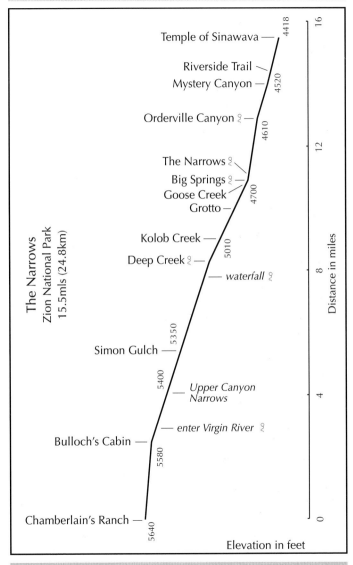

The Narrows
Zion National Park
15.5mls (24.8km)

Temple of Sinawava — 4418
Riverside Trail
Mystery Canyon — 4520
Orderville Canyon ⚲ — 4610
The Narrows ⚲
Big Springs ⚲ — 4700
Goose Creek
Grotto —
Kolob Creek — 5010
Deep Creek ⚲ —
— *waterfall* ⚲
Simon Gulch — 5350
5400
— *Upper Canyon Narrows*
— *enter Virgin River* ⚲
Bulloch's Cabin — 5580
Chamberlain's Ranch — 5640

Distance in miles

Elevation in feet

walk in the river bed until you reach the end of the road. Heading west you pass through a pastoral setting amidst grazing cattle. After 2.5 miles you pass old Bulloch's cabin and, still on the old road, you begin to criss-cross the river from bank to bank. As soon as the road begins to fade, a well-worn trail marks your route along the shore, dotted with ponderosa pines. Slowly, cliffs begin to close in the river bed.

After 2 miles more you come to the first true narrow section of the canyon. If you were planning to see only narrows below Big Springs, this part may come as a surprise. By now you are wading in the river and the red walls soar 500 feet above you. Six and a half miles from the start, Simon Gulch, breaking up the continuous canyon walls, enters from the north. Now the canyon becomes more and more enclosed by the towering walls. After 7.5 miles you meet a waterfall; take the passage on its south side. After 5-6 hours from the start, the canyon widens and you encounter Deep Creek where the water level rises significantly. Most of the designated campsites are located on benches above the river, below this confluence. Look carefully for the campsite markers.

Now beyond Deep Creek, measure your progress downstream by noting the side streams that join the Virgin River Canyon. Kolob Creek joins from the west 3 miles below the confluence with Deep Creek. One-half mile from Kolob Creek along, you pass The Grotto, an overhanging alcove used for a campsite. Next, 0.5 mile farther on and easy to miss, narrow Goose Creek enters from the north. One mile more and you come to the impressive Big Springs as it pours over boulders, moss and other plants, the spring gurgling water at a rapid rate.

From Big Springs, south, you enter the true Narrows. There is no high ground for 2 miles until Orderville Canyon. Occasional flash floods rampage through this canyon; undercut canyon side walls and debris attest to their power. Little sunlight graces this hidden area as the sculptured canyon side walls rise over 1,000 feet above your head. Be careful as the deepest pools exist here. Look carefully for sandbars and visually scour the bottom as you place your feet. Enjoy the solitude and splendour of the narrow, fluted canyon walls.

Orderville Canyon, a fine side canyon to explore, joins the Virgin River from the east, 2 hours below Big Springs. After 1 mile, deep

Looking east from Bryce Canyon National Park

pools and a waterfall block your way. From Orderville Canyon, south, you will meet day-hikers walking up the Virgin River from the Temple of Sinawava. One mile below Orderville Canyon, a stream of water from Mystery Canyon splashes down the canyon walls from the east side. Two miles more brings you the Riverside Trail. Finish with the last mile on the concrete trail that ends at the car park. The section between Orderville Canyon and the Temple of Sinawava is described in section 13.

EAST RIM TRAIL VIA CABLE AND DEERTRAP MOUNTAINS

Start:	East Entrance (5,740 feet/1,750 metres)
End:	Weeping Rock (4,360 feet/1,329 metres)
Distance, one way:	20.4 miles (32.6 kilometres)
Times, one way:	10 hours or 2 days
Maps:	The Barracks, Temple of Sinawava, Springdale East (United States Geological Survey 7.5'); Zion National Park, (TI)
Season:	April and May, September to November
Water:	Stave Spring
Rating:	moderate

This trip can be completed in one day or as an overnight, backpacking trip. It combines the East Rim Trail with visits to Cable and Deertrap mountains. The Zion shuttle bus will take you to the trailhead next to the Park's East Entrance. Finish at the Weeping Rock car park. The only water available is at Stave Spring.

You will find individual trail descriptions in chapter 16.

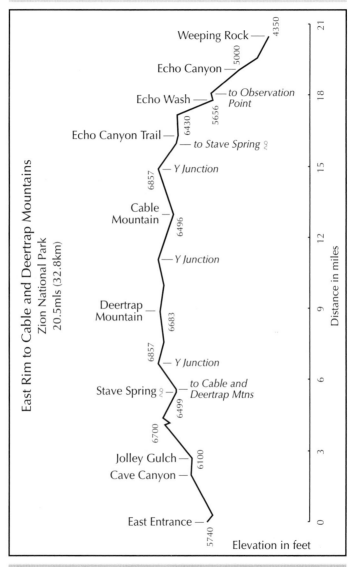

East Rim to Cable and Deertrap Mountains
Zion National Park
20.5mls (32.8km)

Weeping Rock — 4350

5000

Echo Canyon

Echo Wash — — *to Observation Point*

5656

Echo Canyon Trail — 6430

— *to Stave Spring*

— *Y Junction*

6857

Cable Mountain

6496

— *Y Junction*

Deertrap Mountain

6683

6857

— *Y Junction*

Stave Spring — — *to Cable and Deertrap Mtns*

6499

6700

Jolley Gulch — 6100

Cave Canyon —

East Entrance — 5740

Distance in miles

Elevation in feet

21
18
15
12
9
6
3
0

CHAPTER 19

VISITING BRYCE CANYON NATIONAL PARK

It's a hell of a place to lose a cow.
Ebenezer Bryce, 1875

Introduction

Your first gaze over the rim into Bryce Canyon National Park comes as a surprise. The multi-coloured collections of spires spread endlessly into the depths of the far distance and defy what you can imagine. Far away views spread out over three states. It is hard to capture the many coloured hues with the amateur's photographic lens; memories are best preserved in the mind of the observer. Years of erosion, rain, snow and ice have shaped the limestone cliffs into acres of spires, towers and hoodoos coloured by red, rose and pink overtones. ("Hoodoos" is the collective name given to the colourful limestone and sandstone formations.) The green ponderosa pines and spruce forests accent these colours; the blue sky rounds out the magnificent vistas.

In winter, when the trails are closed with snow, you can enjoy the park only from its viewpoints. The canyon trails are usually closed by snow from November through to April. When a dusting of snow coats the ground, a magnificent contrast occurs between the blue sky, the red-pink walls and the green conifers. From late spring to the autumn, the walker can experience the true feel of Bryce Canyon on foot. The true depth of the colour can be best appreciated early morning or late afternoon.

The small, 56 square mile park, made up of a series of horseshoe shaped amphitheatres, opens year round. Lodging and visitor services operate from April through to October. An 18 mile Rim Drive passes thirteen overlooks; four spur roads provide access to its most distant points.

Getting there

Visits to Bryce Canyon National Park are often combined with trips to Zion National Park and the North Rim (mid-May to mid-October) and the South Rim (open all year) of the Grand Canyon National Park. The best way to get around this area of the United States is to rent a car. There is no public transportation into the park.

Bryce Canyon National Park is 270 miles or 6 hours by car from Las Vegas and 256 miles or 6 hours from Salt Lake City by car. Zion National Park is a 78 mile, 2 hour car ride. The North Rim of the Grand Canyon is a 152 mile, 3 hour ride from Bryce Canyon and the South Rim of the Grand Canyon is 300 miles.

Commercial airlines serve the major airports of Las Vegas (270 miles) and Salt Lake City (270 miles) and the smaller cities of Cedar City (87 miles) and St. George (150 miles).

From Panguitch, Utah take Utah 12, east, 7 miles south to Utah 63. Turn south on Utah 63 and travel 3 miles to the park entrance. From the east via Capitol Reef National Park and Escalante National Monument, take Utah 12 to Utah 63 and turn south to the park entrance.

Getting around

Renting a car offers the most flexibility when travelling in this part of the United States. Depending on your route, rental cars are available in Page, Flagstaff and Phoenix, Arizona and Las Vegas, Cedar City, Salt Lake City, and St. George, Utah.

Weather and seasons

Bryce Canyon National Park opens all year. However, from late autumn into early spring many access roads and walking trails remain closed by snow. Road maintenance and snowploughing may lead to temporary road closures during the winter and early spring. Spring weather brings intermittent rain storms and some muddy trails. Night-time temperatures remain below freezing well into May. Pleasant summer temperatures predominate due to the park's high elevation. Much of the yearly precipitation occurs in July and August in the form of thundershowers. Autumn may be the best season to visit Bryce. The temperatures remain cool, the summer visitors have departed and the golden aspen trees accent the park's green and red background.

Snow, averaging 100 inches per year, blankets the area from early November to early May. Winter visits to the park can be rewarding

Average Rim Temperatures and Precipitation
Bryce Canyon National Park

	Max °F (°C)		Min °F (°C)		Precp ins (cm)	
January	39	(3)	9	(-12)	1.7	(4.3)
February	41	(5)	13	(-10)	1.4	(3.6)
March	46	(8)	17	(-9)	1.4	(3.6)
April	56	(13)	25	(-4)	1.2	(3.0)
May	66	(19)	31	(1)	0.8	(2.0)
June	76	(25)	38	(3)	0.6	(1.5)
July	83	(28)	47	(9)	1.4	(3.6)
August	80	(27)	45	(7)	2.2	(5.7)
September	74	(23)	37	(2)	1.4	(3.6)
October	63	(18)	29	(-2)	1.4	(3.6)
November	51	(11)	19	(-7)	1.2	(3.0)
December	42	(6)	11	(-11)	1.6	(4.1)

although temperatures can be very cold. Visitors are low and rates at local motels are discounted. Snow blocks the main park walking trails but some snowshoe and cross-country ski trails invite visitors. The Park Service ploughs the main road all the way to Rainbow Point and viewpoints remain open.

Lodging

AmFac Parks and Resorts handles cabin and room reservations at Bryce Canyon Lodge. The historic lodge, renovated in 1989 to its early 1930s style, is located off the park road between Sunrise and Sunset Points. You'll find a dining room, lounge and gift shop.

Ruby's Inn, just north of the park entrance, offers lodging all year. This sprawling complex, complete with pools, spas, convention centre, a Post Office, gift shop, art gallery, horseback riding and ski rentals provides the only available lodging near the park. Limited lodging can be found in nearby Panguitch and Tropic; all are full to capacity in the summer.

Camping

North and Sunset campgrounds offer pleasant shaded first-come first-served sites inside the park. Campgrounds fill early in the busy summer months. One group campsite is available by reservation only. Campground openings in the winter months may be variable; check with park headquarters before you arrive. Several private, National Forest and State Park campgrounds operate near the park.

Visitor services

The Bryce Visitor Centre, located near the park entrance, presents exhibits, a slide show and gift shop. Backcountry permits may be obtained here. Hours are extended during the summer, spring and autumn.

Interpretative programmes

Campfire programmes, offered by the National Park Service (NPS) during the summer, are held at North and Sunset campgrounds.

Bryce Canyon Natural History Association

Bryce Canyon Natural History Association, a non-profit organization, publishes educational materials, maps and slides about the park. Membership entitles you to the groups publications as well as discounts at any National Park or National Monument store throughout the country.

Other facilities
A grocery store, The General Store, a laundromat and showers, located next to Sunrise Point, operate during the summer season. AmFac Parks and Resorts runs the dining room and gift shop in the Bryce Canyon Lodge.

Shuttle services
A shuttle service is planned to relieve traffic congestion, improve road maintenance and allow for backcountry access. The shuttle, which may charge a small fee, will operate during the peak periods of late spring through autumn. The shuttle will serve the main viewpoints frequently and Rainbow Point on a limited basis.

Times zones
The state of Utah, including Zion National Park and Bryce Canyon National Park, operates on Mountain Standard Time (MST). Daylight Savings Time, (MDT or Mountain Daylight Time), when the clocks are pushed ahead 1 hour, stays in effect between early April and October.

CHAPTER 20

WALKING IN BRYCE NATIONAL PARK

Though we travel the world over to find the beautiful,
we must carry it with us or we find it not.
Ralph Waldo Emerson

Introduction

Day-hikers and backcountry walkers find a number of options for exploration in Bryce Canyon National Park. The walks in the park's northern section, such as the Fairyland Loop, and in its central section, such as the Peekaboo Loop, give the visitor a splendid look at the park in a short half-day or whole-day-walk. If time is short, try the Navajo Loop in combination with the Queen's Garden Loop; alternatively, just stroll along the 5.5 mile Rim Trail. Views of Bryce National Park's hoodoos and spires and expansive amphitheatres are most impressive in the northern and central sections of the park.

Overnight trips are limited to the 23 mile Under the Rim Trail or the short, 8 mile Riggs Spring Loop. The Under the Rim Trail, though less congested than trails in the northern section of the park, supports only limited views of the park's geologic formations and travel may be handicapped by lack of reliable water sources.

Walking permits

Day-walking requires no permits. Free overnight permits for all backpacking in Bryce National Park may be obtained at the visitor centre. Reservations are not accepted.

Groups

Backcountry group camping sites support a limited number of walkers in only a few group sites.

Maps

The Trails Illustrated (TI) 1:37270 topographical map *Bryce Canyon National Park* provides all the information you will need in a handy waterproof casing. It can be purchased at local stores and at the park visitor centre. The United States Geological Survey (USGS 7.5') maps

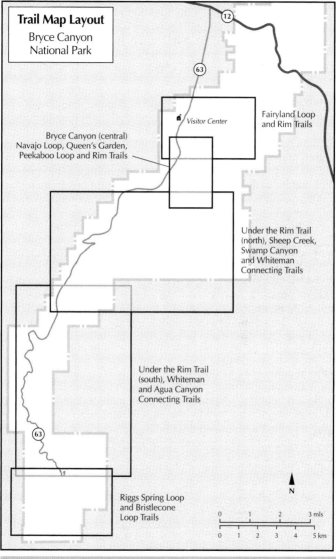

Trail Map Layout
Bryce Canyon
National Park

(12)

(63)

Visitor Center

Fairyland Loop
and Rim Trails

Bryce Canyon (central)
Navajo Loop, Queen's Garden,
Peekaboo Loop and Rim Trails

Under the Rim Trail
(north), Sheep Creek,
Swamp Canyon
and Whiteman
Connecting Trails

Under the Rim Trail
(south), Whiteman
and Agua Canyon
Connecting Trails

(63)

Riggs Spring Loop
and Bristlecone
Loop Trails

N

| 0 | 1 | 2 | 3 mls |
| 0 | 1 | 2 | 3 | 4 | 5 km |

listed show more detail and are available through mail order from the USGS Denver office.

Weather and seasons
The park trails open for backpacking and walking once the snow has melted, usually May through to October. Cool nights, many below freezing, predominate for over 200 nights per year. Winter visits are limited to driving along the main road, viewing the park from the automobile pull-outs and snow shoeing and cross-country skiing.

Water sources
Water at Bryce National Park is limited; the National Park provides information on water sources. All backcountry water should be treated. Check with the National Park Service for up-to-date information on water availability and conditions. You may have to carry all the water you will need for your overnight trips.

Waymarking
Prominent signs mark all trail junctions in the backcountry and along day routes.

Flash floods
Flash floods are not a danger in Bryce as they are in Zion and in some parts of Grand Canyon National Park. However, use good judgement and common sense when entering narrow canyons and creek beds.

Insects, reptiles and mammals
Mule deer graze along the park roads in the evening. Marmots and squirrels, usually looking for a handout, may visit your campsite. Skunks and gophers inhabit the surrounding hills. Please do not feed any of these visitors. Red hills follow crumbs of food and deliver a nasty lingering sting if they get too close. Try to avoid coming into close contact with them.

The Great Basin Rattlesnake blends in well with the park's surroundings; be careful where you place your hands and feet. Leave these and other reptiles to their own meandering and they will return the same.

CHAPTER 21

BRYCE CANYON NATIONAL PARK: CANYON AND RIM TRAILS

*As long as there are canyons,
man will be drawn to them.*
Anonymous

CANYON AND RIM TRAILS

Trail	Distance Miles One way	Distance Kilometres One Way	Rating
Fairyland Loop	7.9	12.6	Moderate
Queen's Garden Trail	0.9	1.5	Moderate
Navajo Loop	1.3	2.1	Moderate
Rim Trail	5.5	8.8	Easy
Peekaboo Loop	5.5	8.8	Moderate
Bristlecone Loop	1.0	1.6	Easy
Riggs Spring Loop	8.8	14.1	Moderate

FAIRYLAND LOOP

Start:	Fairyland Point (7,770 feet/2,368 metres)
End:	Fairyland Point (7,770 feet/2368 metres)
Distance, loop:	7.9 miles (12.6 kilometres)
Time, one way:	4 hours
Maps:	Bryce Canyon, Bryce Point (United States Geological Survey 7.5′); Bryce Canyon National Park (TI)
Season:	May through to October
Water:	none
Rating:	moderate

The Fairyland Loop can be accessed from Fairyland Point, North

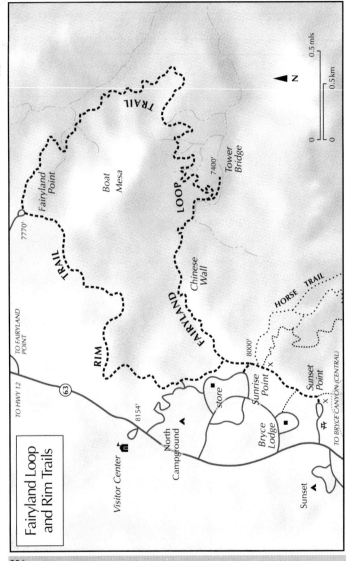

Fairyland Loop
and Rim Trails

TO HWY 12

TO FAIRLAND POINT

63

8154'

Visitor Center

North Campground

store

Bryce Lodge

Sunrise Point

Sunset Point

TO BRYCE CANYON (CENTRAL)

Sunset

8000'

HORSE TRAIL

RIM TRAIL

FAIRYLAND LOOP

FAIRYLAND TRAIL

Chinese Wall

Tower Bridge

7400'

Boat Mesa

Fairyland Point

7770'

N

0   0.5 km

0   0.5 mls

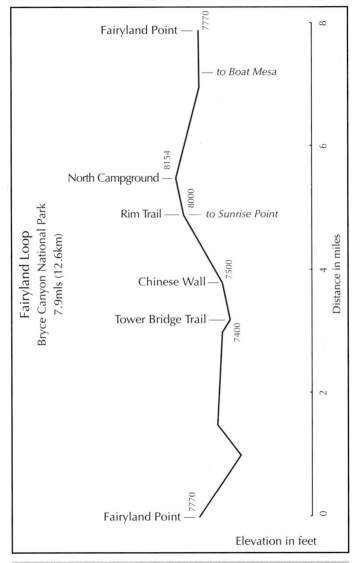

Fairyland Point — 7770

— to Boat Mesa

North Campground — 8154

Rim Trail — 8000 — to Sunrise Point

Chinese Wall — 7500

Tower Bridge Trail — 7400

Fairyland Point — 7770

Fairyland Loop
Bryce Canyon National Park
7.9mls (12.6km)

Distance in miles

Elevation in feet

Campground or Sunrise Point. To begin from Fairyland Point, drive north of the visitor centre for 1 mile and turn east on the spur road, proceeding 1 mile on the road to Fairyland Point. This road doubles as a cross-country ski trail in the winter. To begin from North Campground, drive 100 yards south from the visitor centre along Highway 63 and turn east on the road to North Campground. Proceed past the check-in station and continue into the campground. If you wish to begin your walk at Sunrise Point, continue 0.4 mile south past the visitor centre to the Sunrise Point Road that branches east. Turn left and drive to the end of the road to the car park for Sunrise Point.

Starting from Fairyland View, North Campground or Sunrise Point, this 8 mile loop or 5.7 mile shuttle trip covers much of the significant area in the northern section of the park.

Directions
From Fairyland Loop Trailhead at Fairyland Point, proceed northeast along the track and descend gradually on the north side of Boat Mesa. The trail drops to the floor of Fairyland Canyon as views of the Sinking Ship open up. Boat Mesa looms in the south-west. The trail ascends as it crosses several draws. Turning west after some more ups and downs, the trail switchbacks into Campbell Canyon to reach the Tower Bridge Trail. This short, 200 yard detour gives close up views of Tower Bridge and makes a nice lunch stop. Back on the trail, you begin your return ascent to the rim past the Chinese Wall as you cut through a break in the hoodoos. Your final ascent heads back up to the rim to meet the Rim Trail just south of North Campground. Turning right and joining the Rim Trail, in 5 minutes you pass North Campground and after 2 miles a spur trail east leads you to the top of Boat Mesa. To close the loop, another 0.7 miles brings you back to Fairyland Point.

(handwritten: ✱ Combined Loop r Peekaboo Loop)
(handwritten: ⬙ w/ Navajo Loop)

QUEEN'S GARDEN TRAIL

Start:	Sunrise Point (8,000 feet/2438 metres)
End:	Sunrise Point (8,000 feet/2438 metres)
Distance, one way:	0.9 miles (1.5 kilometres)
Time, one way:	20 minutes
Maps:	Bryce Canyon, Bryce Point (USGS 7.5');
	Bryce Canyon National Park (TI)

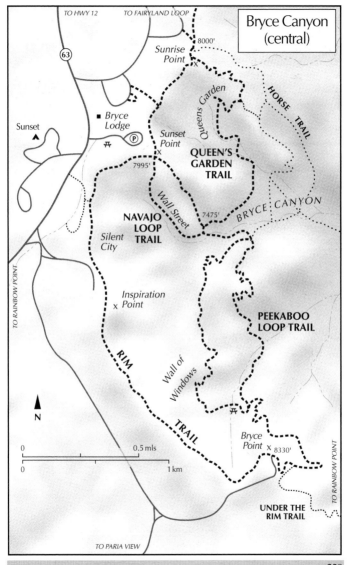

Bryce Canyon (central)

TO HWY 12
TO FAIRLAND LOOP
63
8000'
Sunrise Point
X

■ *Bryce Lodge*
Sunset
▲
⚲
P
Sunset Point
X
7995'
QUEEN'S GARDEN TRAIL

Queen's Garden

HORSE TRAIL

NAVAJO LOOP TRAIL
Wall Street
7475'
BRYCE CANYON

Silent City

Inspiration Point
X

PEEKABOO LOOP TRAIL

RIM

Wall of Windows

N

TRAIL

⚲
Bryce Point
X 8330'

TO RAINBOW POINT

TO RAINBOW POINT

0   0.5 mls
0   1 km

UNDER THE RIM TRAIL

TO PARIA VIEW

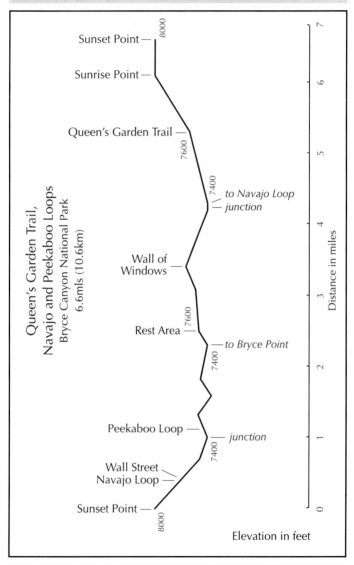

Queen's Garden Trail,
Navajo and Peekaboo Loops
Bryce Canyon National Park
6.6mls (10.6km)

Sunset Point — 8000

Sunrise Point —

Queen's Garden Trail — 7600

7400

*to Navajo Loop
junction*

Wall of
Windows

Rest Area — 7600

7400

to Bryce Point

Peekaboo Loop — 7400 *junction*

Wall Street
Navajo Loop —

Sunset Point — 8000

Distance in miles

Elevation in feet

Season:	May through to October
Water:	none
Rating:	moderate

The Queen's Garden Loop can be accessed from either Sunrise Point or Sunset Point. To reach Sunrise Point, proceed 0.4 mile south of the visitor centre on Highway 63 and turn east on the spur road to Sunrise Point. To reach Sunset Point continue 1.2 miles south on the park road from the entrance station to the turn-off east to Sunset Point.

The Queen's Garden Trail, not a loop itself, best combines with the Navajo Loop or Peekaboo Loop. I recommend a 6 hour walk that descends to the canyon bottom via Wall Street on the Navajo Loop, then circles the Peekaboo Loop and returns to the rim via the Queen's Garden Loop. (See the route profile for Queen's Garden Trail, Navajo and Peekaboo Loops for a mile by mile elevation profile of this walk and the other book descriptions below of the Navajo Loop and Peekaboo Loop.)

Directions
To walk just the Queen's Garden Trail from Sunrise Point, walk a short way south to the Queen's Garden trailhead, the easiest of the trails that reaches the canyon floor. At first the trail descends below Sunrise Point heading east and then switchbacks 320 feet into the canyon. Views of Sinking Ship, Boat Mesa and Aquarius Plateau open up to the north-east. When you meet the first junction, bear right. The trail continues to descend through a tunnel passing by numerous hoodoos. Turn east at the next trail junction to reach a viewpoint of the Queen Victoria formation. Retrace your steps back to the main trail. The most direct path to the rim turns north and returns the way you came.

To combine this walk with the Navajo Loop, turn right at the main trail and take the Queen's Garden Connecting Trail 1 mile to meet the Navajo Loop. You will pass through several tunnels before you join the Navajo Loop Trail. Turn right to ascend the Navajo Loop and, after reaching the rim, turn south at the Rim Trail and proceed 0.5 mile back to Sunrise Point.

NAVAJO LOOP

Start:	Sunset Point (7,995 feet/2,437 metres)
End:	Sunset Point (7,995 feet/2,437 metres)
Distance, loop:	1.3 miles (2.1 kilometres)
Time, one way:	45 minutes
Maps:	Bryce Canyon, Bryce Point (USGS 7.5'); Bryce Canyon National Park (TI)
Season:	May through to October
Water:	none
Rating:	moderate

To reach Sunset Point, drive 1.5 miles south of the visitor centre on Highway 63, then turn east and drive to the end of the spur road to the parking area.

The Navajo Loop, combined with the Queen's Garden Trail, make up the most popular of Bryce Canyon's walks. Best walked in combination, or better yet, with the Peekaboo Loop, the two or three trails together provide direct access into the central hoodoo area.

Directions
From Sunset Point, drop off the rim onto the upper Navajo Loop and take the right fork towards Wall Street. Pass through the notch of hoodoos above Silent City with its 200 foot high cliffs. Twenty-nine short switchbacks drop steeply for 0.7 mile down 520 feet as the trail criss-crosses through many tall hoodoos. These spires are reminiscent of New York's Wall Street towering skyscrapers. At the bottom enter Wall Street itself through a narrow passage and break out into a sunlit, forested drainage on the other side of the passageway. Turn right at the four-way junction to head for the Peekaboo Loop (see below). To remain on the Navajo Trail turn left, climb north-west into a canyon to the Two Bridges. Above Two Bridges, the Navajo Loop continues upwards over switchbacks past the Sentinel and the obvious Thors Hammer. Finally, you reach the rim as you reach your starting point at Sunset Point.

RIM TRAIL

Start:	Fairyland Point (7,770 feet/2,368 metres)
End:	Bryce Point (8,330 feet/2,539 metres)

Distance, one way:	5.5 miles (8.8 kilometres)
Time, one way:	2.5 hours
Map:	Bryce Canyon, Bryce Point (USGS 7.5′);
	Bryce Canyon National Park (TI)
Season:	May through to October
Water:	none
Rating:	easy

From the Bryce Canyon visitor centre, drive north for 0.7 mile and turn east onto the Fairyland Loop road and proceed to the parking area at the end of this road.

The popular Rim Trail, connecting Fairyland Point with Bryce Point, can be walked in sections or in its entirety. Access the trail from anywhere along its route: Fairyland Point, North Campground, Sunrise Point, Sunset Point, Inspiration Point or Bryce Point. Pavement allows wheelchair access between Sunset and Sunrise Points. If you don't want to retrace your steps, you'll need to arrange for a ride back to the start if a shuttle service is not operating.

Directions

From Fairyland Loop, the trail proceeds southward along the Rim and then winds in and out, away from the rim through a forested area. Northward views include Boat Mesa and Aquarius Plateau; to the east you can see Navajo Mountain. The trail continues to wind in and out along the rim past the turn-off to Boat Mesa, then passes North Campground. Finally it reaches the junction to the southern end of Fairyland Loop. Continue right on the Rim Trail to reach Sunrise Point as you can point out Boat Mesa and Sinking Sink on the horizon. Climbing a small hill to Sunrise Point you meet the Queen's Garden Trail. Continue veering right along the Rim Trail.

In 0.5 mile you reach Sunset Point, just north, past the junction to the Navajo Loop. A spur trail leads through the forest to the lodge and to Sunset Campground. You climb a bit at first and then level off. Silent City predominates to the north and the Wall of Windows is visible to the south-east.

Now the trail, perhaps in its most beautiful section, climbs steadily to Inspiration Point. As you pass from point to point, the

Wall of Windows becomes more prominent. Next the Bryce Canyon amphitheatre dominates the views. This is one of the best views of the park's largest amphitheatres. Silent City and the Wall of Windows are well seen from here to the north-west; Tropic, Utah can be seen to the south-west.

A narrow trail now meanders in various directions along the way to Bryce Point. The section of the trail is less used than its northern section. Undulating along the rim splendid views of the Bryce amphitheatres line the horizon. Finally you meet the trail to the Peekaboo Loop and the trail's end at Bryce Point.

PEEKABOO LOOP

Start:	Bryce Point (8,280 feet/2,524 metres)
End:	Bryce Point (8,280 feet/2,524 metres)
Distance, loop:	5.5 miles (8.8 kilometres)
Time, one way:	3 hours
Maps:	Bryce Point (USGS 7.5'); Bryce Canyon National Park (TI)
Season:	May through to October
Water:	none
Rating:	moderate

From the Bryce Canyon visitor centre, drive 1.6 miles south on Highway 63 to the turn-off to Inspiration and Bryce points. Turn east and follow the signs to Bryce Point, the starting point for this loop. The actual Peekaboo Loop itself measures 3.5 miles long but if you join the loop from Bryce Point you'll walk 5.5 miles. One of my favourite park hikes, do not be put off by the trail's relentless ups and downs and the smell of horses.

Directions

From Bryce Point, head north-east toward the Hat Shop to the junction with the Under the Rim Trail. Turn north, descend steeply for 1 mile on switchbacks through a tunnel to the junction with the Peekaboo Connector Trail. Turn west at the junction and proceed around the Peekaboo Loop in a clockwise direction. Soon Bryce Point towers 400 feet above you. Turn west at the next junction and you come shortly to a resting point for the horses with a picnic area and pit toilets.

Continuing west you rise up a series of switchbacks and pass through a small cavern. Soon you traverse the Wall of Windows, the highlight of the trail. Looking up you can see several windows in the red walls. Descending to a draw, you come to the Navajo Connecting Trail. Turn east to stay on the loop and then, in a few minutes, turn south back on the Peekaboo Loop. The trail drops up and down passing cliffs of hoodoos and looping under small arches with scattered pine and juniper trees. Next you meet the Bryce Point Connecting Trail; bear south for your climb back to the rim.

A longer, highly recommended day-hike starting at Sunset Point combines the Navajo Loop descending to the canyon bottom via Wall Street, connects to the Peekaboo Loop and then ascends to the rim via the Queen's Garden Loop. (See the Route Profile: Queen's Garden Trail, Navajo and Peekaboo Loops.)

BRISTLECONE LOOP

Start:	Rainbow Point (9,015 feet/2,748 metres)
End:	Rainbow Point (9,015 feet/2,748 metres)
Distance, loop:	1 mile (1.6 kilometres)
Time, one way:	20 minutes
Maps:	Rainbow Point (USGS 7.5'); Bryce Canyon National Park (TI)
Season:	May through to October
Water:	none
Rating:	easy

From the Bryce Canyon Visitor Centre, take Highway 63 16.8 miles south to the end of the road at Rainbow Point.

Directions
From the trailhead near the parking area, the Bristlecone Loop winds south-east through a forest of fir and pine. You should be able to recognize bristlecone pines by the tuft of needles at the end of their limbs. These hearty trees, known to be some of the oldest living things on earth, survive in windy, desolate climates. Approaching the canyon rim you loop back north at the viewpoint near a lovely bristlecone pine. Returning to Rainbow Point in the counter-clockwise direction, you pass the Under the Rim Trail.

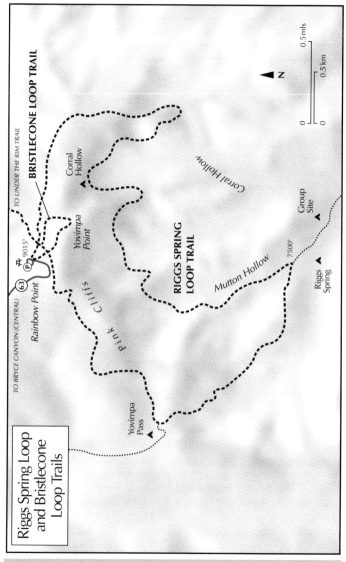

Riggs Spring Loop
and Bristlecone
Loop Trails

BRISTLECONE LOOP TRAIL

TO UNDER THE RIM TRAIL

TO BRYCE CANYON (CENTRAL)

Rainbow Point

63

9015'

Yovimpa Point

Corral Hollow

Corral Hollow

RIGGS SPRING
LOOP TRAIL

Group
Site

Mutton Hollow

7500'

Riggs
Spring

Pink Cliffs

Yovimpa
Pass

N

0   0.5 mls

0   0.5 km

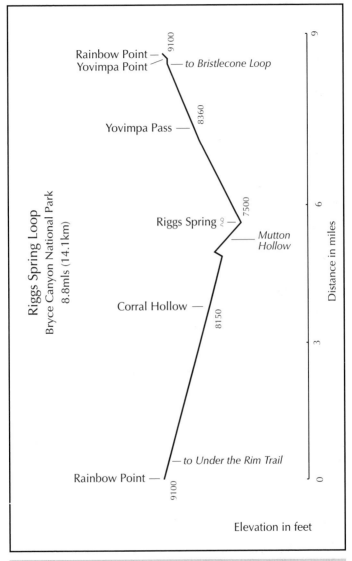

Riggs Spring Loop
Bryce Canyon National Park
8.8mls (14.1km)

Rainbow Point —
Yovimpa Point
— *to Bristlecone Loop*
9100

Yovimpa Pass —
8360

Riggs Spring —
7500
— *Mutton Hollow*

Corral Hollow —
8150

— *to Under the Rim Trail*
Rainbow Point —
9100

Distance in miles

Elevation in feet

RIGGS SPRING LOOP

Start:	Rainbow Point (9,015 feet/2,748 metres)
End:	Rainbow Point (9,015 feet/2,748 metres)
Distance, loop:	8.8 miles (14.1 kilometres)
Time, loop:	4 hours
Maps:	Podunk Creek, Rainbow Point (USGS 7.5');
	Bryce Canyon National Park (TI)
Season:	June through to October
Rating:	moderate

Drive 16.3 miles south of the visitor centre on Highway 63 to the end of the road at Rainbow Point. If you are planning to camp overnight, you must first obtain a backcountry permit at the visitor centre and check on the availability of water sources. For backpackers, the Riggs Springs Trail offers a pleasant and shorter alternative to the longer Under the Rim Trail. The trail can be walked as a day trip as well.

This southern section of the park, seen by many fewer visitors than its northern counterpart, offers fewer spires and hoodoos to admire. The pleasant, cool forest that beckons during the hot summer day blocks some of the views along the trail. Rainbow Point itself, at the start of this walk, boasts some of the finest park views.

Directions
From Rainbow Point, follow the Bristlecone Loop going east to join the Under the Rim Trail and turn north at the junction. Descend to the next junction and turn south onto the Riggs Spring Loop. The trail now descends east and then south and then loops back north. After 3.5 miles you reach the Corral Hollow Campsite. Then you turn south and follow the Mutton Hollow Drainage for 0.8 miles to the Riggs Spring Campsite, a lovely spot, shaded by tall pine trees. The spring nearby gurgles behind a fence.

Now turning north you ascend 900 feet in 1.6 miles to the Yovimpa Pass Campsite. Next turn north-east, crossing above the Pink Cliffs back to Rainbow Point. Fine views of the Pink Cliffs and Mutton Hollow grab your attention along this traverse until you reach your starting point at Rainbow Point.

CHAPTER 22

BRYCE CANYON NATIONAL PARK: LONG DISTANCE AND CONNECTING TRAILS

Here you find the elemental freedom
to breathe deep of unpoisoned air,
to experiment with solitude and stillness,
to gaze through a hundred miles of untrammelled atmosphere,
across red-rock canyons, beyond blue mesas
Edward Abbey

LONG DISTANCE TRAIL

Trail	Distance Miles One way	Distance Kilometres One Way	Rating
Under the Rim Trail	22.8	36.5	Strenuous

UNDER THE RIM TRAIL

Start:	Bryce Point (8,280 feet/2,524 metres)
End:	Rainbow Point (9,015 feet/2,748 metres)
Distance, one way:	22.8 miles (36.5 kilometres)
Time, one way:	10–12 hours, 2 days
Maps:	Bryce Point, Tropic Reservoir, Rainbow Point (USGS 7.5'); Bryce Canyon National Park (TI)
Season:	June through to October
Rating	moderate

The Under the Rim Trail and the Riggs Spring Loop (section 21) make up the only backpacking trails in Bryce Canyon National Park. The Under the Rim Trail, remaining below the rim for its length, travels through the less-visited southern half of the park. First, obtain a backcountry permit from

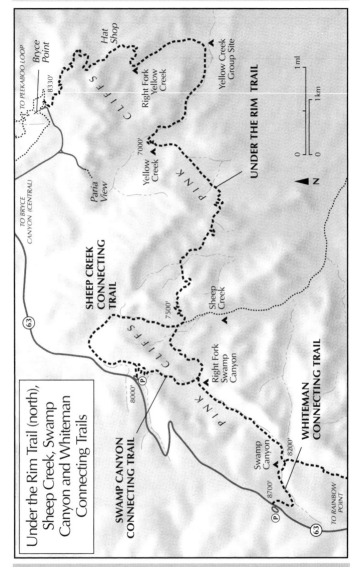

Under the Rim Trail (north), Sheep Creek, Swamp Canyon and Whiteman Connecting Trails

Bryce Point

Hat Shop

TO PEEKABOO LOOP

8330'

Right Fork Yellow Creek

Yellow Creek Group Site

CLIFFS

UNDER THE RIM TRAIL

7000'

Yellow Creek

PINK

Paria View

TO BRYCE CANYON (CENTRAL)

N

1 ml

1 km

0

0

SHEEP CREEK CONNECTING TRAIL

63

7500'

Sheep Creek

CLIFFS

WHITEMAN CONNECTING TRAIL

8000'

P

Right Fork Swamp Canyon

PINK

SWAMP CANYON CONNECTING TRAIL

8200'

Swamp Canyon

8700'

P

63

TO RAINBOW POINT

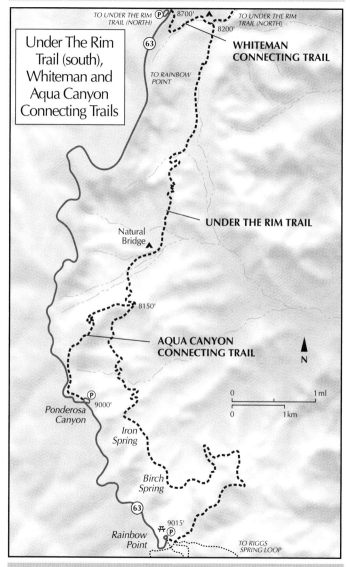

Under The Rim Trail (south), Whiteman and Aqua Canyon Connecting Trails

TO UNDER THE RIM TRAIL (NORTH)

8700'

8200'

TO UNDER THE RIM TRAIL (NORTH)

WHITEMAN CONNECTING TRAIL

63

TO RAINBOW POINT

UNDER THE RIM TRAIL

Natural Bridge

8150'

AQUA CANYON CONNECTING TRAIL

N

0   1 ml

0   1 km

9000'

Ponderosa Canyon

Iron Spring

Birch Spring

63

9015'

Rainbow Point

TO RIGGS SPRING LOOP

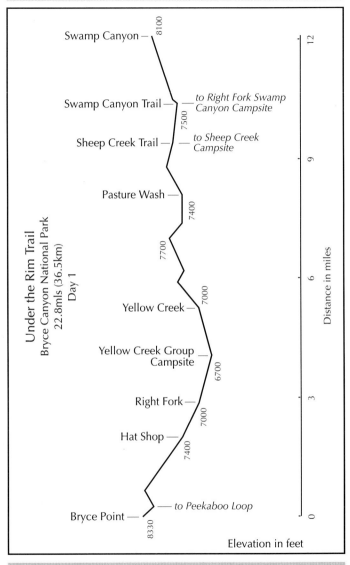

Under the Rim Trail
Bryce Canyon National Park
22.8mls (36.5km)
Day 1

Swamp Canyon — 8100

Swamp Canyon Trail — 7500 — *to Right Fork Swamp Canyon Campsite*

Sheep Creek Trail — *to Sheep Creek Campsite*

Pasture Wash — 7400

7700

Yellow Creek — 7000

Yellow Creek Group Campsite — 6700

Right Fork — 7000

Hat Shop — 7400

Bryce Point — *to Peekaboo Loop*
8330

Distance in miles

12

9

6

3

0

Elevation in feet

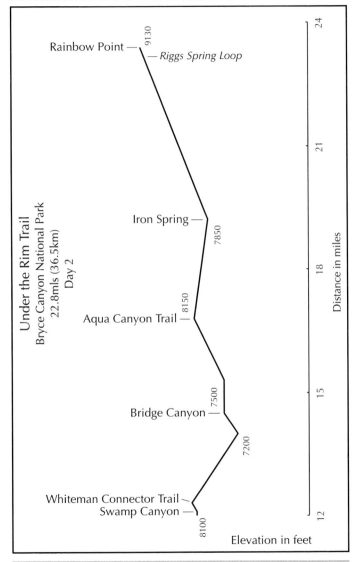

Under the Rim Trail
Bryce Canyon National Park
22.8mls (36.5km)
Day 2

Rainbow Point — 9130
— *Riggs Spring Loop*

Iron Spring — 7850

Aqua Canyon Trail — 8150

Bridge Canyon — 7500
7200

Whiteman Connector Trail
Swamp Canyon — 8100

Distance in miles

Elevation in feet

the visitor centre. You'll need to check on water availability and be sure to bring water purification tablets with you.

Directions

Heading south-east from the Bryce Point car park you soon reach the Peekaboo Connector Trail. Turn south onto the Under the Rim Trail. Switchbacking down to some level ground you'll see hoodoos rise to the south-east. The Table Cliffs and glimpses of Tropic, Utah highlight the views to the north-east. In 2 miles you reach the "Hat Shop" where cap-rocks or "hats" accent numerous pillars of rocks.

Now you descend into the Right Fork of Yellow Creek and pass its campsite. The trail turns south-west and heads to the main fork of Yellow Creek and crosses the turn-off to the Yellow Creek Group campsite. Continuing north-west you can see the Pink Cliffs. Next, pass the Yellow Creek campsite with its outstanding views of the amphitheatre as a backdrop. Leaving the campsite you gain 400 feet with the Pink Cliffs providing stimulating views to encourage you on the ascent. Topping out at the saddle at 7,700 feet you descend to near the Pink Cliffs and views of Rainbow Point open up. Now you descend steadily into Pasture Wash and climb again to another saddle.

At a four-way junction, the Sheep Creek campsite can be found a short way down a spur trail to the south. The Sheep Creek Connecting Trail ascends north to the park road. The Under the Rim Trail goes straight ahead towards Swamp Canyon. A bit farther on, the Swamp Creek campsite and Swamp Canyon campsite are popular in summer with visitors descending from the rim for an overnight stay.

From the Sheep Creek Connecting Trail ascend another small saddle and descend into Swamp Canyon. Soon you come upon the Swamp Canyon Connector Trail heading north to the park road. The Under the Rim Trail continues to head west into Swamp Canyon, soon passing the Right Fork Swamp Canyon campsite. Shortly onward you come to the Swamp Canyon Connector Trail veering up to the rim.

Now the trail leaves Swamp Canyon and soon you pass Swamp Camp located on a wooded terrace above the trail. You reach the junction with the Whiteman Connector Trail; veer south at the junction. Descending into Willis Creek, Canyon Butte lines the skyline to the east. Soon you climb to a saddle and descend into the next basin as the Natural Bridge marks the skyline to the west. At the bottom you pass Natural Bridge Camp and enter Aqua Canyon. Getting out of Aqua Canyon you climb up a slope dotted with pine trees to the junction of the Aqua Canyon Connecting Trail.

Descending from the junction into Ponderosa Canyon you pass several creeks and Iron Spring. Now the trail loops around to the north and east beginning its final climb to Rainbow Point. Views spread all the way north to Bryce Point. Rounding a corner, the climb becomes steeper and then crosses a narrow ridge as it overlooks the Pink Cliffs. Finally, the Under the Rim Trail ends at Rainbow Point.

CONNECTING TRAILS: INTRODUCTION
The Bryce National Park Connecting trails link up the only automobile road in the park, Highway 63, with the Under the Rim Trail. The four connecting trails, described here from north to south, Sheep Creek, Swamp Canyon, Whiteman and Aqua Canyon, depart from the main road between Bryce Point and Rainbow Point. These trails can be used on day or overnight walks to meet the Under the Rim Trail. You may wish to loop back to another parking area. Views are often obscured by trees and there are fewer hoodoos than in the northern section. As a result, this part of the park is much less used than its northern section.

CONNECTING TRAILS

Trail	Distance Miles One way	Distance Kilometres One Way	Rating
Sheep Creek Connecting Trail	2.0	3.2	Moderate
Swamp Canyon Connecting Trail	0.9	1.4	Moderate
Whiteman Connecting Trail	0.9	1.4	Moderate
Aqua Canyon Connecting Trail	1.6	2.6	Moderate

SHEEP CREEK CONNECTING TRAIL

Take Highway 63, 5 miles south of the visitor centre and park in the turnout on the east side of the road. This parking area is the road head for both the Swamp Canyon and Sheep Creek Connecting trails.

Directions
From the parking area the path heads east, downhill, for a short way and after 0.14 mile meets the connecting point of the two trails. To take the Sheep Creek Connector, turn north at the junction through pine studded slopes. The trail soon turns south-east in a draw and crosses a saddle spotted with juniper. Hoodoos line the views to the south-east. Now the trail turns south and descends below the rim through a break in the pink cliff walls. As you reach the bottom of the canyon you meet the Under the Rim Trail. Continue south on the trail for 0.1 mile to meet the Sheep Creek Trail and if you are going to Sheep Creek Campground, proceed straight ahead 0.5 mile. Turn west onto the Under the Rim Trail to reach Swamp Camp.

SWAMP CANYON CONNECTING TRAIL

From the parking area 5 miles south of the visitor centre park in the turnout on the east side of the road. This parking area is the road head for both the Swamp Canyon and Sheep Creek Connecting trails.

Directions
Begin by walking 0.14 mile north-east to the junction with the Sheep and Swamp Connecting trails. Turn south onto the Swamp Connecting Trail. Descend steeply for 1 mile between limestone cliffs to reach the Under the Rim Trail. The South Canyon Butte lines the skyline to the south. A turn north heads you towards Bryce Point on the Under the Rim Trail and a turn south takes you to Rainbow Point.

WHITEMAN CONNECTING TRAIL

To reach the Whiteman Connecting Trail from the Bryce Canyon Visitor Centre, drive 9 miles south to the parking area on the east side of the road.

Hoodoos, Bryce Canyon National Park

Directions

From the Rim, follow the trail south through the juniper until you reach a wash. Turn north-east and remain along the wash as you descend to the Under the Rim Trail and the Swamp Canyon campsite.

AQUA CONNECTING TRAIL

The Aqua Connecting Trail departs from the Ponderosa Canyon Viewpoint, 13.7 miles south of the Bryce Canyon Visitor Centre.

Directions

Head north through forest, paralleling the road for 0.5 mile. Begin your descent, remaining in trees for another 0.5 mile. Soon the views open up to the gorgeous Pink Cliffs above; the canyon looms below you. The trail then switchbacks down a slippery slope into the canyon to meet the Under the Rim Trail.

APPENDIX A

LONG DISTANCE ROUTES SUMMARY TABLES

Estimated times allow for carrying a 40 pound pack under good weather conditions. Times are affected by walker's fitness, the overall strength of the party, temperature, terrain and the direction travelled.

GRAND CANYON NATIONAL PARK

Boucher Trail to Hermit Trail Loop

Distance:	*23 miles (36.8 kilometres)*
Days:	*3–4*
Start:	*Hermit Trailhead at Hermits' Rest*

30mins	Waldron Trail
30mins	Dripping Springs Trail
45mins	Boucher Trailhead
1hr	Yuma Point
1hr 15mins	Travertine Canyon
1hr	Whites Butte Saddle
1hr	Tonto Trail
15mins	Boucher Creek
45mins	Tonto Trail
1hr 15mins	Travertine Canyon
1hr 25mins	Hermit Creek
45mins	Tonto Trail to Hermit Trail
1hr 30mins	Cathedral Stairs
2hr 30mins	Santa Maria Spring
45mins	Waldron Trail
45mins	Hermits' Rest

Hermit Trail to Bright Angel Trail Loop

Distance:	*22.9 miles (36.6 kilometres)*
Days:	*3–4*
Start:	*Hermit Trailhead at Hermits' Rest*

35mins	Waldron Trail
10mins	Dripping Springs Trail Junction
30mins	Cathedral Stairs
30mins	Hermit Trail to Tonto Trail junction
30mins	Hermit Creek Trailhead
1hr	Hermit Rapids
1hr	Hermit Creek Trailhead
20mins	Hermit Trail to Tonto Trail junction
30mins	Monument Creek
45mins	Granite Rapids
50mins	Monument Creek
30mins	Cedar Spring
45mins	Salt Creek
1hr 45mins	Horn Creek
1hr 15mins	Indian Garden
45mins	Three Mile Resthouse
1hr 10mins	Mile-and-a-Half Resthouse
1hr 10mins	Bright Angel Trailhead at Kolb Studio

North to South Rim: Cross Canyon North Kaibab Trailhead to Bright Angel Trailhead

Distance:	*23.3 miles (37.2 kilometres)*
Days:	*2–3*
Start:	*North Kaibab Trailhead*
10mins	Coconino Overlook
45mins	Supai Tunnel
1hr	Roaring Springs
1hr 15mins	Cottonwood Camp
30mins	Ribbon Falls Turnoff
2hr	Clear Creek Trail
10mins	Phantom Ranch
5mins	Bright Angel Campground
5mins	Colorado River at Silver Suspension Bridge
1hr	River Resthouse
1hr 15mins	Indian Garden
45mins	Three Mile Resthouse
1hr 10mins	Mile-and-a-Half Resthouse
1hr 10mins	Bright Angel Trailhead at Kolb Studio

South Kaibab Trail to Bright Angel Trail

Distance:	*16.3 miles (26.1 kilometres)*
Days:	*2–4*
Start:	*South Kaibab Trailhead at Yaki Point*

15mins	Oh Hah Point
40mins	Cedar Ridge
25mins	O'Neill Butte
30mins	Skeleton Point
40mins	The Tipoff
45mins	Silver Suspension Bridge
10mins	Phantom Ranch
5mins	Bright Angel Campground
5mins	Colorado River at Silver Suspension Bridge
1hr	River Resthouse
1hr 15mins	Indian Garden
45mins	Three Mile Resthouse
1hr 10mins	Mile-and-a-Half Resthouse
1hr 10mins	Bright Angel Trailhead at Kolb Studio

Grandview Trail to South Kaibab Trail

Distance:	*27.8 miles (44.4 kilometres)*
Days:	*4–5*
Start:	*Grandview Trailhead at Grandview Point*

1hr 30mins	Horseshoe Mesa
45mins	Cottonwood Creek
2hr	Grapevine Creek
3hr	Boulder Creek
1hr 30mins	Lonetree Creek
2hr	Cremation Creek (south arm)
20mins	Cremation Creek (south-west arm)
15mins	Cremation Creek (west arm)
1hr	The Tipoff
1hr	Skeleton Point
1hr	Cedar Ridge
1hr	South Kaibab Trailhead

Escalante Route: Tanner Trail to Grandview Trail

Distance:	*33 miles (52.8 kilometres)*
Days:	*5–7*
Start:	*Tanner Trailhead at Lipan Point*

1hr	Seventyfive Mile Saddle
1hr	Escalante Butte
45mins	Cardenas Butte
15mins	Top of Redwall
4hr	Tanner Rapids
1hr	Unkar Delta
2hr	Escalante Creek
1hr	River at Escalante
30mins	Head of Seventyfive Mile Creek
30mins	Nevills Rapids
30mins	above Papago Creek
30mins	Papago Creek
1hr	Overlook
30mins	Colorado River
30mins	Red Canyon
30mins	Mineral Canyon
30mins	Shady Overhang
2hr	Hance Creek
45mins	Miner's (Page) Spring
1hr 15mins	Horseshoe Mesa
3hr	Grandview Trailhead

Kanab Canyon to Thunder River Route

Distance:	*50.5 miles (80.8 kilometres)*
Days:	*7–9*
Start:	*Sowats Point*

1hr	South Arm Kwagunt Hollow at cottonwood trees
3hr	Jumpup Canyon
1hr	Indian Hollow
1hr 45mins	Kanab Creek
1hr 15mins	Pencil Spring
45mins	Showerbath Spring
45mins	Scotty's Hollow
1hr	Cave on north side of Kanab Creek

3hr	Whispering Falls
2hr 30mins	Kanab Creek
6hr	Fishtail Rapids
3hr 30mins	Deer Creek Falls
20mins	Deer Creek Narrows
5mins	Deer Creek Camping
30mins	Deer Creek Spring
1hr	Surprise Valley
1hr	Surprise Valley Rim above Thunder River
10mins	Thunder River Spring
20mins	Return to Surprise Valley above Thunder River
1hr 45mins	Surprise Valley Rim
2hr	Bill Hall Trailhead
1hr	Esplanade Camp
3hr	Indian Hollow

ZION NATIONAL PARK

Across Zion via Hop Valley and the West Rim

Distance:	*37.6 miles (60.2 kilometres)*
Days:	*4–5*
Start:	*La Verkin Creek Trailhead at Lee Pass*

1hr	Shuntavi Butte
1hr	Corral
1hr 30mins	Kolob Arch Trail
10mins	Beatty Spring
5mins	Hop Valley and Willis Creek Trail junction
40mins	High Point
40mins	Hop Valley fence #1
30mins	Langston Canyon
1hr 15mins	Hop Valley fence #2
20mins	Connector Trail
2hr	to Wildcat Canyon Trailhead
5mins	to Northgate Spur Trail
1hr 15mins	Wildcat Spring
10mins	Wildcat Canyon Creek
30mins	West Rim Trail near Lava Point
10mins	to Sawmill Spring

2hr	Potato Hollow
1hr 15mins	West Rim Trail and Telephone Canyon Trail junction via West Rim Trail
1hr 15mins	Cabin Spring
1hr 30mins	bridge
20mins	Scout Lookout and Angels' Landing Trail junction
1hr 15mins	Grotto picnic area

The Zion Narrows

Distance:	*15.5 miles (24.8 kilometres)*
Days:	*2*
Start:	*Chamberlain's Ranch*

1hr	Bulloch's Cabin
2hr 30mins	First Narrows
1hr	Waterfall
1hr	Deep Creek
45mins	Kolob Creek
15mins	Grotto
35mins	Goose Creek
45mins	Big Springs
2hr 45mins	Orderville Canyon
1hr 45mins	Riverside Trail
20mins	Temple of Sinawava

East Rim Trail via Cable and Deertrap mountains

Distance:	*20.4 miles (32.6 kilometres)*
Days:	*2*
Start:	*East Entrance*

45mins	Cave Canyon
15mins	Rise
20mins	Jolley Gulch
1hr 10mins	High Point
10mins	Stave Spring
1min	Stave Spring Junction to Deertrap and Cable mountains
20mins	Y-junction
15mins	Knoll above Deertrap Mountain

45mins	Deertrap Mountain
35mins	Return to signed Y-junction
30mins	Cable Mountain
20mins	Return to signed Y-junction
15mins	Return to Stave Spring Junction
5mins	Spur to East Boundary
20mins	Above Echo Canyon
15mins	Echo Canyon Wash
10mins	Observation Point Trail
15mins	Hidden Canyon Trail
15mins	Weeping Rock picnic area

BRYCE CANYON NATIONAL PARK

Riggs Spring Loop

Distance:	*8.8 miles (14.1 kilometres)*
Days:	*1–2*
Start:	*Rainbow Point*
1hr 15mins	Corral Hollow
1hr	Riggs Spring
45mins	Yovimpa Pass Campground
30mins	Yovimpa Point
5mins	Bristlecone Loop
5mins	Rainbow Point

Under the Rim Trail

Distance:	*22.8 miles (36.5 kilometres)*
Days:	*2–3*
Start:	*Bryce Point*
5mins	Peekaboo Loop
1hr	Hat Shop
20mins	Right Fork Camping
30mins	Yellow Creek Group Site
30mins	Yellow Creek Camping
30mins	Saddle
1hr	Pasture Wash
20mins	Divide
30mins	Sheep Creek Trail

30mins	Swamp Canyon Connecting Trail
5mins	Right Fork Swamp Canyon Camp
40mins	Swamp Canyon Camp
10mins	Whiteman Connect Trail
1hr 10mins	Bridge Canyon Camp
40mins	Aqua Canyon Connecting Trail
1hr	Iron Spring Camping
2hr	Rainbow Point

APPENDIX B

USEFUL ADDRESSES

GRAND CANYON NATIONAL PARK
Grand Canyon National Park, PO Box 129, Grand Canyon, Arizona 86023 (520) 638-7888

Grand Canyon National Park: www.thecanyon.com/nps

Grand Canyon National Park Lodges, PO Box 699, Grand Canyon, Arizona (Same day hotel reservations only) 86023 (520) 638-2631

Grand Canyon National Park, advance hotel reservations: see AmFac Parks and Resorts below

Grand Canyon Association, PO Box 399, Grand Canyon, Arizona 86023 (520) 638-2481 Fax: (520) 638-2484

Grand Canyon Association: www.grandcanyon.org

Grand Canyon Field Institute, PO Box 399, Grand Canyon, Arizona 86023 (520) 638-2485 Fax: (520) 638-2484

Grand Canyon Field Institute: www.thecanyon.com/fieldinstitute

Grand Canyon Chamber of Commerce, PO Box 3007, Grand Canyon, Arizona 86023 (520) 638-2901

Backcountry Ranger Office (BRO): Grand Canyon National Park, PO 129, Grand Canyon, Arizona 86023-0129 (520) 638-7875 (1pm to 5pm MST) Fax: (520) 638-2125

Backcountry Ranger Office: Grand Canyon National Park: www.thecanyon.com/nps/backcountry

Bright Angel Lodge Transportation Desk: (Phantom Ranch Reservation confirmation and reservations 3 days ahead) 86023 (520) 638-3283 or (520) 638-2631, Ext. 6015

Campground reservations (North and South Rim): (800) 365-2267; International calls: (301) 722-1257

Campground reservations: www.reservations.nps.gov

North Kaibab Ranger District, PO Box 248, Fredonia, Arizona 86022 (520) 643-7395

Transcanyon Shuttle, PO Box 348, Grand Canyon, Arizona 86023 (520) 638-2820

Tusayan Shuttle (Serves Grand Canyon Airport, South Rim): 86023 (520) 638-0821

South Rim Taxi 86023 .(520) 638-2822 or (520) 638-2631, Ext. 6563

Gray Line of Flagstaff, Nava-Hopi Tours, PO Box 339, Flagstaff, Arizona (520) 774-5003 Fax: (520) 774-7715

Grand Canyon Railway, 518 East Bill Williams Avenue, Williams, Arizona (800) 843-8724; International calls to: (520) 773-1976

ZION NATIONAL PARK
Zion National Park, Springdale, Utah 84767 (435) 772-3256

Zion National Park web site: www.nps.gov/zion

Zion Natural History Association, Zion National Park, Springdale, Utah 84767 (435) 772-3265

Zion Canyon Chamber of Commerce, PO Box 331, Springdale, Utah 84767

Zion National Park, Zion Canyon Visitor Centre 84767 (435) 772-3256

Zion National Park, Kolob Canyons Visitor Centre 84767 (435) 586-9548

Campground reservations (Watchman Campground) (800) 365-2267; International calls: (301) 722-1257

Campground reservations: www.reservations.nps.gov

Hiker's Shuttle: Zion Lodge, Transportation Desk 84767 (435) 772-3213

The Zion Adventure Company, 36 Lion Blvd., Springdale, Utah 84767 (435) 772-1001

BRYCE CANYON NATIONAL PARK

Bryce Canyon National Park, Bryce Canyon, Utah 84717 (435) 834-5322

Bryce Canyon National Park: www.nps.gov/brca/

Bryce Canyon Lodge, Bryce Canyon, Utah 84717 (April through to October) (435) 834-5631

Bryce Canyon Natural History Association, Bryce Canyon, Utah 84717 (435) 834-5322

Best Western Ruby's Inn, PO Box 1, Bryce, Utah 84764 (435) 834 5341

Garfield County Travel Council, PO Box 200, Panguitch, Utah 84759

General Store at Bryce Canyon (435) 834-5361

LODGE RESERVATIONS

Zion Lodge, Bryce Canyon Lodge, Grand Canyon Lodges (North and South Rim) and Phantom Ranch: AmFac Parks and Resorts, 14001 East Iliff Drive, Suite 600, Aurora, Colorado 80014 (303) 297-2757 Fax: (303) 297-3175

AmFac Parks and Resorts: www.amfac.com

MAPS

United States Geological Survey (USGS), Box 25286, Denver, Colorado 80225. Order by Fax: (303)202-4693; Information: 1-800-USA-MAPS

Zion Natural History Association, Zion National Park, Springdale, Utah 8476784767 (435) 772-3265

Grand Canyon Association, PO Box 399, Grand Canyon, Arizona,

86023 (520) 638-2481 Fax: (520) 638-2484

Trails Illustrated, PO Box 4357, Evergreen, Colorado 80439-3746 (800) 962-1643; International calls: (303) 670-3457

Trails Illustrated: www.colorado.com/trails

APPENDIX C

LOCAL FACILITIES

A synopsis of facilities available at the three national parks and their surrounding communities is provided below. "Full supplies" means that a wide range of food and camping supplies are available. "Limited supplies" means that some camping and backpacking gear and food supplies are sold, but with a limited choice. "Very limited supplies" means that only a few camping and backpacking items can be purchased and their may be only one small grocery store.

Abbreviations:
BCNP: Bryce Canyon National Park
GCN: Grand Canyon National Park, North Rim
GCS: Grand Canyon National Park, South Rim
ZNP: Zion National Park

Bryce Canyon National Park (BCNP): lodging, camping, very limited supplies, Bryce Canyon National Park Visitor Centre: laundromat, Post Office (in Bryce Lodge)

Cameron, Arizona (GCS): lodging, petrol, very limited supplies

Cedar City, Utah (BCNP, ZNP): lodging, petrol, full supplies, bank, Post Office, laundromat, airport, bus station

Desert View, Grand Canyon National Park (GCS): camping (seasonal), petrol (seasonal)

Flagstaff, Arizona (GCS): lodging, petrol, full supplies, bank, Post Office, laundromat, airport, train station, bus station

Fredonia, Arizona (GCN): petrol, North Kaibab Ranger Station, lodging (very limited)

Grand Canyon, North Rim (GCN): lodging, petrol, very limited supplies, camping, laundromat, showers, Post Office (in Bright Angel Lodge), visitor centre; backcountry reservations

Grand Canyon, South Rim (GCS): lodging, petrol, limited supplies, camping, bank, laundromat, showers, medical clinic, dog kennel, train station, airport, taxi, Post Office, bus service, backcountry reservations

Hatch, Utah (BCNP, ZNP): petrol, no supplies

Hurricane, Utah (ZNP): lodging, petrol, limited supplies, bank, Post Office, laundromat

Jacob Lake, Arizona (GCN): lodging, petrol, camping, North Rim Ranger Station

Kanab, Utah (BCNP, GCN, ZNP): lodging, petrol, limited supplies, bank, Post Office, laundromat

Las Vegas, Nevada (BCNP, GCN, GCS, ZNP): lodging, petrol, full supplies, bank, Post Office, laundromat, airport

Long Valley Junction, Utah (BCNP, ZNP): lodging, petrol

Mt. Carmel Junction, Utah (BCNP, ZNP): lodging, petrol

Page, Arizona (GCN): lodging, petrol, full supplies, bank, Post Office, laundromat, airport

Panguitch, Utah (BCNP): lodging, petrol, limited supplies, bank, Post Office, laundromat

Phantom Ranch (GCN, GCS): lodging, camping, mail service

Phoenix, Arizona (GCS): lodging, petrol, full supplies, bank, Post Office, laundromat, airport

Rockville, Utah (ZNP): Post Office, lodging (very limited)

Springdale, Utah (ZNP): lodging, petrol, limited supplies, camping, bank, Post Office, laundromat, showers (at campground)

St. George, Utah (ZNP): lodging, petrol, full supplies, bank, Post Office, laundromat, airport

Tropic, Utah (BCNP): lodging, petrol, limited supplies

Tusayan, Arizona (GCS): lodging, petrol, limited supplies, camping, Post Office, Grand Canyon airport

Williams, Arizona (GCS): lodging, petrol, limited supplies, bank, Post Office, train station (limited service), bus station

Zion National Park (ZNP): lodging, camping, Zion Canyon Visitor Centre, Post Office (in Zion Lodge)

APPENDIX D

AUTHOR'S FAVOURITE WALKS

GRAND CANYON NATIONAL PARK

Day-walks, South Rim
Boucher Trail to Dripping Springs via Hermit Trail
Grandview Trail to Horseshoe Mesa
Hermit Trail to Santa Maria Spring or Cathedral Stairs
Rim Trail
Shoshone Point
South Kaibab Trail to Cedar Mesa, O'Neill Butte or Skeleton Point

Day-walks, North Rim
Bright Angel Point
Cape Final
Cape Royal
Ken Patrick Trail from Point Imperial

Overnight or long distance tips
Boucher to Hermit Loop (South Rim)
Escalante Route, Tanner Trail to Grandview Trail (South Rim)
Grandview Trail to Horseshoe Mesa (South Rim)
Kanab Canyon to Thunder River (North Rim)

ZION NATIONAL PARK

Day-walks
Angel's Landing
East Rim Trail
Hop Valley Trail to Kolob Arch Trail
Northgate Peaks Trail
Observation Point
West Rim Trail
Up The Narrows to Orderville Canyon

Overnight or long distance walks:
Across Zion
East Rim Trail to Cable and Deertrap mountains
The Zion Narrows
West Rim Trail from Lava Point to Grotto picnic area

BRYCE CANYON NATIONAL PARK

Day-walks
Fairyland Loop
Navajo Loop to Peekaboo Loop to Queen's Garden Trail
Rim Trail

APPENDIX E

INDEX OF CHARTS AND ROUTE PROFILES

WATER TEMPERATURE AND RAINFALL

Average South Rim Temperatures and Precipitation, Grand Canyon 36
Average North Rim Temperatures and Precipitation, Grand Canyon 37
Year Round Water Sources, Grand Canyon 50
Average Inner Canyon Temperatures and Precipitation, Grand Canyon 53
Average Valley Temperatures and Precipitation, Zion.............156
Average Rim Temperatures and Precipitation, Bryce..............229

GRAND CANYON

South Bass Trail...59
Boucher Trail 63
Hermit Trail 65
Bright Angel Trail...69
South Kaibab Trail..72
Grandview Trail...76
New Hance Trail..79
Tanner Trail 82
Thunder River and Bill Hall Trails 88
North Bass Trail 93
North Kaibab Trail 97
Nankoweap Trail...101
Boucher to Hermit Loop 134
Hermit to Bright Angel Loop 136
North Kaibab to Bright Angel Trail 138
South Kaibab to Bright Angel Trail 140
Grandview Trail to South Kaibab Trail 141
Tanner Trail to Grandview Trail...143
Kanab Canyon to Thunder River (Days 1–3) 148
Kanab Canyon to Thunder River (Days 4–7)..............................149

ZION NATIONAL PARK

La Verkin Creek and Wills Creek Route 168
Hop Valley Trail...174
Connector Trail and Wildcat Canyon Trail................................179
West Rim Trail...183
East Rim Trail..206
Chinle Trail 213
Across Zion National Park..217
The Narrows 223
East Rim to Cable and Deertrap Mountains 226

BRYCE NATIONAL PARK

Fairyland Loop 237
Queen's Garden Trail, Navajo and Peekaboo Loops 240
Riggs Spring Loop..247
Under the Rim Trail (Day 1) 252
Under the Rim Trail (Day 2) 253

APPENDIX F

INDEX OF MAPS

GENERAL MAPS

Grand Canyon, Zion and Bryce Canyon National Parks...........12
Western United States...22

GRAND CANYON

Trail Map Layout...41
South Bass Trail..58
Boucher and Hermit Trails..62
Bright Angel and South Kaibab Trails 68
South Kaibab and Grandview Trails 74
New Hance and Tanner Trails..80
Thunder River, Bill Hall and Deer Creek Trails 87
North Bass Route..91
North Kaibab Trail 96
Nankoweap Trail 100
Tonto Trail (east) and Escalante Route.....................................106
Tonto Trail (central)...110
Tonto Trail (west)...114
Clear Creek Trail 117
Rim Trail 120
Cape Final, Cape Royal and Cliff Spring Trails.......................125
Ken Patrick, Uncle Jim, Transept and Widforss Trails..............128
Kanab Creek Route (north)..146
Kanab Creek Route (south)..147

ZION CANYON

Trail Map Layout...161
La Verkin Creek, Taylor Creek, Timber Creek Overlook and
 Kolob Arch Trails 167
Willis Creek Route..171

Hop Valley Trail...173
Connector, Wildcat Canyon (west) and Northgate Peaks
  Trails 178
Wildcat Canyon Trail...180
West Rim Trail (north) 184
West Rim Trail (south), Telephone Canyon and Riverside
  Trails..185
Angels' Landing and Weeping Rock Trails.................192
Observation Point, Hidden Canyon and East Mesa Trails 194
Court of the Patriarchs, Sand Bench and Emerald Pools
  Trails..198
Canyon Overlook, Par'us and Watchman Trails.......201
East Rim, Cable and Deertrap Mountain Trails........205
Chinle Trail...212
The Narrows (north)...220
The Narrows (south)...221

BRYCE CANYON

Trail Map Layout..233
Fairyland Loop and Rim Trails 236
Bryce Canyon (central) 239
Riggs Spring Loop and Bristlecone Loop Trails 246
Under the Rim Trail (north), Sheep Creek, Swamp Canyon
  and Whiteman Connecting Trails...............................250
Under the Rim Trail (south), Whiteman and Aqua
  Canyon Connecting Trails 251

CICERONE GUIDES

WALKING AND TREKKING IN THE ALPS

WALKING IN THE ALPS *Kev Reynolds* The popular author of many of our Alpine guide-books now draws on his vast experience to produce an outstanding comprehensive volume. Every area covered. Not for over half a century has there been anything remotely comparable. Fully illustrated. *ISBN 1 85284 261 X Large format Case bound 496pp*

CHAMONIX TO ZERMATT - The Walker's Haute Route *Kev Reynolds* The classic walk in the shadow of great peaks from Mont Blanc to the Matterhorn. In 14 stages, this is one of the most beautiful LD paths in Europe. *ISBN 1 85284 215 6 176pp*

THE GRAND TOUR OF MONTE ROSA *C.J. Wright*

Vol 1: - MARTIGNY TO VALLE DELLA SESIA (via the Italian valleys) *ISBN 1 85284 177 X 216pp*

Vol 2: - VALLE DELLA SESIA TO MARTIGNY (via the Swiss valleys) *ISBN 1 85284 178 8 182pp* The ultimate alpine LD walk which encircles most of the Pennine Alps.

TOUR OF MONT BLANC *Andrew Harper* One of the world's best walks - the circum-navigation of the Mont Blanc massif. 120 miles of pure magic, split into 11 sections. Reprinted and updated. *ISBN 1 85284 240 7 144pp PVC cover*

100 HUT WALKS IN THE ALPS *Kev Reynolds* 100 walks amid dramatic mountain scenery to high mountain huts, each with a map, photograph and route description. A fine introduction to Europe's highest mountains in France, Italy, Switzerland, Austria and Slovenia. *ISBN 1 85284 297 0*

FRANCE, BELGIUM AND LUXEMBOURG

WALKING IN THE ARDENNES *Alan Castle* 53 circular walks in this attractive area of gorges and deep cut wooded valleys, caves, castles and hundreds of walking trails. Easily accessible from the channel. *ISBN 1 85284 213 X 312pp*

SELECTED ROCK CLIMBS IN BELGIUM AND LUXEMBOURG *Chris Craggs* Perfect rock, good protection and not too hot to climb in summer. *ISBN 1 85284 155 9 188p A5*

THE BRITTANY COASTAL PATH *Alan Castle* The GR34, 360 miles, takes a month to walk. Easy access from UK means it can be split into several holidays. *ISBN 1 85284 185 0 296pp*

CHAMONIX - MONT BLANC - A Walking Guide *Martin Collins* In the dominating presence of Europe's highest mountain, the scenery is exceptional. A comprehensive guide to the area. *ISBN 1 85284 009 9 192pp PVC cover*

THE CORSICAN HIGH LEVEL ROUTE - Walking the GR20 *Paddy Dillon* The most challenging of the French LD paths - across the rocky spine of Corsica. *ISBN 1 85284 100 1 (2001)*

WALKING THE FRENCH ALPS: GR5 *Martin Collins* The popular trail from Lake Geneva to Nice. Split into stages, each of which could form the basis of a good holiday. *ISBN 1 85284 051 X 160pp*

WALKING THE FRENCH GORGES *Alan Castle* 320 miles through Provence and Ardèche, includes the famous gorges of the Verdon. *ISBN 1 85284 114 1 224pp*

FRENCH ROCK *Bill Birkett* THE guide to many exciting French crags! Masses of photo topos, with selected hit-routes in detail. *ISBN 1 85284 113 3. 332pp A5 size*

WALKING IN THE HAUTE SAVOIE *Janette Norton* 61 walks in the pre-Alps of Chablais, to majestic peaks in the Faucigny, Haut Giffre and Lake Annecy regions. *ISBN 1 85284 196 6 312pp*

TOUR OF THE OISANS: GR54 *Andrew Harper* This popular walk around the Dauphiné massif and Écrins national park is similar in quality to the celebrated Tour of Mont Blanc. A two week suggested itinerary covers the 270km route. *ISBN 1 85284 157 5   120pp PVC cover*

TOUR OF MONT BLANC *see Walking and Trekking in the Alps, above*

WALKING IN PROVENCE *Janette Norton* 42 walks through the great variety of Provence - remote plateaux, leafy gorges, ancient villages, monuments, quiet towns. Provence is evocative of a gentler life. *ISBN 1 85284 293 8 248pp*

THE PYRENEAN TRAIL: GR10 *Alan Castle* From the Atlantic to the Mediterranean at a lower level than the Pyrenean High Route. 50 days but splits into holiday sections.   *ISBN 1 85284 245 8 176pp*

WALKS AND CLIMBS IN THE PYRENEES *Kev Reynolds   See entry under FRANCE/SPAIN*

THE TOUR OF THE QUEYRAS *Alan Castle* A 13 day walk which traverses wild but beautiful country, the sunniest part of the French Alps. Suitable for a first Alpine visit.   *ISBN 1 85284 048 X 160pp*

THE ROBERT LOUIS STEVENSON TRAIL *Alan Castle* 140 mile trail in the footsteps of Stevenson's *Travels with a Donkey* through the Cevennes, from Le Puy to St Jean du Gard. This route is ideal for people new to walking holidays. *ISBN 1 85284 060 9 160pp*

ROCK CLIMBS IN THE PYRENEES *Derek Walker See entry under FRANCE/SPAIN*

WALKING IN THE TARENTAISE AND BEAUFORTAIN ALPS *J.W. Akitt* The delectable mountain area south of Mont Blanc includes the Vanoise National Park. 53 day walks, 5 tours between 2 and 8 day's duration, plus 40 short outings. *ISBN 1 85284 181 8 216pp*

ROCK CLIMBS IN THE VERDON - An Introduction *Rick Newcombe* An English-style guide, which makes for easier identification of the routes and descents.   *ISBN 1 85284 015 3 72pp*

TOUR OF THE VANOISE *Kev Reynolds* A 10-12 day circuit of one of the finest mountain areas of France, between Mt. Blanc and the Écrins. The second most popular mountain tour after the Tour of Mont Blanc. *ISBN 1 85284 224 5 120pp*

WALKS IN VOLCANO COUNTRY *Alan Castle* Two LD walks in Central France, the High Auvergne and Tour of the Velay, in a unique landscape of extinct volcanoes. *ISBN 1 85284 092 7 208pp*

THE WAY OF ST JAMES *Two titles - see below*

FRANCE/SPAIN

ROCK CLIMBS IN THE PYRENEES *Derek Walker* Includes Pic du Midi d'Ossau and the Vignemale in France, and the Ordesa Canyon and Riglos in Spain. *ISBN 1 85284 039 0 168pp PVC cover*

WALKS AND CLIMBS IN THE PYRENEES *Kev Reynolds* Includes the Pyrenean High Level Route. Invaluable for any backpacker or mountaineer who plans to visit this still unspoilt mountain range. (3rd Edition) *ISBN 1 85284 133 8 328pp   PVC cover*

THE WAY OF ST JAMES: Le Puy to Santiago - A Cyclist's Guide *John Higginson* A guide for touring cyclists follows as closely as possible the original route but avoids the almost unrideable sections of the walkers' way. On surfaced lanes and roads. *ISBN 1 85284 274 1 112pp*

THE WAY OF ST JAMES: Le Puy to Santiago - A Walker's Guide *Alison Raju* A walker's guide to the ancient route of pilgrimage. Plus the continuation to Finisterre. *ISBN 1 85284 271 7 264pp*

SPAIN AND PORTUGAL

WALKING IN THE ALGARVE *June Parker* The author of *Walking in Mallorca* turns her expert attention to the Algarve, with a selection of walks to help the visitor explore the true countryside. *ISBN 1 85284 173 7 168pp*

ANDALUSIAN ROCK CLIMBS *Chris Craggs* El Chorro and El Torcal are world famous. Includes Tenerife. *ISBN 1 85284 109 5 168pp*

COSTA BLANCA ROCK *Chris Craggs* Over 1500 routes on over 40 crags, many for the first time in English. The most comprehensive guide to the area. *ISBN 1 85284 241 5 264pp*

MOUNTAIN WALKS ON THE COSTA BLANCA *Bob Stansfield* An easily accessible winter walking paradise to rival Mallorca. With rugged limestone peaks and warm climate. This guide includes the 150 km Costa Blanca Mountain Way. *ISBN1 85284 165 232pp*

ROCK CLIMBS IN MAJORCA, IBIZA AND TENERIFE *Chris Craggs* Holiday island cragging at its best. *ISBN 1 85284 189 3 240pp*

WALKING IN MALLORCA *June Parker.* The 3rd edition of this great classic guide, takes account of rapidly changing conditions. Revised reprint for 1999. *ISBN 1 85284 250 4 288pp PVC cover*

BIRDWATCHING IN MALLORCA *Ken Stoba* A complete guide to what to see and where to see it. *ISBN 1 85284 053 6 108pp*

THE MOUNTAINS OF CENTRAL SPAIN *Jaqueline Oglesby* Walks and scrambles in the Sierras de Gredos and Guadarrama which rise to 2600m and remain snow capped for 5 months of the year. *ISBN 1 85284 203 2 312p*

ROCK CLIMBS IN THE PYRENEES *Derek Walker See entry under FRANCE/SPAIN*

THROUGH THE SPANISH PYRENEES: GR11 *Paul Lucia* An updated new edition of the long distance trail which mirrors the French GR10 but traverses much lonelier, wilder country. With new maps and information. *ISBN 1 85284 307 1 232pp*

WALKING IN THE SIERRA NEVADA *Andy Walmsley* Spain's highest mountain range is a wonderland for the traveller and wilderness backpacker alike. Mountain bike routes indicated. *ISBN 1 85284 194 X 160pp*

WALKS AND CLIMBS IN THE PICOS DE EUROPA *Robin Walker* A definitive guide to these unique mountains. Walks and rock climbs of all grades. *ISBN 1 85284 033 1 232pp PVC cover*

SWITZERLAND - including parts of France and Italy

ALPINE PASS ROUTE, SWITZERLAND *Kev Reynolds* Over 15 passes along the north ern edge of the Alps, past the Eiger, Jungfrau and many other renowned peaks. A 325 km route in 15 suggested stages. *ISBN 1 85284 069 2 176pp*

THE BERNESE ALPS, SWITZERLAND *Kev Reynolds* Walks around Grindelwald, Lauterbrunnen and Kandersteg dominated by the great peaks of the Oberland. *ISBN 1 85284 243 1 248pp PVC cover*

CENTRAL SWITZERLAND - A Walking Guide *Kev Reynolds* A little known but delightful area stretching from Luzern to the St Gotthard, includes Engelberg and Klausen Pass. *ISBN 1 85284 131 1 216pp PVC cover*

CHAMONIX TO ZERMATT *— see entry under Walking and Trekking in the Alps*

THE GRAND TOUR OF MONTE ROSA Vols 1 & 2 *See entry under Walking and Trekking in the Alps*

WALKS IN THE ENGADINE, SWITZERLAND *Kev Reynolds* The superb region to the south-east of Switzerland of the Bregaglia, Bernina Alps, and the Engadine National Park. *ISBN 1 85284 003 X 192pp PVC cover*

THE JURA: WALKING THE HIGH ROUTE *Kev Reynolds and* **WINTER SKI TRAVERSES** *R. Brian Evans.* The High Route is a long distance path along the highest crest of the Swiss Jura. In winter it is a paradise for cross-country skiers. Both sections in one volume. *ISBN 1 85284 010 2 192pp*

WALKING IN TICINO, SWITZERLAND *Kev Reynolds* Walks in the lovely Italian part of Switzerland, little known to British walkers. *ISBN 1 85284 098 6 184pp PVC cover*
THE VALAIS, SWITZERLAND - A Walking Guide *Kev Reynolds* The splendid scenery of the Pennine Alps, with such peaks as the Matterhorn, Dent Blanche, and Mont Rosa providing a perfect background. *ISBN 1 85284 151 6 224pp PVC cover*

GERMANY, AUSTRIA AND EASTERN EUROPE

MOUNTAIN WALKING IN AUSTRIA *Cecil Davies* An enlarged second edition. 25 mountain groups, 98 walks from half a day to a good week. *ISBN 1 85284 239 3 126pp*
WALKING IN THE BAVARIAN ALPS *Grant Bourne & Sabine Korner-Bourne* 57 walks of variety in the Allgau, Ammergau, Wetterstein, Tegernsee, Chiemgau and Berchtesgarden Alps on the German-Austrian border. *ISBN 1 85284 229 6 184pp*
WALKING IN THE BLACK FOREST *Fleur & Colin Speakman* Above the Rhine valley, the Ortenauer Wine path (64km) and the Clock Carriers Way (10 day circular walk) are described, together with practical walking advice for the area in general. *ISBN 1 85284 050 1 120p*
GERMANY'S ROMANTIC ROAD A Guide for Walkers and Cyclists *Gordon McLachlan* 423km past historic walled towns and castles of southern Germany. *ISBN 1 85284 233 4 208pp*
WALKING IN THE HARZ MOUNTAINS *Fleur & Colin Speakman* 30 walks in Germany's most northerly mountains, some from the narrow gauge steam railway. *ISBN 1 85284 149 4 152pp*
KING LUDWIG WAY *Fleur and Colin Speakman* Travels the Bavarian countryside from Munich to Füssen. King Ludwig was responsible for the fabulous castle of Neuschwanstein and sponsored Wagner's operas. *ISBN 0 902363 90 5 80pp*
KLETTERSTEIG - Scrambles in the Northern Limestone Alps *Paul Werner Translated by Dieter Pevsner* Protected climbing paths similar to the Via Ferrata in the German/Austrian border region. *ISBN 0 902363 46 8 184pp PVC cover*
THE MOUNTAINS OF ROMANIA *James Roberts* A definitive guide to the newly accessible Carpathian mountains. Potentially one of the best walking destinations in Europe, with mountain wilderness and friendly people. *ISBN 1 85284 295 4 296pp*
WALKING THE RIVER RHINE TRAIL *Alan Castle* A spectacular 170mile (273km) walk along Germany's most famous river from Bonn to Alsheim near Worms. Excellent public transport assists the walker. *ISBN 1 85284 276 8 176pp*
WALKING IN THE SALZKAMMERGUT *Fleur and Colin Speakman* Holiday rambles in Austria's Lake District. Renowned for its historic salt mines. *ISBN 1 85284 030 7 104pp*
HUT TO HUT IN THE STUBAI ALPS *Allan Hartley* The Stubai Rucksack Route and The Stubai Glacier Tour, each around 10 days. Easy peaks and good huts make it a good area for a first Alpine season. *ISBN 1 85284 123 0 128pp*
THE HIGH TATRAS *Colin Saunders & Renata Narozna* A detailed guide to the Tatras, popular area between Poland and Slovakia. *ISBN 1 85284 150 8 248pp PVC cover*

SCANDINAVIA

WALKING IN NORWAY *Constance Roos* 20 walking routes in the main mountain areas from the far south to the sub-arctic regions, all accessible by public transport. *ISBN 1 85284 230 X 200pp*

ITALY AND SLOVENIA

ALTA VIA - HIGH LEVEL WALKS IN THE DOLOMITES *Martin Collins* A guide to some of the most popular mountain paths in Europe - Alta Via 1 and 2. *ISBN 0 902363 75 1 160pp PVC cover*

THE CENTRAL APENNINES OF ITALY - Walks, Scrambles and Climbs *Stephen Fox* The mountainous spine of Italy, with secluded walks, rock climbs and scrambles on the Gran Sasso d'Italia and some of Italy's finest sport climbing crags. *ISBN 1 85284 219 9 152pp*

WALKING IN THE CENTRAL ITALIAN ALPS *Gillian Price* The Vinschgau, Ortler and Adamello regions. Little known to British walkers, certain to become popular. *ISBN 1 85284 183 4 230pp PVC cover*

WALKING IN THE DOLOMITES *Gillian Price* A comprehensive selection of walks amongst spectacular rock scenery. By far the best English guide to the area. *ISBN 1 85284 079 X PVC cover*

WALKING IN ITALY'S GRAN PARADISO *Gillian Price* Rugged mountains and desolate valleys with a huge variety of wildlife. Walks from short strolls to full-scale traverses. *ISBN 1 85284 231 8 200pp*

LONG DISTANCE WALKS IN THE GRAN PARADISO *J.W. Akitt* Includes Southern Valdotain. Supplements our Gran Paradiso guide by Gillian Price. Describes Alta Via 2 and the Grand Traverse of Gran Paradiso and some shorter walks. *ISBN 1 85284 247 4 168pp*

THE GRAND TOUR OF MONTE ROSA *C.J. Wright*
See entry under Walking and Trekking in the Alps

ITALIAN ROCK - Selected Climbs in Northern Italy *Al Churcher.* Val d'Orco and Mello, Lecco and Finale etc. A good introduction to some great crags. *ISBN 0 902363 93 X 200pp PVC cover*

WALKS IN THE JULIAN ALPS *Simon Brown* Slovenia contains some of Europe's most attractive mountain limestone scenery. 30 walks as an introduction to the area, from valley strolls to high mountain scrambles. *ISBN 1 85284 125 7 184pp*

WALKING IN TUSCANY *Gillian Price* 50 itineraries from brief strolls to multi-day treks in Tuscany, Umbria and Latium. *ISBN 1 85284 268 7 312pp*

VIA FERRATA SCRAMBLES IN THE DOLOMITES *Höfler/Werner Translated by Cecil Davies* The most exciting walks in the world. Wires, stemples and ladders enable the 'walker' to enter the climber's vertical environment. *ISBN 1 85284 089 7 248pp PVC cover*

WALKING IN SICILY *Gillian Price* Year-round walking on this sunny island takes you to ancient Greek temples, olive groves, citrus orchards and many volcanoes. Good transport, accommodation and eating. 42 graded walks. *ISBN 1 85284 305 5 240pp*

OTHER MEDITERRANEAN COUNTRIES

THE ATLAS MOUNTAINS *Karl Smith* Trekking in the mountains of north Africa. Practical and comprehensive. *ISBN 1 85284 258 X 136pp PVC cover*

WALKING IN CYPRUS   *Donald Brown*   Without a guide getting lost in Cyprus is easy. Donald Brown shares undiscovered Cyprus with 26 easy to moderate routes for walkers. *ISBN 1 85284 195 8 144pp*

THE MOUNTAINS OF GREECE - A Walker's Guide *Tim Salmon*   Hikes of all grades from a month-long traverse of the Pindos to day hikes on the outskirts of Athens.   *ISBN 1 85284 108 7 PVC cover*

CRETE - THE WHITE MOUNTAINS *Loraine Wilson* Describes 49 walks graded from modest to demanding, in this spectacularly beautiful range of mountains in the west of Crete. Includes Samaria gorge, high mountains up to 2500 metres, and glorious coastal walks. *ISBN 1 85284 298 9 152pp*

THE MOUNTAINS OF TURKEY *Karl Smith* Over 100 treks and scrambles with detailed route descriptions of all the popular peaks. Includes Ararat. *ISBN 1 85284 161 3   184pp PVC cover*

TREKS AND CLIMBS IN WADI RUM, JORDAN *Tony Howard*   The world's foremost desert climbing and trekking area. Increasingly popular every year as word of its quality spreads. *ISBN 1 85284 254 7   252pp   A5 Card cover*

JORDAN - Walks, Treks, Caves, Climbs, Canyons in Pella, Ajlun, Moab, Dana, Petra and Rum *Di Taylor & Tony Howard*   The first guidebook to the superlative routes found in Jordan's recently formed Nature Reserves. These are walks, treks, caves and climbs described in this little known landscape by the authors of our Wadi Rum guide. *ISBN 1 85284 278 4 192pp A5*

THE ALA DAG, Climbs and Treks in Turkey's Crimson Mountains *O.B. Tüzel* The best mountaineering area in Turkey.   *ISBN 1 85284 112 5   296pp   PVC cover*

HIMALAYA

ADVENTURE TREKS IN NEPAL *Bill O'Connor*
ISBN 1 85223 306 0 160pp   large format

ANNAPURNA - A Trekker's Guide *Kev Reynolds*   Includes Annapurna Circuit, the Annapurna Santuary and the Pilgrim's Trail, with lots of good advice. *ISBN 1 85284 132 X 184pp*

EVEREST - A Trekker's Guide *Kev Reynolds* A new second edition of this guide to the most popular trekking region in the Himalaya. Lodges, tea-house, permits, health - all are dealt with in this indispensible guide. With updated information, clear mapping and superb photography, including detailed descriptions of approach routes from both Nepal and Tibet. *ISBN 1 85284 306 3 184pp*

GARHWAL AND KUMAON - A Trekker's and Visitor's Guide *K.P. Sharma* Almost at the centre of the Himalayan chain culminating in Nanda Devi. Garhwal consists of rugged mountains and valleys, Kumaon is more gentle. *ISBN 1 85284 264 4 200pp*

KANGCHENJUNGA - A Trekker's Guide *Kev Reynolds* Known as the Five Treasures of the Snows because of its five summits, Kangchenjunga is the world's third highest peak (8586m). The trek to base camp is regarded by many as the most beautiful walk in the world. Various options are described by one of the best of current guide book writers. *ISBN 1 85284 280 6 184pp*

LANGTANG, GOSAINKUND & HELAMBU - A Trekker's Guide *Kev Reynolds* Popular area, easily accessible from Kathmandu. *ISBN 1 85284 207 5*

MANASLU - A Trekker's Guide *Kev Reynolds* A guide to the world's sixth highest mountain, currently only open to trekking parties. Details and descriptions never detract from the sense of discovery and wonder that the trekker experiences. *ISBN 1 85284 302 2 172pp*

OTHER COUNTRIES

MOUNTAIN WALKING IN AFRICA 1: KENYA *David Else* Detailed route descriptions and practical information. *ISBN 1 85365 205 9 180pp   A5 size*

OZ ROCK - A Rock Climber's Guide to Australian Crags *Alastair Lee* An overall view of Oz rock with details of each crag and how to get there. *ISBN 1 85284 237 7 184pp A5 size*

TREKKING IN THE CAUCAUSUS *Yuri Kolomiets & Aleksey Solovyev* The great mountains once hidden behind the Iron Curtain. 62 walks of which half demand basic climbing skills. Included are the walks to the highest tops in Europe, the summits of Mt Elbrus. *ISBN 1 85284 129 X 224pp PVC cover*

ROCK CLIMBING IN HONG KONG *Brian J. Heard* Great climbing for both locals and travellers. *ISBN 1 85284 167 2 136pp A5 size*

TREKKING IN THE CAUCAUSUS *Yuri Kolomiets & Aleksey Solovyev* The great mountains once hidden behind the Iron Curtain. 62 walks of which half demand basic climbing skills. Included are the walks to the highest tops in Europe, the summits of Mt Elbrus. *ISBN 1 85284 129 X 224pp PVC cover*

ADVENTURE TREKS WESTERN NORTH AMERICA
Chris Townsend ISBN 1 85223 317 6 160pp large format

CLASSIC TRAMPS IN NEW ZEALAND *Constance Roos* The 14 best long distance walks in both islands. Each "tramp" takes between 2-7 days. ISBN 85284 118 4 208pp PVC cover